The Construction
of
Racial Identities
in
China and Japan

Historical and
Contemporary Perspectives

EDITED BY
FRANK DIKÖTTER

CONSULTING EDITOR
BARRY SAUTMAN

HURST & COMPANY, LONDON

First published in the United Kingdom by
C. Hurst & Co. (Publishers) Ltd.,
38 King Street, London WC2E 8JZ
© Frank Dikötter, 1997
All rights reserved.
Printed in Hong Kong

ISBNs
1-85065-287-2 (cased)
1-85065-353-4 (paper)

ACKNOWLEDGEMENTS

Four of the chapters in this book were first presented at the 'International Conference on Racial Identities in East Asia' held in Hong Kong on 25-26 November 1994. The conference was organised by Frank Dikötter and Barry Sautman and sponsored by the School of Oriental and African Studies, University of London, and the Hong Kong University of Science and Technology.

The editor of this book would like to thank all the participants of the conference, in particular Michael Banton (University of Bristol), Grant Evans (University of Hong Kong), Andrew Gerstle (SOAS), Richard Tanter and Wang Gungwu (University of Hong Kong). Special thanks are extended to Barry Sautman (Hong Kong University of Science and Technology), who served as a consulting editor, and to Geremie Barmé (Australian National University, Canberra) for invaluable advice and help.

London, March 1997   F. D.

CONTENTS

Contents

THE CONTRIBUTORS

Chow Kai-wing is Associate Professor in History at the University of Illinois at Urbana-Champaign.

Frank Dikötter is Senior Lecturer in History and Wellcome Research Fellow at the School of Oriental and African Studies, University of London.

David Goodman is Professor in the Department of East Asian Languages and Cultures at the University of Illinois at Urbana-Champaign.

Kazuki Sato is Assistant Professor at Sophia University, Tokyo.

Barry Sautman is Lecturer in Politics at the Hong Kong University of Science and Technology.

Richard Siddle is Research Fellow at the University of Sheffield, England.

Michael Weiner is Senior Lecturer at the University of Sheffield, England.

Kosaku Yoshino is Associate Professor in Sociology at the University of Tokyo.

Louise Young is Associate Professor in History at New York University.

Xun Zhou is a doctoral candidate in Religious Studies at the School of Oriental and African Studies, University of London.

INTRODUCTION

Frank Dikötter

'This yellow river, it so happens, bred a nation identified by its yellow skin pigment. Moreover, this nation also refers to its earliest ancestor as the Yellow Emperor. Today, on the face of the earth, of every five human beings there is one that is a descendant of the Yellow Emperor.'[1]

If, in contemporary Germany, a leading intellectual were to identify the people of that country according to physical features ('blond hair and blue eyes') and represent them as a homogeneous descent group ('the Aryans'), he would be considered to be contributing to the invention of a German racial identity. Unlike other group identities, racial discourse essentialises presumed biological features. Racial theories attempt to root culture in nature, to equate social groups with biological units, and give primacy to the imagined or real congenital endowments of people. In Su Xiaokang's recent definition of China given above, human beings do not have a common descent: 'Of every five human beings there is one that is a descendant of the Yellow Emperor.' 'Chineseness' is seen primarily as a matter of biological descent, physical appearance and congenital inheritance. Cultural features such as 'Chinese civilisation' or 'Confucianism' are thought to be the product of that imagined biological group: they are secondary and can be changed, reformed or even eradicated. Confucian scholar or socialist cadre, Hunanese peasant or Hong Kong entrepreneur, one will always, according to Su Xiaokang, be 'Chinese' by virtue of one's blood.

Because it is considered politically embarrassing, the importance

---

[1] Su Xiaokang, 'River Elegy' in *Chinese Sociology and Anthropology*, 24, no. 2 (winter 1991-2), p. 9.

of racialised identities in East Asia has so far been deliberately
ignored. However, far from being a negligible aspect of contemporary identities, racialised senses of belonging have often been
the very foundation of national identity in East Asia in the twentieth
century. In their opposition to the systematic investigation of
racial discourses and practices in East Asia, some social scientists
have argued that 'racism', however defined, cannot be found
in 'Asian culture'.[2] For instance, the anthropologist Charles Stafford
maintains that 'race' is not a 'Chinese' concept, hence 'racism'
can only occur in 'the West'.[3] Let us take an example. Kang
Youwei (1858-1927), one of the most acclaimed philosophers
of the late nineteenth century, judged that Africans, 'with their
iron faces, silver teeth, slanting jaws like a pig, front view like
an ox, full breasts and long hair, their hands and feet dark black,
stupid like sheep or swine', should be whitened by intermarriage,
although he feared that no refined white girl would ever agree
to mate with a 'monstrously ugly black'. 'Whites' and 'yellows'
who married 'blacks' as a contribution to the purification of
mankind should therefore be awarded a medal with the inscription
'Improver of the race', whereas 'browns or blacks whose characteristics are too bad, whose physical appearance is too ugly
or who carry a disease should be given a sterilising medication
to stop the perpetuation of their race.'[4] In his description of
Africans, Kang Youwei used the terms *renzhong* ('human breed',
'human race') and *zhongzu* ('breed', 'race') but, according to Charles
Stafford, 'to translate these [terms] as race is to impose a Western
reading on what are supposed to be Chinese cultural constructs.'[5]
The virulent racial discourse of a prominent reformer has been
transformed into an inconsequential utterance which does not
'belong' to 'Chinese culture'. 'Racism', it is argued, like 'human
rights' is a 'Western concept' with no equivalent in China. At
recent meetings in Geneva of the United Nations Committee
for the Elimination of Racial Discrimination Chinese delegates
have upheld precisely the same argument, a rhetorical strategy

[2] For instance David Y.F. Ho, 'Prejudice, colonialism, and interethnic relations: An
East-West dialogue', *Journal of Asian and African Studies*, 20 (1985), pp. 224-5.
[3] Charles Stafford, 'The discourse of race in modern China', *Man: The Journal of the Royal
Anthropological Institute*, 28, no. 3 (Sept. 1993), p. 609.
[4] Kang Youwei, *Datongshu* (One World), Beijing: Guji chubanshe, 1956, pp. 118-22.
[5] Stafford, 'The discourse', p. 609.

used to delay the introduction of clear definitions of racial discrimination into the country's legal system.

However, racial discourse cannot be reduced to the mere appearance of the word 'race'. In English, for instance, the word has had a number of very different meanings and connotations since the Middle Ages; only during the nineteenth century did it begin to refer to alleged biological differences between groups of people.[6] Nor is it a necessary precondition to use the word 'race' in order to construct racial categories of thought. At the turn of the century, many authors in Britain used the word 'nation' to sustain racial frames of analysis; the 'nation' was thought to correspond to a biologically homogeneous unit which could be improved through selective breeding. In Nazi Germany, German citizens were often described as a '*Volk*', whereas 'racial hygiene' was called '*Volksgesundheit*'. No historian would deny that the term '*Volk*' has a variety of ambiguous meanings, but it would take a bigot to argue that these terms did not contribute to the invention of 'the Aryans' as a biologically integrated group of people.

Similarly, many terms were used in China and Japan from the late nineteenth century onwards to represent these countries as biologically specific entities: *zu* ('lineage', 'clan'), *zhong* ('seed', 'breed', 'type', 'race'), *zulei* ('type of lineage'), *minzu* ('lineage of people', 'nationality', 'race'), *zhongzu* ('breed of lineage', 'type of lineage', 'breed', 'race') and *renzhong* ('human breed', 'human race') in Chinese, and *jinshu* ('human breed', 'human race'), *shuzoku* ('breed of lineage', 'type of lineage', 'breed', 'race') and *minzoku* ('lineage of people', 'nationality', 'race') in Japanese. All acquire different meanings in different contexts. The question a historian should ask is what type of identity is shaped by these different terms in specific circumstances. *Minzu*, to take a notorious example, is often simply translated as 'nationality', but it means different things for a variety of authors in China throughout the twentieth century. Between 1902 and 1911 *minzu* as a term was used to promote symbolic boundaries of blood and descent: 'nationalities' as political units were equated with 'races' as biological units. In nationalist theories of the 1900s, *minzu* was thought to be based on a quantifiable number of people called 'Chinese', a

[6] Michael Banton, *Racial Theories*, Cambridge University Press, 1987.

group with clear boundaries by virtue of imagined blood ties, kinship and descent. As Sun Yatsen (1866-1925), the principal proponent of a Chinese *minzu,* put it in his famous *Three Principles of the People,* 'The greatest force is common blood. The Chinese belong to the yellow race because they come from the blood stock of the yellow race. The blood of ancestors is transmitted by heredity down through the race, making blood kinship a power-ful force.'[7] In Japan, increasing numbers of intellectuals after the First World War defined the *minzoku* as a distinct people with shared physical attributes and pure blood whose origins could be traced back to the palaeolithic period. Ethnicity continued to be identified with biological descent in the period between the two World Wars, while cultural and racial characteristics con-stantly overlapped in political, anthropological and medical litera-ture. Throughout the twentieth century, in fact, the notion of *minzu* in China and *minzoku* in Japan has consistently conflated ideas of culture, ethnicity and race in efforts to represent cultural features as secondary to, and derivative of, an imagined biological essence. Racial definitions have constantly been deployed in order to account for cultural differences. The historian of racial identities, in short, is not interested in a philological examination of a few terms for their own sake, but in the analysis of different texts in which authors attempt to naturalise cultural differences between population groups.

While the reality of racial discourse and practice in East Asia is sometimes recognised, it is often argued that the social scientist needs 'a' definition of racism, as if there were only one model of racism which is universal in its origins, causes, meanings and effects. By imposing a definition of an ideal type of 'racism', racial discourses which do not conform to the imposed model are ignored, marginalised or trivialised. For instance, when racial discourse is defined in terms of features which are specific to a European context ('white racism'), the specific articulations which have emerged in China and Japan are seen as 'special cases' which threaten to deconstruct the ideal type.[8] Far from being fixed

[7] Sun Wen (Sun Yatsen), *Sanminzhuyi* (The Three Principles of the People), Shanghai: Shangwu yinshuguan, 1927, pp. 4-5.

[8] For a more detailed discussion of essentialism in explanations of racism, see the excellent article of Philip Cohen, "It's racism what dunnit": Hidden narratives in theories of racism' in James Donald and Ali Rattansi (eds), *'Race', culture and difference,* London: Sage, 1992, pp. 83-4.

or static entities, the adaptability of racial theories in different historical circumstances should be recognised if their enduring appeal is to be understood. There is, nonetheless, a common thread to different forms of racism in that they all primarily group human populations on the basis of some biological signifier, be it skin colour, body height, hair texture or head-shape. In different cultural and historical contexts, racial discourse combines in varying degrees with ethnocentrism, where groups of people are defined primarily in cultural terms, and furthermore intersects with discourses of gender, sexuality, social status, region and age to produce different meanings. Socially constructed 'races', in other words, are population groups which are imagined to have boundaries based on immutable biological or other inherent characteristics, and can be contrasted to socially constructed 'ethnicities', which are groups thought to be based on culturally acquired characteristics: the ways in which boundaries are created and maintained are distinct, although they clearly overlap in many cases.

Racial definitions of difference, of course, are not specific to East Asia only. Although genetic research has long established that there are only trivial biological differences between population groups defined as 'races', differential and inequitable treatment in the West has been justified on arbitrary scientific grounds ever since the rise of biological theories in the nineteenth century. The number of genes involved in surface traits (melanine, hair and stature) is insignificant, and the diversity and variations between individuals are so enormous that the entire concept of 'race', however defined, has become utterly meaningless. Genetic diversity is more or less evenly distributed over the entire human species, and there is no justification to support the view that socially significant groups are grounded on genetic differences. In some European countries, however, racial discourses and practices were produced by political groups and scientific institutions until the end of the Second World War, while racial discrimination persisted at an official level in the United States until a few decades ago. More recently, the transformation of political economies and cultures in the West has led to the emergence of new motives for discrimination, in particular in Britain, France, Germany and the United States.

Although a considerable body of scholarly work has highlighted the historical and contemporary dimensions of racialised identities in the West, almost nothing is known about the invention, articulation and deployment of racial frames of reference in East Asia. However, official policies endorsing racial discrimination and leading to abuses of human rights can be found in most East Asian states. Myths of origins, ideologies of blood and theories of biological descent have formed a central part in the cultural construction of identity in China and Japan since the nationalist movements of the late nineteenth century. Naturalised as a pure and homogeneous 'Yamato race' in Japan, or as a biological descent group from the 'Yellow Emperor' in China, political territories have been conflated with imaginary biological entities by nationalist writers. As the different contributions to this volume emphasise, modernising élites in East Asia endowed foreign cultural repertoires with indigenous meanings. Cultural intermediaries – educators, journalists, academics, doctors and scientists – appropriated the language of science, indigenised evolutionary theories, reinterpreted racial ideologies and actively reconstructed their own definitions of identity. They often constructed racial discourse on the basis of more stable notions of purity and descent. In Japan, for instance, the language of blood, expressing a notion of immutable difference, was strengthened through the selective appropriation of evolutionary theories, in particular from Arthur de Gobineau and other nineteenth-century racial theorists. Ideas of purity and pollution, an integral part of folk models of identity in Japan, were also reconfigured in the propagation of ideas about the divine origins of the imperial line and the racial and cultural homogeneity of the Japanese people. Established modes of representation centred on the lineage (*zu*) in China and the family (*ie*) in Japan were also fundamental to cultural processes of articulating and defining the nature of difference. Folk notions of patrilineal descent in China were reconfigured into a racial discourse which thrived on the semantic similarity between *zu* as lineage and *zu* as race: *huangzhong* as a new racialised identity invented by the reformers at the end of the nineteenth century meant both 'lineage of the Yellow Emperor' and 'yellow race'. In both countries, moreover, Confucian social hierarchies underwent a permutation into new racial taxonomies: binary distinctions between 'superior races' (*liangzhong*) and 'inferior races' (*jianzhong*) were often extrapolated from existing social hierarchies, which had divided 'common people' (*liangmin*) from 'mean people' (*jianmin*) in China until their legal abolition by the Yongzheng emperor in 1723 (social discrimination persisted until the twentieth century). Africans were referred to in China and Japan as the 'black slave race' until the end of the 1920s. The opening sentence of a textbook written in 1918 by China's first Professor in Anthropology put it concisely: 'Anthropology studies all races, from the Chinese and the English down to the dwarf slave [i.e. the Japanese] and the black slave.'[9] Different population groups were thus assigned a low social status as 'slaves': their social inequality was made to appear permanent and immutable through a discourse of race which firmly located these social differences inside the body.

Cultural definitions of 'civilisation' versus 'barbarism' – widespread in the Confucian symbolic universe – were also racialised into binary oppositions between 'advanced' and 'backward' groups of people: in the popular imagery of twentieth-century Japan, China was portrayed as an exotic and different 'race' in stark contrast to the cultural and biological uniqueness of Japan. Scientific literature on the superior physical attributes which distinguished the Japanese in tropical climates was paralleled by the spread of woodblock prints in which 'darker races' were portrayed as short yellow-skinned figures or dark thick-lipped cannibals. In the context of colonial expansion to Korea and China, it was assumed that the differences in economic and political capacities of the peoples of East Asia were the result of natural or biological laws: colonial populations were regularly contrasted with Japanese modernity. 'Spiritual and physical purity' were said to be the attributes which marked the Japanese as the 'leading race' in their divine mission in Asia. In war-time Japan, a sense of unique purity – both moral and genetic – was central to the notion of racial separateness in which other population groups were dehumanised as beasts and ultimately as demons. In both China and Japan, other population groups were also ranked according to their presumed physical attributes.

Since evolution was interpreted as an inevitable ascent through a preordained hierarchy of stages, modernising élites in East Asia not only deployed racial hierarchies in which 'savage tribes' were

---

[9] Chen Yinghuang, *Renleixue* (Anthropology), Shanghai: Shangwu yinshuguan, (1st edn 1918) 1928, p. 5.

represented as throwbacks on the evolutionary scale, but also portrayed women and children as the lower stages of evolutionary growth. The different social roles of men and women were increasingly thought to be firmly grounded in inescapable biological laws, and gender hierarchy was represented as the natural result of an unequal endowment. New gender distinctions, based on presumed biological characteristics such as the quality of blood, the size of the pelvis, the structure of the brain and general stature, established a hierarchical relationship in which women were represented as inferior and passive versions of men. Portrayed as the guardians of the 'race', women were excluded from having a public role and were assigned a primary responsibility over the reproductive health of the nation.

Racial discourse, in other words, appealed to and was supported by a diversity of people precisely because it was based on common folk models of identity, in particular patrilineal descent and common stock. While it is undoubtedly true the state was instrumental in the deployment of racial theories and disseminating them among the general public by means of school textbooks, anthropology exhibitions and travel literature, a degree of reciprocal interaction between popular culture and official discourse could be suggested. More stable folk notions of patrilineal descent, widespread in late imperial China, were reconfigured in the twentieth century into a discourse of 'racial strength', 'genetic inheritance' and 'sexual hygiene'. Scientised by cultural intermediaries, indigenous notions of identity were reinforced and enriched by the use of new biological vocabularies. Racial discourse in China and Japan thrived and evolved over time because it reconfigured pre-existing notions of identity and simultaneously appealed to a variety of groups, from popular audiences to groups of scientists.

Most contributors to this volume underline the importance of 'power' in the articulation of racial taxonomies. From the subordination of colonised populations in prewar Japan to the dispossession of so-called 'national minorities' of natural resources in China today, racial knowledge has been deployed to subordinate and dominate entire groups of people. Political power, social privilege and economic exploitation have all been legitimised by the invention of racial boundaries, in particular in China and Japan. However, domination and subjugation need not necessarily figure at the centre of racial discourse. Beyond the direct economic and political power that may be gained in the racialisation of social relations, the drawing of racial boundaries between Self and Other is often about imagined inclusions and exclusions. 'Race' was seen by many nationalists in China as the only concept capable of including both peasant and emperor. The revolutionary Zou Rong greeted the 'peasants with weatherbeaten faces and mudcaked hands and feet' as the proud descendants of the Yellow Emperor:[10] blood was thought to overarch gender, lineage, class and region to integrate the nation's citizens into a powerful community. The power of inclusion unleashed by racial discourse was a fundamental part of its appeal, in particular for social groups which had traditionally been marginalised (youth were acclaimed as the vanguard of the race, women were celebrated as the guardians of future generations, farmers were hailed for their physical vigour). At the same time as racial discourse created and shaped racially defined inclusions, it produced racially excluded Others, notably 'Blacks' or 'Jews', although these may not have had a significant presence in Asia comparable to Europe and the United States. However, as some of the chapters in this book attest, they are central in the racial taxonomies devised in China and Japan throughout the twentieth century. Less the result of a social encounter conditioned by political domination, their invention is more part of a network of symbolic relations which fulfill contradictory and ambiguous roles: harbingers of decline ('the stateless Jews') or repositories of hope ('Jewish international finance'), their real object has been the construction of the self in which racialised others remain distant mirrors. Racial discourse, which has sometimes been more about imagined cultural inclusions than about real social encounters, has shaped the identity of millions of people in East Asia: although it is a historically contingent object which is constantly rearticulated in adaptations to changing environments, its fundamental role in creating both Self and Other has given it a particular kind of resilience so that it often survives social, economic and political changes.

The construction of symbolic boundaries between racially constituted categories has gone through many transformations in China

[10] Tsou Jung, *The revolutionary army: A Chinese nationalist tract of 1903*, intro. and transl. by J. Lust, Paris: Mouton, 1968, p. 72.

and Japan in the twentieth century, but the attempt to mark, naturalise and rank real or imagined differences between population groups remains widespread. However, in East Asia, in contrast to other regions, there is no clear sign that the hierarchies of power maintained through racial discourse are being questioned by the cultural centres of authority. Notions of racial homogeneity continue today to inform debates about 'Japaneseness' (*nihonjinron*), punctuated by ideas about 'Japanese blood' and claims for a 'Japanese-length intestine'. Racialised representations of foreigners also remain relatively widespread: from the first encounter with black sailors sent by Commodore Perry in 1853 to Taisuke Fujishima's recent essay entitled 'We Cannot Marry Negroes', blackness has become a symbol of the savage Other in Japan. The recent influx of foreign workers into Japan has also led to expressions of fear of cultural or racial contamination. The Japanese government, in fact, decided not to ratify the International Convention on the Elimination of Racial Discrimination. In China too, the racialisation of identity has recently increased both within government circles and within relatively independent intellectual spheres, particularly since the erosion of communist authority after the Tiananmen events in 1989. Imagined as an inferior species, African students are periodically subjected to racial attacks on the university campuses of the People's Republic of China.

Theories of racial purity have combined with dubious studies in anthropometry in official efforts to legitimise discrimination against social groups such as the Tibetans and the Uighurs. The official promotion of China as the 'homeland of the Modern Yellow Race' has far-reaching consequences not only for minority groups inside the political boundaries of the PRC. Outer Mongolia, for instance, has recently been portrayed as an 'organic and integral part' of the 'Chinese race'. Racial nationalism arising in a potentially unstable empire with an embattled Communist Party could have grave consequences for regional stability in that vital part of the world. Similar to the first decades of the twentieth century, moreover, the multiplication of regional identities and the emergence of cultural diversity could prompt a number of political figures to appeal to racialised senses of belonging in order to overcome internal divisions. In contrast, multiple identities, free choice of ethnicity and ambiguity in group membership are not likely to appear as viable alternatives to more essentialist models

of group definition. The racialisation of identity, it should finally
be underlined, has often led to the rejection of hybridity, fluidity
and heterogeneity in contemporary East Asia.

The construction of racial identities has become particularly
important since the rise of nationalist movements in the late
nineteenth century, but primordial senses of belonging based on
blood remain as salient in East Asia as they are in Europe and
in the United States. In an era of economic globalisation and
political depolarisation, racial identities and racial discrimination
have increased in East Asia, affecting both the human rights of
marginalised groups and collective perceptions of the world order.
Official policies endorsing racial discrimination and leading to
abuses of human rights can be found in most East Asian states.
Efforts to reduce or eliminate all forms of discrimination on an
international scale will not succeed without the active support
of a part of the world which accounts for a quarter of mankind.
Racialised identities and their effect on human rights in East
Asia are a serious and potentially explosive issue of the last decade
of the twentieth century which needs to be fully addressed. However, as the result of an excessively narrow frame of analysis
which has reduced the formation of racialised identities in the
contemporary world to a uniquely 'Western' phenomenon, the
current state of the field and the available expertise on these
issues is dangerously underdeveloped. The aim of this volume
is to open up that field and point to a number of possible avenues
for future research. It does not pretend to offer a unitary and
integrated perspective, nor does it compare in any systematic way
the racial identities forged in East Asia. Its contributors are located
at different level of research, some focusing on specific authors
or particular periods, others offering more general overviews of
the field. However fragmentary the state of our knowledge may
be in this early stage, it is hoped that the book will stimulate
further interest in the historical dimensions of the construction
of racial identities in China and Japan.

Part I. CHINA

RACIAL DISCOURSE IN CHINA
CONTINUITIES AND PERMUTATIONS

Frank Dikötter

Was the notion of a 'yellow race' imposed on China by Europeans in the late nineteenth century? The term only appeared in Europe at the end of the seventeenth century, probably in response to Jesuit reports on the symbolic significance of the colour yellow in China. It did not exist in the ancient world, and was not used by travellers of the Middle Ages such as Marco Polo, Pian del Carpini, Bento de Goes or any of the Arab traders. In 1655 the first European mission to the Qing described the Chinese as having a white complexion, 'equal to the Europeans', except for some southerners whose skin was 'slightly brown'.[1] When a young inhabitant of the Celestial Kingdom was presented at the court of Louis XIV in 1684, he was described as a 'young Indian'. The first scientific work in which the notion of a 'yellow race' appeared was François Bernier's 'Étrennes adressées à Madame de la Sablière pour l'année 1688'.[2] In China, however, the symbolic meanings ascribed to the colour yellow placed it in a privileged position in the construction of social identities. Yellow, one of the five 'pure' colours in China, had long been symbolic of grandeur and of the emperor. In both popular and literate culture, yellow was the colour of the Emperor of the Middle Kingdom, ancestral home of the 'descendants of the Yellow Emperor' who, it was claimed, had originated in the valley of the Yellow River. Wang

---

[1] Jan Nieuhof, *Het gezantschap der Neerlandtsche Oost-Indische Compagnie aan den Grooten Tartarischen Cham den tegenwoordigen Keizer van China*, Amsterdam: Jacob van Meurs, 1665, p. 173.

[2] Pierre Huard, 'Depuis quand avons-nous la notion d'une race jaune?', *Institut Indochinois pour l'Etude de l'Homme*, 4 (1942), pp. 40-1.

Fuzhi (1619-92), a seventeenth-century scholar who wrote after the fall of the Ming and the invasion of China by the Manchus, entitled one of his more important works the *Yellow Book* (*Huangshu*) (1656): the last chapter contrasted the imperial colour yellow to 'mixed' colours, and named China the 'Yellow Centre' (*huang-zhong*).[3] On more popular discursive registers, legends circulated about the origins of mankind in which noble people were said to be made out of yellow mud and ignoble people of vulgar rope.[4] These folk accounts were appropriated and rearticulated into a racial identity by scholars in the late nineteenth century. Huang Zunxian (1848-1905), for instance, recorded in his diary when aged twenty that 'all men are fashioned out of yellow mud'. At the age of fifty-four, as one of the most outstanding reformers and an important architect in the racialisation of identity, he publicly wondered 'Why is the yellow race not the only race in the world?'[5] Far from being a negative label imposed on Chinese scholars by the 'cultural hegemony' of 'imperialism', the notion of a 'yellow race' was a positive symbol of imperial nobility which was actively mobilised by reformers who transformed it into a powerful and effective means of identification. The only sector of the social field which denounced the reformers' use of terms like 'yellow race' (*huangzhong*) and 'white race' (*baizhong*) were conservative scholars, mainly because it undermined imperial cos-mologies on which their power and knowledge was predicated.[6]

Chinese reformers in the 1890s were active agents who par-ticipated in the invention of their identities. They were not the passive recipients of a 'derivative discourse', but creative individuals who selectively appropriated elements of foreign thought systems in a process of cultural interaction. More important, the reform movement which contributed so much to the invention of racial identities in China was largely the product of complex interactions

---

[3] E. Vierheller, *Nation und Elite im Denken von Wang Fu-chih (1619-1692)*, Hamburg: Gesellschaft für Natur- und Völkerkunde Ostasiens, 1968, pp. 30 and 124.

[4] *Taiping yulan* (Song encyclopaedia), quoting the Later Han work 'Fengsutong', Taipei: Xinxing shuju, 1959, p. 1693 (360: 5a). See also Zhou Jianren, 'Renzhong qiyuan shuo' (Legends about the origins of human races), *Dongfang zazhi*, 16, no. 11 (June 1919), pp. 93-100.

[5] Noriko Kamachi, *Reform in China: Huang Tsun-hsien and the Japanese model*, Cambridge, MA: Harvard University Press, 1981, pp. 15, 141.

[6] Charles M. Lewis, *Prologue to the Chinese revolution: The transformation of ideas and institutions in Hunan Province, 1891-1907*, Cambridge, MA: Harvard University East Asian Research Centre, 1976, pp. 64-5.

and fusions of different indigenous schools of thought, such as New Text Confucianism, statecraft scholarship (*jingshi*), classical non-canonical philosophies (*zhuzixue*) and Mahayana Buddhism, all of which had virtually nothing to do with Western learning. In other words, racial identities during the late imperial period were created through cultural interaction with a variety of schools of thought by a group of reformers who actively responded to the decline of imperial cosmology. Far from being a 'derivative discourse' of a more 'authentic' form of 'white racism', narratives of blood and descent in China had an internal cohesion which was based on the active reconfiguration of indigenous modes of representation. Lineage discourse was perhaps one of the most prominent elements in the construction of symbolic boundaries between racially defined groups of people.[7]

THE RECONFIGURATION OF LINEAGE DISCOURSE AND THE EMERGENCE OF RACIAL TAXONOMIES

The racial categories of analysis which first emerged in China with the rise of nationalism were largely constructed on the basis of indigenous modes of representation, in particular lineage discourse. The Qing era was marked by a consolidation of the cult of patrilineal descent, centre of a broad movement of social reform that had emphasised the family and the lineage (*zu*) since the collapse of the Ming.[8] Considerable friction arose between lineages throughout the nineteenth century in response to heightened competition over natural resources, the need to control market towns, the gradual erosion of social order and organisational disorders caused by demography pressures.[9] Lineage feuds as well as interethnic conflicts (*fenlei xiedou*) prevailed throughout the empire, but were more common in the south-east, where the institution of the lineage had grown more powerful than in the north. The militarisation of powerful lineages reinforced folk

---

[7] The following sections are discussed in much greater detail in Frank Dikötter, *The discourse of race in modern China*; London: C. Hurst; Stanford University Press; Hong Kong University Press, 1992.

[8] Kai-wing Chow, *The rise of Confucian ritualism in late imperial China: Ethics, Classics, and lineage discourse*, Stanford University Press, 1994.

[9] See H.J. Lamley, 'Hsieh-tou: The pathology of violence in south-eastern China', *Ch'ing-shih Wen-t'i*, 3, no. 7 (Nov. 1977), pp. 1-39.

models of kinship solidarity, forcing in turn more loosely organised associations to form a unified descent group under the leadership of the gentry. At court level, too, ideologies of descent became increasingly important, in particular with the erosion of a sense of cultural identity among Manchu aristocrats. Racial identity through patrilineal descent became important in the Qianlong period (1736-95), when the court progressively turned towards a rigid taxonomy of distinct descent lines (*zu*) to distinguish between Han, Manchu, Mongol or Tibetan.[10] Within three distinct social levels – popular culture, gentry society and court politics – the deployment of more stable folk notions of patrilineal descent became widespread in the creation and maintenance of group boundaries.

The racialisation of lineage discourse during the last decade of the nineteenth century was largely the work of the 1898 reformers, who championed a radical transformation of imperial institutions and orthodox ideology. In contrast to their precursors, they promoted an alternative body of knowledge which derived its legitimacy independently from the official examination system. It was the product of a fusion between different indigenous strains of knowledge and foreign discursive repertoires, with the principal object of political attention being the species. The scientific category of 'race' and the administrative category of 'population' were heralded as objects worthy of systematic investigation. Folk models of shared kinship and élite notions of belonging were the two most dominant variations of lineage discourse: popular culture and élite culture stressed patrilineal descent in the creation and maintenance of group boundaries. Cultural intermediaries like Liang Qichao and Kang Youwei selectively appropriated scientific knowledge from foreign discursive repertoires, actively manipulated evolutionary theories to bolster theories of pure origins; they reconfigured folk notions of patrilineal descent into a racial discourse which represented all inhabitants of China as the descendants of the Yellow Emperor. The semantic similarity between *zu* as lineage and *zu* as race was rearticulated in a new racialised identity called *huangzhong*, meaning both 'lineage of the Yellow Emperor' and 'yellow race'. Extrapolating from an indigenous vision of

---

[10] Pamela Kyle Crossley, 'The Qianlong retrospect on the Chinese-martial (*hanjun*) banners', *Late Imperial China*, 10, no. 1 (June 1989), pp. 63-107, and 'Thinking about ethnicity in early modern China', *Late Imperial China*, 11, no. 1 (June 1990), p. 20.

Frank Dikötter

lineage feuds, which permeated the social landscape of late imperial China, the reformers ordered mankind into a racial hierarchy of biological groups where 'yellows' competed with 'whites' over degenerate breeds of 'browns', 'blacks' and 'reds'. Thriving on its affinity with lineage discourse, 'race' thus gradually emerged as the most common symbol of national cohesion, permanently replacing more conventional emblems of cultural identity. The threat of racial extinction (*miezhong*), a powerful message of fear based on more popular anxieties about lineage extinction (*miezu*), was often raised to bolster the reformers' message of change: 'They will enslave us and hinder the development of our spirit and body.... The brown and black races constantly waver between life and death, why not the 400 million of yellows?'[11] In the reformers' symbolic network of racialised Others, the dominating 'white' and 'yellow races' were opposed to the 'darker races', doomed by hereditary inadequacy to racial extinction. Liang Qichao rearticulated traditional social hierarchies into a new racial taxonomy of 'noble' (*guizhong*) and 'low' (*jianzhong*), 'superior' (*youzhong*) and 'inferior' (*liezhong*), 'historical' and 'ahistorical races' (*youlishi de zhongzu*). The widespread distinction between 'common people' (*liangmin*) and 'mean people' (*jianmin*) that had officially characterised late imperial China up till the early eighteenth century also found an echo in Tang Caichang (1867–1900), who opposed 'fine races' (*liangzhong*) to 'mean races' (*jianzhong*). He phrased it in evenly balanced clauses reminiscent of the classical language: 'Yellow and white are wise, red and black are stupid; yellow and white are rulers, red and black are slaves; yellow and white are united, red and black are scattered.'[12]

The myth of blood was further sealed by the turn of the century when the revolutionaries created a national symbol out of the Yellow Emperor. Liu Shipei (1884–1919), to take but one example, advocated the introduction of a calendar in which the foundation year corresponded to the birth of the Yellow Emperor. 'They [the reformers] see the preservation of religion as a handle, so they use the birth of Confucius as the starting date of the calendar; the purpose of our generation is preservation

---

[11] Yan Fu, *Yan Fu shiwen xuan* (Selected poems and writings of Yan Fu), Beijing: Renmin wenxue chubanshe, 1959, p. 22.

[12] Tang Caichang, *Juedianmingzhai neiyan* (Essays on political and historical matters), Taibei: Wenhai chubanshe, 1968, p. 468.

of the race, so we use the birth of the Yellow Emperor as a founding date.'[13] Early twentieth-century revolutionaries like Chen Tianhua (1875-1905) infused kin terms, previously deployed in lineage discourse, into racial frames of reference to foster the much needed bonds of national loyalty: 'The racial feeling comes from birth onwards. For the members of one's own race, there is surely mutual intimacy and love; for the members of a foreign race, there is surely mutual savagery and killing.'[14] The first issue of the *Tides of Zhejiang*, a nationalist journal published in Japan by Chinese students, stated that 'those who are able to group their own tribe into an organised body able to resist other groups will survive.' In an era dominated by 'racial competition', the key to survival lay in the cohesive force of the group (*qunli*). Nationalism fostered unity, as it 'erects borders against the outside and unites the group inside'.[15] A contributor to the journal *Yunnan* attributed the decline of the 'barbarian red and the savage black races' to their ignorance of the racial principles of nationalism: a nation needed a 'group strategy and group strength'.[16] World politics were expounded in terms of racial cohesion. India, for instance, had been conquered by the 'white race' because its class system inhibited racial homogeneity.[17] Russians were a 'crossbreed between Europeans and Asians and nothing else', another polemicist claimed. A cranial analysis and a detailed racial investigation revealed that the Russians had Asian blood running in their veins. This racial mix was responsible for Russia's inability to group.[18] The naval superiority of the United States, on the other hand, was ascribed to its racial quality: were not the Americans an inch taller than the English?[19] Culture, nation and race had

---

[13] Liu Shipei, 'Huangdi jinian shuo' (About a calendar based on the Yellow Emperor), *Huangdi hun* (The soul of the Yellow Emperor), 1904, p. 1; reprinted, Taibei: Zhonghua minguo shiliao congbian, 1968.

[14] Chen Tianhua, *Chen Tianhua ji* (Collected works of Chen Tianhua), Changsha: Hunan renmin chubanshe, 1982, p. 81.

[15] Yuyi, 'Minzuzhuyi lun' (On nationalism), *Zhejiangchao*, 1 (Feb. 1903), p. 3.

[16] *Yunnan*, 1 (Aug. 1906), pp. 7-12.

[17] 'Yindu miewang zhi yuanyin' (The reasons for the extinction of India), *Zhejiangchao*, 1 (Feb. 1903), pp. 4-6.

[18] Feisheng, 'Eren zhi xingzhi' (The Russians' nature), *Zhejiangchao*, 1 (Feb. 1903), pp. 4-5, 2 (March 1903), pp. 77-9.

[19] Taosheng, 'Haishang de Meiren' (The Americans on the sea), *Zhejiangchao*, 6 (Aug. 1903), p. 2.

become coterminous in the symbolic universe of China's revolutionaries.

RACIAL DISCOURSE IN REPUBLICAN CHINA

The imperial reformers failed to secure the power necessary to implement their vision of change. However, the promotion of racial definitions of identity would become widespread after the fall of the Qing empire in 1911, a momentous political event which was marked by a number of important developments. First came the rapid transformation of the traditional gentry into powerful new élites, such as factory managers, bankers, lawyers, doctors, scientists, educators and journalists – the result of new economic opportunities created through contacts with foreign traders and the closer integration of the country into a global economy. The gradual emergence of new social formations was particularly pronounced in the large metropolises of the coast. Based on a common ground of social values, a sophisticated network of relations webbed intellectuals, urban notables and financial élites together into a modernising avant-garde. Secondly, with the collapse of the imperial system, neo-Confucian knowledge rapidly lost its credibility and authority. Previously imagined as a purposeful whole, a benevolent structure which could not exist independently from ethical forces, 'nature' was now conceptualised as a set of impersonal forces that could be objectively investigated. No longer were physical bodies thought to be linked to the cosmological foundations of the universe: bodies were produced by biological laws inherent in 'nature'. With the decline of conformity to the moral imperatives enshrined in a canon of Confucian texts, a growing number of people believed 'truth' to be encoded in a nature which only science could decipher: identity, ancestry and meaning were buried deep inside the body. Embryology or genetics could establish differences between population groups, not philology or palaeography. Human biology replaced imperial cosmology as the epistemological foundation for social order. Thirdly, private printing houses, run by private associations of merchants, greatly profited from increased demand for new books and the general growth in literacy after the fall of the empire, and rapidly grew into huge publishing companies. The printed pages which poured forth from the vernacular press greatly facilitated the accessibility of new cultural modes to a larger public of consumers.

Shared consumption of cultural products which heralded the demise of 'primitive races' and the regeneration of the 'yellow race' contributed to the construction of imagined boundaries based on blood. The epistemic shift from cosmology to biology was particularly evident in studies in anthropometry, craniology and raciology. Racial categories of analysis were consolidated by endless references to science. Folk notions of biological discontinuity, of course, had long existed in popular culture. To this day, for instance, the Cantonese describe the Tanka, a population group of boat-dwellers in South China, as people with six toes on each foot: they are claimed to be of non-Han descent.[20] The small toenails of the Mongols are said by the Han to be cloven,[21] while minorities in Hainan have long been alleged to have a tail. A variety of cultural intermediaries – social reformers, professional writers, medical researchers, university professors – scientised these folk notions of common stock and legitimised racial discourse through appeals to the authority of science. Chen Yucang (1889-1947), director of the Medical College of Tongji University and a secretary to the Legislative Yuan, boldly postulated that cranial weight was the only indicator of the degree of civilisation: 'If we compare the cranial weights of different people, the civilised are somewhat heavier than the savages, and the Chinese brain is slightly heavier than the European brain.'[22] Liang Boqiang, in an oft-quoted study on the 'Chinese race' published in 1926, took the blood's 'index of agglutination' as an indicator of purity,[23] while the absence of body hair came to symbolise a biological boundary of the 'Chinese race' for a popular writer like Lin Yutang (1895-1976), who even proclaimed that 'On good authority from medical doctors, and from references in writing, one knows

---

[20] Barbara E. Ward, 'Varieties of the conscious model: The fishermen of South China' in Michael Banton (ed.), *The relevance of models for social anthropology*, London: Tavistock, 1965, p. 118.

[21] Naran Bilik, 'Mongols: Moral Authority, Nationality and Racial Metaphor', and Pang Kong-feng, 'The Structuration of Racism: Theory and Practice', papers presented at the International Conference on Racial Identities, Hong Kong, 25-26 November 1994.

[22] Chen Yucang, *Renti de yanjiu* (Research on the human body), Shanghai: Zhengzhong shuju, 1937, p.180.

[23] Liang Boqiang, 'Yixueshang Zhongguo minzu zhi yanjiu' (Medical research on the Chinese race), *Dongfang zazhi* (Eastern miscellany), no. 13 (July 1926), pp. 87-100.

that a perfectly bare *mons veneris* is not uncommon in Chinese women.'[24] Archaeologists, too, sought evidence of human beginnings in China. Like many of his contemporaries, Lin Yan cited the discovery of Peking Man at Zhoukoudian as evidence that the 'Chinese race' had existed on the soil of the Middle Kingdom since the earliest stage of civilisation. Excavations supported his hypotheses by demonstrating that migrations had taken place only within the empire. It was concluded that China was inhabited by 'the earth's most ancient original inhabitants'.[25]

If 'Chineseness' was thought to be rooted in every part of the body, cultural differences between groups of people were also claimed to be solidly grounded in nature, in particular in the case of Africans. The *Great Dictionary of Zoology* (1923), the first reference work of its kind, contended that the 'black race' had 'a rather long head, many protruding teeth and a quite low forehead, so that their face is inclined towards the back. This type of people have a shameful and inferior way of thinking, and have no capacity to shine in history.'[26] In a popular introduction to the 'human races of the world', professor Gu Shoubai wrote that black people could be recognised by their smell. They had a 'protruding jaw, very thick lips, a narrow forehead' and emitted an offensive stench.[27] Professor Gong Tingzhang claimed that even the slightest physical contact with a black person was enough for the olfactory organs to be repelled by an 'amazing stench'.[28] The presumed inferiority of African people was made to appear permanent and immutable through a discourse of race which firmly located social differences inside the body: the use of the term 'black slave race', common in China until the 1920s, most clearly expressed the conflation of social and racial differences. Chen Jianshan, the popular evolutionist, classified the 'black slave' with the chimpanzees, gorillas and Australians as a branch of

[24] Lin Yutang, *My country and my people*, New York: John Ray, 1935, p. 26.

[25] Lin Yan, *Zhongguo minzu de youlai* (Origins of the Chinese race), Shanghai: Yongxiang yinshuguan, 1947, p. 27.

[26] Du Yaquan et al. (eds), *Dongwuxue da cidian* (Great dictionary of zoology), Shanghai: Shangwu yinshuguan, 1927 (1st edn 1923), p. 15.

[27] Gu Shoubai, *Renleixue dayi* (Main points of anthropology), Shanghai: Shangwu yinshuguan, 1924, p. 51.

[28] Gong Tingzhang, *Renlei yu wenhua jinbu shi* (History of the progress of mankind and culture), Shanghai: Shangwu yinshuguan, 1926, pp. 1 and 55.

the propithecantropus.[29] A popular zoology textbook first published in 1916 included a paragraph on the differences between man and ape. The 'inferior races' (*liedeng zhongzu*) had a facial index similar to that of the orang-utan. The 'black slave' was classified in the gorilla branch, and Malays were represented as descendants of the orang-utan.[30]

Racialised senses of identity also permeated lower levels of education after the foundation of the Republic in 1911. The opening sentence of a chapter on 'human races' in a 1920 textbook for middle schools declared that 'among the world's races, there are strong and weak constitutions, there are black and white skins, there is hard and soft hair, there are superior and inferior cultures. A rapid overview shows that they are not of the same level.'[31] Even in primary schools, readings on racial politics became part of the curriculum: 'Mankind is divided into five races. The yellow and white races are relatively strong and intelligent. Because the other races are feeble and stupid, they are being exterminated by the white race. Only the yellow race competes with the white race. This is so-called evolution [...] Among the contemporary races that could be called superior, there are only the yellow and the white races. China is the yellow race.'[32] Although it is clear that individual writers, political groups and academic institutions had different ideas about the meanings of physical features, many people in China had come to identify themselves and others in terms of 'race' by the end of the Republican period. The success of racial discourse in China, in short, was the result of a significant degree of convergence between popular culture and officially sponsored discourses of race, of the scientisation of folk models of identity and of the reconfiguration of more stable notions of descent, lineage and genealogy.

[29] Chen Jianshan, 'Shi renlei' (Explaining mankind), *Minduo zazhi*, 5, no.1 (March 1924, p.7.

[30] Chen Darong, *Dongwu yu rensheng* (Animals and life), Shanghai: Shangwu yinshuguan, 1928 (1st edn 1916), pp. 8-13. The author thus echoed the 'polyphyletic theory' first expounded by Carl Vogt in 1865, in which he identified a different anthropoid ape with each human race; see Léon Poliakov, *Le mythe aryen. Essai sur les sources du racisme et des nationalismes*, Bruxelles: Editions Complexe, 1987, p. 316.

[31] Fu Yunsen, *Renwen dili* (Human geography), Shanghai: Shangwu yinshuguan, 1914, pp. 9-15.

[32] Léon Wieger, *Moralisme officiel des écoles, en 1920*, Hien-hien, 1921, p.180, original Chinese text.

Some isolated voices in China openly contested the existence
of a racial taxonomy in mankind: Zhang Junmai, for instance,
wisely excluded 'common blood' from his definition of the nation.[33]
Qi Sihe also criticised the use of racial categories of analysis in
China, and pointed out how 'race' was a declining notion in
the West.[34] Generally, however, racial discourse was a dominant
practice which cut across most political positions, from the fascist
core of the Guomindang to the communist theories of Li Dazhao.[35]
Its fundamental role in the construction of racialised boundaries
between Self and Other, its powerful appeal to a cultural sense
of belonging based on presumed immutable links of blood, its
authoritative worldview in which social differences could be explained in terms of stable biological laws, all these aspects provided
racial discourse with a singular resilience: it shaped the identity
of millions of people in Republican China, as it had done for
people in Europe and the United States.

Conflicting feelings of superiority and inferiority were part of
the racialisation of social encounters. As Hong Yuan observed
in 1930, 'Most of the [Chinese] people, however, continue to
think of our race as inherently superior to that of our neighbours
of lighter or darker skin. Indeed there is very often a set of
superiority and inferiority complexes stirring within those who
have constant or occasional contacts with foreigners. He constantly
persuades himself of his unexplainable superiority over the foreigner, but frequently has to rationalize in order to disperse the
inferiority complex'.[36] Racial classifications between different
population groups were so important that they often preceded
and shaped real social encounters. The poet Wen Yiduo, for
instance, sailed for the United States in 1922, but even on board
his courage ebbed away as he felt increasingly apprehensive of
racial discrimination in the West. In America he felt lonely and
homesick: he described himself as the 'Exiled Prisoner'. Wen
Yiduo wrote home: 'For a thoughtful young Chinese, the taste

---

[33] Zhang Junmai, *Minzu fuxing zhi xueshu jinchu* (The scientific foundations for national revival), Beijing: Zaishengshe, 1935, pp. 10, 22.

[34] Qi Sihe, 'Zhongzu yu minzu' (Race and nationality), *Yugong*, 7, nos 1-2-3 (April 1937), pp. 25-34.

[35] See Maurice Meisner, 'Class, nation, and race' in *Li Ta-chao and the origins of Chinese Marxism*, New York: Atheneum, 1970, pp. 188-94.

[36] Frederick Hung (Hong Yuan), 'Racial superiority and inferiority complex', *The China Critic*, 9 Jan. 1930, p. 29.

of life here in America is beyond description. When I return home for New Year, the year after next, I shall talk with you around the fire, I shall weep bitterly and shed tears to give vent to all the accumulated indignation. I have a nation, I have a - history and a culture of five thousand years: how can this be inferior to the Americans?'[37] His resentment against 'the West' cumulated in a poem entitled 'I am Chinese':

> *I am Chinese, I am Chinese,*
> *I am the divine blood of the Yellow Emperor,*
> *I came from the highest place in the world,*
> *Pamir is my ancestral place,*
> *My race is like the Yellow River,*
> *We flow down the Kunlun mountain slope,*
> *We flow across the Asian continent,*
> *From us have flowed exquisite customs.*
> *Mighty nation! Mighty nation.*[38]

It is undeniable that some Chinese students genuinely suffered from racial discrimination abroad, although undoubtedly an element of self-victimisation and self-humiliation entered into the composition of such feelings. More important, however, they often interpreted their social encounters abroad from a cultural repertoire which reinforced the racialisation of Others. Even social experiences that had the potential to destabilise their sense of identity were appropriated and integrated into a racial frame of reference. Pan Guangdan, the most outspoken proponent of eugenics in China, expressed his disappointment with the unwillingness of a book entitled *The American Negro*, edited by Donald Young in 1928, to speak in terms of racial inequality:

> But to be true to observable facts, in any given period of time sufficiently long for selection to take effect, races *as groups are* different, unequal, and there is no reason except one based upon sentiment why we cannot refer to them in terms of inferiority and superiority, when facts warrant us. It is to be suspected that the Jewish scholars, themselves belonging to

[37] Wen Yiduo, *Wen Yiduo quanji* (Complete works of Wen Yiduo), Hong Kong: Yuandong tushu gongsi, 1968, vol. 1, p. 40.

[38] Wen Yiduo, 'Wo shi Zhongguoren' (I am Chinese), *Xiandai pinglun*, 2, no. 33 (July 1925), pp. 136-7.

a racial group which has long been unjustly discriminated against, have unwittingly developed among themselves a defensive mechanism which is influencing their judgements on racial questions. The reviewer recalls with regret that during his students days [in the United States] he had estranged some of his best Jewish friends for his candid views on the point of racial inequality.[39]

Eugenic ideas, indeed, were also dominant among modernising élites in Republican China. Heredity, descent, sexual hygiene and race became the core themes of medical and eugenic discourses, which thrived on folk ideas of patrilineal descent. In their racialisation of the nation, the discourse of eugenics most clearly endowed the state with a responsibility in the production of a healthy population.[40] Although eugenics in China never achieved legislative expression, in contrast to other countries like the USA and Germany,[41] ideas of race improvement were eagerly appropriated and spread by the new medical professions. As a *Textbook of civic biology* (1924) for middle schools put it, 'the choice of a partner who is unfit harms society and the future of the race. To establish a strong country, it is necessary to have strong citizens. To have strong and healthy citizens, one cannot but implement eugenics. Eugenics eliminate inferior elements and foster people who are strong and healthy in body and mind.'[42] Proponents of eugenics claimed that breeding principles such as assortative mating and artificial selection could prevent further degeneration. Although modernising élites were instrumental in putting forward eugenic views, theories of race improvement circulated among a much wider audience in China. Cheap textbooks on heredity

[39] Pan Guangdan, review of Donald Young (ed.), *The American Negro* (1928) in *The China Critic*, 28 Aug. 1930, p. 838.

[40] The following is taken from Frank Dikötter, *Sex, culture and modernity in China: Medical science and the construction of sexual identities in the early Republican period*, London: C. Hurst; Honolulu: Hawaii University Press; Hong Kong University Press, 1995.

[41] D.J. Kevles, *In the name of eugenics: Genetics and the use of human heredity*, New York: Alfred Knopf, 1985; Michael Burleigh and Wolfgang Wippermann, *The racial state: Germany, 1933-1945*, Cambridge University Press, 1991; Robert N. Proctor, *Racial hygiene: Medicine under the Nazis*, Cambridge, MA: Harvard University Press, 1988; Paul J. Weindling, *Health, race and German politics between national unification and Nazism, 1870-1945*, Cambridge University Press, 1989.

[42] Wang Shoucheng, *Gongmin shengwuxue* (A textbook of civic biology), Shanghai: Shangwu yinshuguan, 1928 (1st edn 1924), p. 52.

and genetics explained to the public the dangers of racial degenera-tion. Primers, self-study manuals, pamphlets and 'ABC' intro-ductions to mainline eugenics were published throughout the 1920s. Hereditary principles, granting sex a biological responsibility for future generations, were thought to highlight further the need for social discipline. Mendelian laws were circulated by popular journalists and commercial writers to underline how genetic factors determined the endowment of an individual. Student magazines urged university students to undertake eugenic research for the sake of advancing the 'race', the state, and the individual.[43] In the 1930s, eugenic arguments became increasingly common in medical circles, 'degeneration' and 'racial hygiene' being the catchwords of the day. Official marriage guides encouraged 'su-perior' people to marry for the regeneration of the 'race',[44] since 'inferior' and 'weak' characteristics were transmitted through sexual congress; a popular guide for women published by the Commercial Press described hereditary diseases as the 'germs' which threatened the nation with degeneration and final extinction (*zhongzu zimie*).[45] Professor Yi Jiayue, a highly respected member of the academic community, made the forceful statement that 'if we want to strengthen the race, there is no time to waste. We should first implement a eugenic program. Strictly speaking, we should not just forbid the sexually diseased, the morons and the insane to marry. For those who abuse the sexual instinct and create a menace to future generations, there can be only one appropriate law of restraint: castration!'[46]

RACIALISED IDENTITIES IN CONTEMPORARY CHINA

Racial frames of reference never disappeared from the People's Republic of China, and have generally increased within popular culture, scientific circles and government publications in the Deng

[43] Wu Zhenzi, 'Women wei shenme yao yanjiu youshengxue' (Why we should study eugenics), *Xuesheng zazhi*, 15, no. 9 (Sept. 1928), pp. 31-6.

[44] For instance Ma Chonggan, *Jiehun zhidao* (Marriage guide), Shanghai: Qinfen shuju, 1931, pp. 11-12.

[45] Zhang Jixiu, *Funü zhuance* (Special handbook for women), Shanghai: Shangwu yinshuguan, 1937, pp. 52-61.

[46] Yi Jiayue, 'Zhongguo de xingyu jiaoyu wenti' (The problem of sex education in China), *Jiaoyu zazhi*, 15, no. 8. (Aug. 1923), p. 22160.

Xiaoping era. University students have been the social group most prominently involved in one of the more recent attempts to promote skin colour as a marker of social status. Physical attacks and demonstrations against African students on the university campuses of the People's Republic throughout the 1980s have been the most widely publicised feature of these racialised practices.[47] Far from being a manifestation of a vestigial form of xenophobia, these events are an intrinsic part of racialised trends of thought which have been diversely deployed in China since the end of the nineteenth century. Articulated in a distinct cultural site (university campuses) by a specific social group (university students) in the political context of the reforms initiated by Deng Xiaoping since 1978, campus racism demonstrates how contradictory discourses of 'race' and 'human rights' can be harnessed together in politicised oppositions to the state: six months after their mass demonstrations against Africans in Nanjing, students were occupying Tiananmen square in the name of 'democracy'.

Images of foreign sexuality have been important in the racialisation of encounters between African and Chinese students, and have played an even greater role in the spread of collective anxieties about sexually transmitted diseases (STDs).[48] On popular levels, the myth of 'international syphilis' (*guoji meidu*) has contrasted the pure blood of Chinese people to the polluted blood of outsiders, said to have become immune to syphilis after centuries of sexual promiscuity. Official discourse and popular culture have also explained AIDS as an evil from abroad, and prostitutes who offered their service to foreigners were singled out for severe punishment in the late 1980s. This official line of thought elicited a law on the mandatory testing of all foreign residents; African students in particular have been singled out for the AIDS test. From calls for the replacement of modern lavatories by Chinese-style toilets in the West, where excrement on toilet seats is claimed to be the main cause of AIDS, to pseudo-scientific studies of the 'Chinese

---

[47] See mini-symposium on 'Racism in China', including Frank Dikötter, 'Racial identities in China: Context and meaning', Barry Sautman, 'Anti-black racism in post-Mao China', Michael J. Sullivan, 'The 1988-89 Nanjing anti-African protests: Racial nationalism or national racism?' in *The China Quarterly*, no. 138 (June 1994), pp. 404-47.

[48] This section is taken from Frank Dikötter, 'A history of sexually transmitted diseases in China' in Scott Bamber, Milton Lewis and Michael Waugh (eds), *A history of sexually transmitted diseases and HIV/AIDS in Asia and the Pacific*, Westport, CT: Greenwood Press, 1997, pp. 67-84.

immune system' (thought to be inherently superior to the damaged bodies of Westerners), dubious theories of cultural and racial superiority articulated by highly prominent voices in the field of medical science have perpetuated a complacent attitude which does little to alert the population to the real dangers of infection. Instead of a virus which can potentially be contracted by every sexually active person, HIV/AIDS is represented as a fair retribution for sexual transgressions which mainly afflicts racial Others. In their racialisation of the disease, many of the publications on STDs produced by government circles and medical institutions carry images of white and black AIDS sufferers; they interpret gay demonstrations in America as a sign of the imminent collapse of 'Western capitalist society'. 'Primitive societies' in Africa are also criticised for their lack of moral fibre, in contrast to the virtues of socialism with Chinese characteristics.

Beyond the popularisation of racial discourse in information pamphlets on STDs, medical circles have also been instrumental in the promotion of a eugenics programme.[49] On 25 November 1988 the Standing Committee of the National People's Congress of Gansu Province passed the country's first law prohibiting 'mentally retarded people' form having children. Further laws for the improvement of the 'gene pool' have been enforced since June 1995: people with hereditary, venereal or reproductive disorders as well as severe mental illness or infectious diseases (often arbitrarily defined) are mandated to be sterilised, undergo abortions or remain celibate in order to prevent 'inferior births'. As Chen Muhua, Vice-President of the Standing Committee of the National People's Congress and President of the Women's Federation, declared a few years ago: 'Eugenics not only affects the success of the state and the prosperity of the race, but also the well-being of the people and social stability.' Although eugenic legislation in itself does not inevitably entail the promotion of racial categories of analysis, since it focuses on the genetic fitness of individuals within a country rather than between population groups, some publications in demography none the less make claims about the 'biological fitness' of the nation and herald the next century as an era to be dominated by 'biological competition' between the 'white

---

[49] For a more detailed analysis of eugenics in the PRC, see Frank Dikötter, *Imperfect conception: Medical knowledge, birth defects and eugenics in China*, London: Hurst (forthcoming).

race' and the 'yellow race'. The mastery of reproductive technologies and genetic engineering is seen as crucial in this future
battle of the genes, and the government has given much support
to medical research in human genetics. A research team was even
set up in November 1993 to isolate the quintessentially 'Chinese
genes' of the genetic code of human DNA.

Racial discourse, as has been illustrated by student demonstrations
against African students, has not been limited to officially sponsored
publications. Even opponents to the regime have been eager to
deploy racial categories of analysis as a unifying concept against
the threat of 'Western culture'. To take but one example, Yuan
Hongbing, a lawyer at Beijing University who was detained in
February 1994 and has become a well-known figure among dissidents, called for a 'new heroicism' in order to save 'the fate
of the race' and for a 'totalitarian' regime which would 'fuse
the weak, ignorant and selfish individuals of the race into a powerful
whole'. According to Yuan, only purification through blood and
fire would provide a solution to China's problems: 'On the battlefield of racial competition the most moving clarion call is the
concept of racial superiority.[...] Only the fresh blood of others
can prove the strength of one race.'[50]

However, scientists have contributed more than others to the
promotion of racial definitions of identity and difference. In their
scientisation of folk notions of patrilineage and descent, many
have represented Peking Man at Zhoukoudian as the 'ancestor'
of the 'mongoloid race'. A great number of hominid teeth, skull
fragments and fossil apes have been discovered from different
sites scattered over China since 1949, and these finds have been
used to support the view that the 'yellow race' today is in a
direct line of descent from its hominid ancestor in China. Although
palaeonthropologists in China acknowledge that the evidence from
fossil material discovered so far points at Africa as the birthplace
of mankind, highly regarded researchers like Jia Lanpo have
repeatedly underlined that man's real place of origin should be
located in East Asia. Wu Rukang, also one of the most respected
palaeoanthropologists in China, has come dangerously close to
upholding a polygenist thesis (the idea that mankind has different

[50] Yuan Hongbing, *Huangyuan feng* (Winds on the plain), Beijing: Xiandai chubanshe, 1990, p. 193, quoted in Geremie Barmé, 'To screw foreigners is patriotic: China's avant-garde nationalists', *China Journal*, 34 (July 1995), pp. 229-30.

origins) in mapping different geographical spaces for the 'yellow race' (China), the 'black race' (Africa) and the 'white race' (Europe): 'The fossils of homo sapiens discovered in China all prominently display the characteristics of the yellow race ... pointing at the continuous nature between them, the yellow race and contemporary Chinese people.'[51] Early hominids present in China since the early Middle Pleistocene (1 million years ago) are believed to be the basic stock from which all the national minorities in the PRC have ultimately emerged. Physical anthropologists have also invoked detailed craniological examinations to provide 'irrefutable evidence' about a continuity in development between early hominids and the 'modern mongoloid race',[52] and detailed studies of prehistoric fossil bones have been carried out to represent the nation's racial past as characterised by the gradual emergence of a Han population into which different minority groups would have merged.[53] As one close observer has noted, 'In the West, scientists treat the Chinese fossil evidence as part of the broad picture of human evolution worldwide; in China, it is part of national history – an ancient and fragmentary part, it is true, but none the less one that is called upon to promote a unifying concept of unique origin and continuity within the Chinese nation.'[54]

Serological studies of population groups defined as 'races' have also been carried out in the PRC. Mainly initiated by Professor Zhao Tongmao, estimations of genetic distance based on gene frequency are claimed to have established that the racial differences between population groups living within China – including Tibetans, Mongols and Uighurs – are comparatively small. Serologists have also observed that the 'Negroid race' and the 'Caucasian race' are closer related to each other than to the 'yellow

[51] Wu Rukang, *Guren leixue* (Palaeoanthropology), Beijing: Wenwu chubanshe, 1989, pp. 205-6; see also Wu Rukang, *Renlei de qiyuan he fazhan* (The origin and evolution of ancient man), Beijing: Kexue chubanshe, 1980.

[52] For instance Yang Qun, 'Kaoguxue yu renleixue' (Archaeology and anthropology) in Zhongguo renlei xuehui (eds), *Renleixue yanjiu* (Studies in anthropology), Beijing: Zhongguo shehui kexue chubanshe, 1987, pp. 288-302.

[53] See for instance Han Kangxin and Pan Qifeng, 'Gudai Zhongguo renzhong chengfen yanjiu' (Research into the racial composition of ancient China), *Kaogu xuebao*, no. 2 (Feb. 1984).

[54] John Reader, *Missing links: The hunt for earliest man*, London: Penguin Books, 1990, p. 111.

race'. Zhao Tongmao put the 'Han race' – represented as the
core group and ultimate point of reference – at the very centre
of his chart, which gradually branched out to include other minority
groups from China in a tree highlighting the genetic distance
between 'yellows' on the one hand and 'whites' and 'blacks'
on the other. A more detailed analysis of gene frequencies revealed
that the Uighurs might share some traits with Europeans but
were ultimately closer to the Han. The author also hypothesised
that the genetic differences within the 'yellow race' could be
divided into a 'northern' and a 'southern' variation, which might
even have different 'origins'. His conclusion underlined that the
Han were the main branch of all the different population groups
in China and that all the minority groups ultimately belonged
to the 'yellow race': the political boundaries of the PRC, in
other words, appeared to be founded on clear biological markers
of genetic distance.[55] The political implications of racial discourse
for minority groups in the PRC are clear in the government's
promotion of China as the 'homeland of the Modern Yellow
Race' (see for instance the Handbook on education in Chineseness
(1990) edited by Wu Jie). Even Outer Mongolia has recently
been portrayed as an 'organic and integral part' of the 'Chinese
race' in a propaganda book called The Inside Story of Outer Mongolia's
Independence.[56]

The missing link between ape and man – symbol of the
phylogenetic continuity between early hominids and the modern
'yellow race' – has also been claimed to exist in China.[57] Officially
sponsored research into the 'mystery of the wild man' became
particularly prominent after the reforms initiated by Deng Xiaoping
in 1978. A string of reports appeared about the 'wild man' (yeren)
from Shennongjia in Fang county, Hubei province, a place where

[55] Zhao Tongmao, Renlei xuexing yichunxue (Genetics of human blood groups), Beijing: Kexue chubanshe, 1987, pp. 351-71; see also Yuan Yida and Du Ruofu, 'Zhongguo shiqige minzu jian de yichuan juli de chubu yanjiu' (Preliminary investigation of the genetic distance between seventeen ethnic groups in China), Yichuan xuebao, 10, no. 5 (1983), pp. 398-405.

[56] William J.F. Jenner, 'Past and Present Political Futures for China', paper presented to the 19th National Conference of the Australian Institute of International Affairs, Sydney, 9 October 1993, p. 13.

[57] This section draws on Frank Dikötter, 'Hairy barbarians, furry primates and wild men: Medical science and cultural representations of hair in China' in Alf Hiltebeitel and Barbara Miller (eds), Hair in Asian cultures: Context and change, Albany, NY: State University of New York Press, 1997.

hairy creatures had been sighted since the Ming dynasty. However, where scattered mentions to hairy otherness had sufficed in imperial ideology, materialist philosophy demanded a full investigation. A China 'Wild Man' Research Society was founded in August 1981 with the support of highly regarded scientists such as anthropologist Wu Dingliang (Fudan University), palaeontologist Jia Lanpo (Chinese Academy of Science), biologist Qian Guozhen (Huadong Normal University) and medical expert Fang Zhongyou (Guangxi Hopital). The wild man was represented as the repository of a lost phylogeny, the 'missing link' between the ape and the human. Portrayed as the vessel of evolutionary traits which had disappeared with civilisation, the scientific analysis of the wild man's hair was thought to reveal prehistoric conditions of life. The findings of a tuft of brown hair in 1980 and remains of more than 3,000 'red hairs' of the 'wild man' from Shennongjia were scrutinised. A book entitled *On the trail of the 'wild man'* provided detailed comparisons of hair between apes and the wild man, whereas the Research Unit for Forensic Medicine of the Wuhan Hospital concluded that the wild man's hair was structurally comparable to human hair: 'We infer that the hair from these "wild men" could belong to an as yet unknown higher primate.' Contrasting 'primitiveness' to 'modernity', popular reports about the wild man became rife during the 1980s, such as a daily newspaper's article about a girl abducted by a wild man who later escaped back to 'civilisation' with her two shaggy children; in 1986, the *Science Evening Paper* even brought to the attention of the public a 'wild boy' coated in hair recently discovered near the Himalaya mountains and kept hidden in a military hospital of Shaanxi province as a living fossil.

In contrast to recent efforts made by some other governments, there is no indication that the hierarchies of power maintained through racial discourse are being contested in any significant way by the cultural centres of authority in China. Critical intellectuals in Hong Kong and Taiwan have also failed to address the issue. Bo Yang's indignant exclamation that 'Chinese racism is far more serious than American racism' remains no more than a gratuitous statement which is never followed by any effort at critical inquiry.[58] In Singapore too, racialised identities have been promoted by the government in the official conflation of notions of culture, ethnicity and race.[59] The desire to consolidate and expand a biologised notion of Chinese identity in mainland China and elsewhere may further be reinforced by the resurgence of overseas networks. Greater China, or the invention of a community that transcends the political boundaries of the People's Republic, can very well be based on the racialisation of 'Chineseness'.

Three conclusions might be drawn from this chapter. First, racialised identities are central, and not peripheral, to notions of identity in China: precisely because of the extreme diversity of religious practices, family structures, spoken languages and regional cultures of population groups that all define themselves as 'Chinese', ideologies of biological descent have emerged as powerful and cohesive forms of identity. Chineseness – in Taiwan, Singapore or mainland China – is primarily defined as a matter of blood and descent: one does not become Chinese like one becomes Swiss or Dutch, since cultural integration (language) or political adoption (passport) are both excluded. Racial discourse, of course, has undergone numerous permutations, reorientations and rearticulations since the end of the nineteenth century. Its flexibility and variability is part of its enduring appeal, as it constantly adapts to different political and social contexts, from the racial ideology of an economically successful city-state like Singapore to the eugenic policies of the communist party in mainland China. It is not suggested here that racialised senses of belonging were the only significant forms of identity available in China. However, it should be underlined that notions of culture, ethnicity and race have consistently been conflated throughout the twentieth century in efforts to portray cultural features as secondary to an imagined biological specificity. Secondly, this chapter has contended that racial discourse thrived largely thanks to, and not in spite of, folk models of identity, based on patrilineal descent

[58] Bo Yang, 'Zhongzu qishi' (Racial discrimination), *Choulou de Zhongguoren* (The ugly Chinese), Taibei: Linbai chubanshe, 1985, pp. 212-14.

[59] Chan Chee Khoon and Chee Heng Leng, 'Singapore 1984: Breeding for Big Brother' in Chan Chee Khoon and Chee Heng Leng, *Designer Genes: I.Q., ideology and biology*, Selangor: INSAN, 1984; John Clammer, 'Sociobiology and the politics of race: "Scientific" knowledge, theories of Chineseness and the management of pluralism in contemporary Singapore', Proceedings of an International Conference on Racial Identities in East Asia held in Hong Kong, 25-26 November 1995.

and common stock. Instead of crude generalisations about the role of 'the state' in the deployment of racial categories which would have been disseminated from top to bottom, or the popular 'cloud to dust' theory of cultural change, a degree of circularity, or reciprocal interaction, between popular culture and officially sponsored discourses of race has been proposed. More stable folk notions of patrilineal descent, which were widespread in late imperial China, were reconfigured from the late nineteenth century onwards. Scientised by cultural intermediaries, indigenous notions of identity were reinforced and enriched by the use of new vocabularies. Moreover, the suggestion that racial narratives inevitably entail a rupture with traditional cultural categories, as is all too common in dominant theories of nationalism, has also been questioned. Thirdly, this chapter has been highly critical of attempts to reduce the complexities of racial discourse in China to so-called 'Western influence'. In contrast to current theories of 'derivation' and 'cultural hegemony', it emphasises how racialised identities have been actively reconstructed and endowed with indigenous meanings that can hardly be explained as 'Westernisation'. Cultural intermediaries in China drew inspiration from foreign cultural repertoires, appropriated the language of science, indigenised notions of 'race', invested new ideas with native meanings, and finally invented their own versions of identity.

IMAGINING BOUNDARIES OF BLOOD

ZHANG BINGLIN AND THE INVENTION OF THE HAN 'RACE' IN MODERN CHINA

Kai-wing Chow

'China's population of one billion includes many nationalities. Over 90% of the population are Han.'[1] This is not only the official view of the People's Republic of China. It is in fact taken for granted by most Chinese that the largest nationality in China is *Hanzu*, literally meaning the 'Han race-lineage' or the 'Han nationality'.[2] Although divided by dialects, those who consider themselves Han Chinese have a sense of belonging to a group which shares more or less the same culture, a history and a vague sense of belonging to the 'yellow race'. They may also believe that they were all descendants of the Yellow Emperor, a mythic figure in the high antiquity of China. This belief in the existence of a huge population called the 'Han race-lineage' (*Hanzu*) or the 'Chinese nation' (*Zhonghua minzu*) is beginning to come under scrutiny as interest in the study of ethnic identities in anthropology and cultural theories spills over into the China field.[3] This chapter

---

[1] I would like to thank Frank Dikötter for his comments and corrections. I am also indebted to colleagues Patricia Ebrey and Kevin Doak for their comments and criticism. I would also like to thank the Center for East Asian and Pacific Studies for its support of this project. The opening statement on the Han given here appeared in Zhu Jiazhen, 'An outline of Chinese history' in Xue Muqiao (ed.), *Almanac of China's economy*, 1981, Beijing: Modern Cultural Company, 1982, p. 3.

[2] Whether the concept of 'ethnicity' is a suitable analytical tool in the study of Chinese history is open to debate, and Pamela Crossley cautions against the hasty adoption of the term 'ethnicity' in studying Chinese social history. P.K. Crossley, 'Thinking about ethnicity in early modern China', *Late Imperial China*, 11. no. 1 (June 1990), pp. 1-30.

[3] See for example the 'Symposium on Ethinicity in Qing China' in *Late Imperial China*, 11, no. 1 (June 1990).

34

is concerned not so much with how the notion of the 'Chinese nation' is defined as with the political, social and cultural origins of the clusters of meanings the concept has acquired. We are interested in the process whereby the constituent symbols of this collective identity were reconfigured and how they came to be accepted by people in China as both a subjective identity and a public symbol. The thought of Zhang Binglin (1869-1936) is the focal point of discussion, as he played a crucial role in constructing and popularising the major components of this new identity that he and the revolutionaries used against the Manchu government. While Zhang was not the only anti-Manchu radical in the wake of the abortive Hundred Days Reform in 1898, his single-mindedness and sharp pen gave shape to the critical discourse against the Manchu regime at a time when the constitutional and revolutionary movements began to separate.[4] As Young-tsu Wong aptly put it, 'If Sun Yatsen was first to advocate overthrowing the Manchu dynasty, Zhang first articulated an anti-Manchu ideology.'[5] Integral to this ideology was the idea that most inhabitants of China belonged to the same race – the Han race. Instead of looking for cultural explanations for the genesis and development of this notion, it can be argued that there were several historical factors contributing to its creation and popularity: the security policy of the Manchu court, the impact of indigenous lineage discourse and practice, and, most important, the debate between the reformists and the revolutionaries in the first decade of the twentieth century. These factors significantly shaped the manner in which Zhang Binglin constructed the notion of the 'Han race-lineage' (*Hanzhong* or *Hanzu*) as the power-welding people of the Chinese nation. The primordial belief in kinship provided the ideological basis for rejecting the culturalist theory of political legitimacy that the Manchu regime had appropriated.

No collective identities remain constant over time and all are contested, reinvented or abandoned. Group identities are imagined and often grounded in historical narratives, literature and myths. Symbols, objects and narratives are invented and appropriated from indigenous as well as foreign sources to articulate and represent

---

[4] Mary Backus Rankin, *Early Chinese revolutionaries: Radical intellectuals in Shanghai and Chekiang, 1902-1911*, Cambridge, MA: Harvard University Press, 1971, p. 56.

[5] Young-tsu Wong, *Search for modern nationalism: Zhang Binglin and revolutionary China, 1869-1936*, Oxford University Press, 1989, p. 61.

group identities. As we shall see, the terms 'Chinese nation' (*Zhong-hua minzu*) and 'Han race-lineage' (*Hanzu*) achieved relative seman-tic stability only after the Manchu regime was overthrown in 1911. Before the end of Manchu rule, the content and the uses of the terms were heatedly debated between the reformers and anti-Manchu revolutionaries.

THE POLITICS OF IMAGINING THE HAN RACE

The Western classification of human groups into different races was introduced into China in the late nineteenth century. Beginning with the early 1890s, the idea that the Chinese belonged to the 'yellow race' was popularised in missionary schools and publications. Charles Darwin's theory of evolution was introduced to China when Yan Fu published his translation of Thomas Huxley's *On Evolution* in 1898. In this translation, the dual meanings of race as lineage and race as type were readily grafted on to the Chinese term *zhong*. The nature of China's resistance to European encroach-ment was understood in terms of a social-Darwinian world view. China's struggle for survival against the European powers was conceptualised as the 'yellow race' competing against the 'white race'.[6] Darwin's ideas of survival of the fittest and natural selection gained popularity as Western learning spread from the city ports to inland cities through the rapid proliferation of reformist journals after 1895.

Zhang Binglin began his career as a political propagandist as a member of the reformist group under the leadership of Kang Youwei, and after 1895 was involved in the *Qiangxuehui* (Society for Learning of Power).[7] Before 1899, Zhang's characterisation of China's struggle against European powers was primarily based on the idea of war between the 'white' and 'yellow' 'races'. Even after his break with the reformist group over intellectual issues in April 1897, his conception of China's crisis did not change immediately.[8] As late as 1899, Zhang still focused his

---

[6] Evolutionary theories and racial thought of this period are analysed in much greater detail in Frank Dikötter, *The discourse of race in modern China*, London: Hurst; Stanford University Press, 1992, in particular chapters 3 and 4 ('Race as Lineage' and 'Race as Nation').

[7] Rankin, *Early revolutionaries*, p. 53.

[8] Jiang Yihua, *Zhang Taiyan sixiang yanjiu* (A study of the thought of Zhang Binglin), Beijing: Renmin chubanshe, 1985, p. 48.

attention on the idea of 'peril of the yellow race'.[9] But the failure of the Hundred Days Reform of 1898 began to polarise political activists into reformists and revolutionaries.

Before that event there was no urgent need for a new corporate identity for the Chinese. But the failure of the Reform Movement and the debacle of the Boxer Uprising in 1900 created a new political situation. Frustration with China's inability to change fast enough to resist foreign aggression had shifted the focus of political discourse to the debate between the reformist supporters of the Manchu regime and the anti-Manchu revolutionaries. For the revolutionaries, the notion of 'race war' was no longer adequate to mobilise a new political struggle against the Manchu government, because the idea of 'yellow race' included the Manchus. The internal conflict between the Manchu court and the revolutionaries demanded a new collective identity narrow enough to exclude the Manchus from the we-group.

The articles contributed by Zhang Binglin to the *Qingyibao* throughout most of the 1890s were reformist in character and showed no explicit hostility towards the Manchu government. In 1897 he explicitly rejected revolution as the solution to China's problem, as internal fighting would only undermine the struggle of the 'yellow race' against the 'white race'.[10] He was supportive of Kang Youwei and even defended him after the coup forced Kang to flee China.[11] But from 1898 onwards, he became increasingly hostile in his political writings towards the Manchus.[12] When he published the article 'On the Guest Emperor' (*Kedi lun*) in May 1899, his sense of alienation and loss of hope in the reformist movement under the leadership of the Manchus were made evident.[13] The title 'Guest emperor' clearly underlined his attempt

[9] In 1899, Zhang published 'Lun huangzhong zhi jianglai' (On the future of the yellow race); see Tang Zhijun, *Zhang Taiyan nianpu changbian* (A detailed chronological biography of Zhang Binglin), Beijing: Zhonghua shuju, 1979, p.105.

[10] Wang Fansen, *Zhang Taiyan de sixiang (1868-1919) ji qi dui ruxue chuantong de chongji* (Zhang Binglin's thought from 1868 to 1919 and his attack on the Confucian tradition), Taibei: Shibao wenhua chuban shiye youxian gongsi, 1985, p. 73.

[11] Tang Zhijun (ed.), *Zhang Taiyan zhenglun xuanji* (Selected writings on politics by Zhang Binglin), vol. 1, Beijing: Zhonghua shuju, 1977, pp. 81-3, 96-7.

[12] In the first month of 1897, Zhang was still calling for reforms and opposed revolution. His anti-Manchu feelings became more pronounced in 1898. See Wang Fansen, *Zhang Taiyan*, pp. 72-4.

[13] In fact, his poems written even before the coup in 1898 already reveal his discontent with and alienation from the Manchu government. Wang Fansen, *Zhang Taiyan*, p. 73.

to redefine the we-group and highlight the historical origin of
the Manchus as the 'outsiders' – the alien 'barbarians' who had
conquered the Chinese people. His assertion that China had no
emperor during the entire period of the Manchu regime was
only one step away from his subsequent call for overthrowing
the Manchus.[14] The debacle of the Boxer Uprising only served
to deepen his concern over imperialist aggressions and his belief
that the Manchus not only failed to provide political leadership
but also stood in the way of China's attempt to build a strong
and modern state.

The publication of *Qiushu* (Book of persecution) in the second
month of 1900 marked the beginning of the public shift of Zhang
from Chinese resistance to European imperialism to overthrowing
the Manchu government.[15] The shift made the rhetoric contained
in the notion of 'race war' ineffective, because the identity of
the 'yellow race' could not be used to exclude the Manchus
who were also regarded as belonging to it. A new identity had
to be imagined to mobilise hatred against the Manchus. It had
to be narrow enough to exclude them and at the same time
be broad enough to integrate the Chinese population.

MOBILISATION OF INDIGENOUS SYMBOLIC RESOURCES

In his attempt to create a new corporate identity for the revolutionary cause, Zhang used indigenous concepts, images and values
– including lineage terminology, classical tradition, historical narratives – as well as newly-acquired knowledge of European social
and natural sciences. The Confucian classics were cited by both
the revolutionaries and reformists in support of their views. While
Kang Youwei depended on the *Gongyang* theory of history (found
in commentaries on the classic *Chunqiu* (Spring and Autumn
Annals), a chronological history of the period 722-481 BC) to
refute the revolutionaries' demand that the Manchus be expelled,
Zhang Binglin pointed to the teaching of the *Zuozhuan* (a different

[14] See the notes by Tang Zhijun, *Nianpu*, vol. 1, pp. 89-90.

[15] Zhu Weizheng thinks that the printing of the first edition of the *Qiushu* without the
appendix was done sometime between February and April of 1900. See Zhu Weizheng,
'Foreword' in Zhang Binglin, *Zhang Taiyan quanji* (Complete works of Zhang Binglin),
Shanghai: Renmin chubanshe, 1980, p. 6.

commentary on the Spring and Autumn Annals). Zhang Binglin was not only confronting the classical rhetoric of Kang Youwei; he was also presented with the difficult task of rejecting the deep-rooted culturalism in traditional political discourse. The theory of political legitimacy, justified in terms of an acceptance of Chinese culture, had been appropriated by the Manchu regime and was a powerful ideological weapon in the reformists' attack on the revolutionaries. To level an effective attack on the reformists' ideas and to challenge the legitimacy of the Manchu regime, Zhang Binglin and the revolutionaries had to combat culturalism with an equally widespread belief found within the Chinese tradition. The kinship bond provided an alternative that could be grafted on to the newly-introduced concept of race. The *Zuozhuan* provided a seemingly racist basis for Zhang's anti-Manchuism,[16] but this appeared inadequate for articulating Zhang's new understanding of a race war between Manchu and European 'barbarians' and a war between the Han and the Manchus.

The shift in the focus of political discourse from race war to the need to overthrow the Manchu regime required the use of different ties in order to create a new sense of identity. In Zhang's attempt to create a new Chinese identity that could be used against the Manchus and the culturalist ideology, he increasingly looked to the primordial values and lineage terminology of the Qing period.[17] He used the term *Hanzu*, meaning 'Han lineage-race'. From 1900 on, the rhetoric of Zhang's political writings shifted from race war to the struggle between the Han 'race' and the Manchu 'race'. Zhang sought to create and promote a Han 'racism' in order to undermine the reformists' ground for continued support of the Manchu regime. To be sure, the conceptualisation of the Manchus and the Chinese as 'Manchu people' (*Manren*) and 'Han people' (*Hanren*) had been a standard practice in the political language of the Qing regime. Both terms denoted no more than loosely related groups of people without specifying the nature of the bond as kinship.

[16] But the idea was that the 'barbarians' were not the same type (*lei*), and the focus of the statement was that as members of different social groups they had different allegiances and were therefore not reliable. It was the suspicion of infidelity or intrigue that was referred to in this statement. It has nothing to do with the idea of racial inferiority.

[17] For a similar analysis based on the writings of the 1898 reformers, see Dikötter, 'Race as Lineage', *Discourse of race*, pp. 61-96.

The importance of lineage discourse in academic circles and lineage practice in the Qing period cannot be overstressed.[18] In the first edition of the *Qiushu*, Zhang continued to use traditional terms to conceptualise the distinction between the Chinese and 'barbarians'.[19] What was notably new was the generous use of lineage terminology to articulate the power relationship between the Manchus and the Han Chinese. In these essays Zhang's anti-Manchu feelings were unmistakable; the language he used to delegitimise the Manchus was a subtle blending of established kinship practice and values. Lineages in China were based on the cult of ancestor worship.[20] As Ernest Renan had long ago remarked, 'Of all cults, that of the ancestors is the most legitimate, for ancestors have made us what we are.'[21] In his arguments against the Manchu government, Zhang used the metaphor of adopting an heir to continue a lineage. In the chapter on the origins of mankind, Zhang argued that the Han Chinese people were descendants of the Yellow Emperor (*Huangdi*) and should not be subject to oppression by other 'tribes' (*buzu*).[22] In another chapter he compared the alien Manchus to people who had usurped the heirship (*zongzi*) of the Chinese lineage.[23] Accepting the rule of the Manchus was similar to worshippers forgetting their 'great descent-line' (*dazong*) in the ancestral hall and adopting someone with a different surname as heir (*yi yixing wei hou*). The use of kinship language and the stress placed on kinship purity served to strengthen the notion of race as lineage. It is common to find rules in Qing genealogies against adopting a son from a different lineage-surname, which was condemned as contaminating the lineage (*luanzong*).[24]

---

[18] Kai-wing Chow, *The rise of Confucian ritualism in late imperial China: Ethics, Classics, and lineage discourse*, Stanford University Press, 1994.

[19] Zhang Binglin, 'Yuanren' in *Qiushu* (1st edn), repr. in Zhang, *Quanji*, pp. 21-4.

[20] For a discussion of how different forms of ancestor worship were closely related to different models of lineage organisations, see Chow, *Confucian ritualism*, chapter 4.

[21] Ernest Renan, 'What is a nation?' in Homi K. Bhabha (ed.), *Nation and narration*, London: Routledge, 1990, p. 19.

[22] Zhang Binglin, 'Yuanren' in *Qiushu* (1st edn), repr. in Zhang, *Quanji*, pp. 21-4.

[23] Zhang, *Quanji*, pp. 78-9.

[24] Taga Akigoro, *An ananlytic study of Chinese genealogical books*, Tokyo: The Toyo Bunko, 1960, pp. 529, 643, 699, 710, 715, 729, 751, 761.

DISTINGUISHING SURNAMES AND THE HAN 'RACE'

Zhang Binglin's quest for a way to exclude the Manchus from the new definition of the Chinese people as a Han 'race' again led him to lineage terminology. He created the term 'race-surname' (*zhongxing*), which could be used to exclude the Manchus from the Chinese.[25] The term is constituted by the two characters *zhong* and *xing*, which were perhaps intended to be the abbreviated forms of 'race-lineage' (*zhongzu*) and 'surname' (*xingshi*). When the *Qiushu* was first printed in 1900, the chapters entitled 'Lineage organisation' (*Zuzhi*), 'Origins of mankind' (*Yuanren*) and 'Making the Korean the emperor' (*Di Han*) contained the term 'race-surname'.[26] In the chapter entitled 'Origins of mankind', Zhang argued that although the Europeans and Americans belonged to the 'white race' (*baizhong*) and the Chinese to the 'yellow race' (*huangzhong*), both were 'intelligent races'. However, the comparison between 'yellow' and 'white races' was used to underline the notion that the Chinese were the most civilised. It was intolerable for the most civilised Chinese to subject themselves to the rule of a less civilised and different race, namely the Manchus.

In these chapters of the *Qiushu*, Zhang used the term 'race-surname' somewhat as a casual synonym of 'tribe' (*buzu*) and 'race-type' (*zhonglei*), and continued to conceptualise different peoples in terms of 'type' (*zhong* or *zhonglei*), 'clan-lineage' (*zu*) or 'race' (*zhongzu*). But in the second edition, which was probably printed several months later, there were two new chapters appended to the main text, one of which was entitled 'Distinguishing surnames' (*Bianshi*).[27] There is reason to believe that Zhang regarded this essay as being so important that it needed to be included in the new reprint to the *Qiushu*, even though he did not have enough time to reorganise the chapters. The significance of these appended essays lies in the importance placed on distinguishing surnames as a method of keeping an accurate record of descent purity. The significance of the essay on 'Distinguishing surnames' needs to be examined in the context of Zhang's growing anti-

---

[25] The term 'race-surname' (*zhongxing*) was used in 'Yuanren' and 'Bianshi', repr. in Zhang, *Quanji*, pp. 21, 110.

[26] Zhang, *Quanji*, pp. 6–7.

[27] According to the editors of Zhang Binglin's collected works, the second edition of the *Qiushu* with the two appendixes was printed sometime in the summer and autumn of 1900. Zhang, *Quanji*, p. 8.

Manchu sentiment and the subsequent debate with Kang Youwei and Liang Qichao.

The writing of this chapter coincided with Zhang Binglin's complete and open rejection of the Manchu government. On July 14, 1900, the allied foreign expeditionary forces seized Tianjin and prepared to advance on Beijing. Tang Caichang founded the Chinese Assembly (*Zhongguo yihui*) on July 29 in Shanghai and with other participants pledged support to the Guangxu emperor; Zhang attended the meeting but was critical of Tang's expression of loyalty. He sent a letter to the Chinese Assembly, requesting a ban on membership for Manchus and Mongols,[28] and on August 3 cut his queue before the participants of the Assembly to express his discontent with the loyalist clause.[29] His anti–Manchu stance drove him away from the reformists, with whom he found it necessary to debate in public about the attitude towards the Manchus.

Since the failure of the Hundred Days in 1898, Liang Qichao had continued to call for reform under the Manchu regime. As soon as he arrived in Japan, he and Kang Youwei, with the support of Chinese merchants, founded the *Qingyibao* in which they continued to publish their political views.[30] One of the issues the reformists underscored was the need for the Manchu court to abandon discriminatory policies against the Han Chinese.[31] In 1900 Liang Qichao published a long essay in the *Qingyibao* explaining China's weaknesses; he exonerated the Manchus from China's plight and rejected an anti–Manchu revolution. In response to Liang's essay, Zhang wrote a piece entitled 'Correct discourse on hatred for the Manchus' (*Zheng chou Man lun*) to explain his position, which he sent to the *Guominbao* (Citizen Journal) to be published in Tokyo. He argued that the reason for expelling the Manchus from China was not so much the massacres of Chinese during their conquest in the mid-seventeenth century as the discriminatory policy they had subsequently pursued against

[28] Zhang claimed that the Mongols had evolved from dogs. In the Manchu government, the Mongols enjoyed better treatment than the Chinese. In fact, there was a separate chapter condemning the Mongols' conquest of China; see 'Menggu xingzui' (The rise and fall of the Mongols), Zhang, *Quanji*, pp. 21-4, 60-3.

[29] Jiang, *Zhang Taiyan*, pp. 139-40.

[30] Ibid., pp. 83-4.

[31] 'Ping Man Han zhi jie' (Eliminating the boundary between the Manchus and the Han), Jiang, *Zhang Taiyan*, pp. 84-5.

the Han. Considered inept and ignorant, the Manchu government was alleged to continue to kill talented and capable Han people. What the revolutionaries wanted, Zhang argued, was not a genocide. They were only interested in taking back the land and other property which the Manchus had confiscated from the Han people; the Manchus would be allowed to move back to Manchuria to continue living under their own regime. Therefore, the anti-Manchu revolution only called for expulsion of the Manchus, not their massacre.[32] Zhang clearly distinguished himself from other revolutionaries like Zhang Shizhao who advocated a genocide of the Manchus.[33]

In 1902, Kang Youwei published a letter he had sent to Chinese merchants in the United States criticising the revolutionaries' hostility to the Manchus. Kang explained that the Guangxu emperor had already taken some important measures to eliminate inequalities between the Manchus and the Han and, most important, the Manchus would change their surnames from multiple characters to a single character like most Han Chinese.[34] Kang's argument appealed to a deep-rooted sense of culturalism, defending the Manchu regime on the basis of its acceptance of Chinese culture. In the same letter, Kang Youwei targeted the revolutionaries' view that the Manchus should be expelled because they belonged to a different 'race' (*zhong*). He insisted that the Manchus and the Mongols belonged to the same 'race' as the Han. Since the Jin period, the emperor of the Northern Wei had adopted Han surnames and their descendants were scattered over China. Furthermore, those people in Fujian, Guangdong and Zhejiang were all Chinese. Since most of the 400 million people in China had Chinese surnames, it was impossible to distinguish Xia descendants from 'barbarians'.[35] Checking the genealogies would not be a

[32] Zhang Nan and Wang Renzhi (eds), *Xinhai geming qian shinian jian shilun xuanji* (Selected writings on current affairs in the decade before the 1911 revolution), vol. 1, part 1, Beijing: Sanlian shudian, 1960, pp. 94–9.

[33] Zhang Shizhao (1881–1973) was a student of Zhang Binglin at the Patriotic College. He became the editor of the *Subao* and began to call for the killing of 'all the Manchus' from June 1903 onwards. Zhang Shizhao, Zhang Binglin, Zou Rong and Zhang Ji were sworn brothers. See Kauko Laitinen, *Chinese nationalism in the late Qing dynasty: Zhang Binglin as an anti-Manchu propaganist*, London: Curzon Press, 1990, p. 91.

[34] Tang, *Nianpu*, vol. 1, p. 222.

[35] Tang Zhijun (ed.), *Kang Youwei zhenglun ji* (Collection of political essays by Kang Youwei), Beijing: Zhonghua shuju, 1981, vol. 1, pp. 487–8.

reliable method for clarifying racial boundaries. Zhang had already
noted that mixing up Han surnames with 'barbarian' ones
throughout a long period of time had gone a long way to confuse
the Han 'race' with 'barbarian races'. The changing of Manchu
surnames to single characters would make it impossible to distinguish Han people from the Manchus.

Zhang argued that the non-Chinese tribes that had mixed with
the Chinese were not the 'masters' and did not consciously fight
with the Chinese as a distinct 'race'. He pointed to the fact
that European countries and the United States allowed naturalisation
of foreigners as national subjects. But the Manchus could not
be considered to be 'naturalised' or 'transformed' Chinese because
they had continued to worship their own deities, wear the queue,
and speak and write their own language. Zhang subsequently
took up the issue of acculturation of the Manchus. For him,
the fact that they respected Confucius and Confucianism should
be taken not as evidence for their transformation into genuine
Chinese, but simply as a strategy for governing the Chinese and
keeping the people ignorant. If one were to speak of the two
as belonging to the same race, it was not that the Manchus were
turned into members of the Han 'race', but that the Han 'race'
was subsumed into the Manchu 'race'.[36]

As Patricia Ebrey points out, people in China have long acquired
the habit of thinking of people with the same surname as sharing
a common ancestry.[37] Their divergence over the Manchu issue
notwithstanding, both Kang Youwei and Zhang Binglin assumed
that surnames were markers of kinship ties. In Kang Youwei's
view, it would be impossible to clarify descent by surnames if
they could be adopted. For Zhang Binglin, pure descent groups
could be identified if the genealogical records were examined.
In fact, lineage rules in Qing genealogies used a similar terminology
of 'distinguishing lineages' (*bian zulei*) as a sanction against adopting
an heir from a different surname.[38] This shared assumption about
the relationship between kinship and surname is evidence for
the same cultural idiom that continued to inform the use of
the new term of 'Han race-lineage' (*Hanzu*) by both reformists

[36] Tang, *Zhenglun*, p. 195.

[37] Patricia Ebrey, 'Surnames and Han Chinese Identity' (forthcoming).

[38] Taka, *Genealogical books*, pp. 734-5, 755, 757.

and revolutionaries. Even when the constituent character *zu* had acquired the European sense of race as type, its usage as lineage often overshadowed other meanings when it came to the method of distinguishing races in China.

The single event that forced many intellectuals to take sides between reformism and revolution was the suppression in 1903 by the Manchu authorities[39] of the *Subao* (Jiangsu Journal) which had become the public forum for revolutionary writers since June of that year.[40] The Manchu court ordered the arrest of Zhang Binglin, Zou Rong and others who published anti-Manchu articles in the *Subao*.[41] Zhang chose to be captured at the risk of his life in order to show his commitment to the revolutionary cause. His arrest and trial in Shanghai the next year had aroused not only widespread sympathy but support for the revolutionary cause;[42] the publicity surrounding his arrest greatly enhanced his status as a major leader of the revolution. In a letter written in prison, he used the term 'Han race' (*Hanzhong*) to refer to all the Chinese who were not Manchus or Mongols.[43]

It was against the view of Kang Youwei that Zhang decided to elaborate his ideas in two chapters entitled 'Ordering races and surnames' (*Xu zhongxing*) (derived from the appendix entitled 'Distinguishing surnames', briefly discussed above) in the second edition of the *Qiushu* published in 1904.[44] Zhang's main goal was to identify Han surnames. In the first edition of the *Qiushu*, the chapter entitled 'Lineage organisation' (*Zuzhi*) showed how Zhang sought to integrate his knowledge of European theories

---

[39] In the entire radicalisation of the intellectuals in Shanghai and Zhejiang, the *Subao* case was not the only important event. But it probably was the one that brought Zhang and Zou Rong a national reputation as the most outspoken and committed revolutionaries. See Rankin, *Early revolutionaries*, pp. 49-50, 88-95.

[40] Rankin, *Early revolutionaries*, p. 70.

[41] As late as June 1903, the *Subao* still published articles by reformists; Rankin, *Early revolutionaries*, pp. 70-1.

[42] Jiang, *Zhang Taiyan*, pp. 192-212.

[43] *Subao*, 6 July 1903, repr. in Luo Jialun (ed.), *Zhonghua minguo shiliao congbian* (Collectanea of historical documents of the Guomindang), Taibei: Tangshi bianzuan weiyuanhui, 1968.

[44] Despite the signal position of the chapters 'Yuanren' and 'Xu zhongxing' in Zhang's *Qiushu*, they were buried among other chapters in the second edition. These two chapters were numbers 17 and 18 in the second edition (Zhang, *Quanji*, pp. 170-90). But when Zhang revised the *Qiushu* and published it with a new title, *Jianlun*, sometime in 1910, the three chapters were moved to the beginning. Their centrality to Zhang's theory of the Han Chinese race is fully established.

of race, genetics, sociology and evolutionary theory with his understanding of the struggle for survival of China. It was primarily
part of his attempt to apply foreign knowledge to the study of
Chinese kinship. There was no attempt to use Han surnames
as a way of excluding the Manchus. But in the chapter on surnames,
distinguishing kinship groups by surname emerged as his central
concern; here Zhang stressed the importance of keeping accurate
records of descent (surname groups) and lamented that records
of descent were corrupted and the lines of descent confused,
especially after the first emperor of the Ming dynasty ordered
the abandonment of 'barbarian' surnames. Once the barbarians
had adopted Chinese surnames, it was no longer possible to distinguish them. Zhang suggested that all the surname groups since
the Jin period be examined and distinguished so that the boundaries
between Chinese and Manchus be strictly established; once this
was done, 'it would be much easier to bring about change in
opinion and mobilise people to fight.'[45]

By appealing to the deep-rooted belief in the 'naturalness' of
kinship bonds and the widespread practice of participation in
lineage activities, Zhang hoped to mobilise the Han against the
Manchu regime. But localised lineages were bound to particular
interests in local society. In order to mobilise different descent
groups collectively against the Manchus, the revolutionaries had
to create a symbol capable of uniting all lineages into a mammoth
kinship group. They found such a symbol in the Yellow Emperor.

THE YELLOW EMPEROR AS THE FIRST ANCESTOR
OF THE HAN 'RACE'

Unlike racial theorists in nineteenth-century Europe, Chinese
revolutionaries did not always focus on grounding racial differences
in biology. It was not so much that the revolutionaries were
not interested in doing so, but few convincing physical differences
could be found between the Manchus and the Han. It is no
surprise then that they looked instead to myths of historical origin
to establish boundaries with which to differentiate 'races'. This
is particularly true of Zhang Binglin's approach. He realised the
importance of establishing the historicity of the Han 'race', which

---

[45] Zhang, *Quanji*, p. 110.

was much easier to achieve than methods of racial science commonly used in Europe. The approach he used was primarily historical and genealogical.

Zhang Binglin clearly pointed out that in modern times the distinction between 'races' was based not on the natural boundaries but on historical ones.[46] It was therefore an important part of his revolutionary rhetoric to provide a historical narrative for this particular view of 'races'. In the *Records of the Historian,* the ancient historian Sima Qian began his account of ancient history with the Yellow Emperor, leaving out the mythical 'Three Kings' (*sanhuang*). He also said that the Yellow Emperor had twenty-five sons, of whom only two had the same surname. He reconstructed the descent line of the Yellow Emperor, including all the important sage-kings.[47] The habit of tracing ancestry back to ancient historical figures, especially to the Yellow Emperor, had been deeply entrenched since Sima Qian's mythical account of the beginning of Chinese history.[48] Sima's ideas were still familiar to most scholars in the Qing period. It is important to note that these ideas were equally accessible to the reformists and the revolutionaries. For example, in his reformist writings, Kang Youwei attempted to apply Western knowledge to the study of Chinese kinship.[49] After arriving in Canada from Japan in early 1899 following the failure of the Hundred Days, he appealed on many occasions to the overseas Chinese for support of his loyalist effort to restore the Guangxu emperor. When he wrote a commemorative essay for a charity school in Victoria, he referred to the 400 million Chinese as the sons and grandsons of the Yellow Emperor (*Huangdi zisun*).[50] This manufactured cultural symbol also appealed to revolutionaries like Zhang Binglin, who argued that the Han Chinese were descendants of the Yellow Emperor.[51] The traditional élite's familiarity

---

[46] Wang, *Zhang Taiyan*, p. 71.

[47] Sima Qian, *Shiji* (Records of Historians), Beijing: Zhonghua shuju, 1973, *zhuan* 1.

[48] Ebrey, 'Surname'.

[49] Tang, *Kang Youwei*, pp. 230, 237-40.

[50] Ibid., p. 401.

[51] But Kang Youwei, in his *Kongzi gaizhi kao,* called into question the reliability of the Yellow Emperor as a historical figure. In the vein of the commentary on the *Book of rites by senior Dai (DaDai Liji),* he argued that statements were attributed to *Huangdi* by the Hundred School philosophers. See Wang Fansen, *Gushi bian yundong di xingqi: yige sixiangshi di fenxi* (The rise of debates on ancient history: An analysis in intellectual history), Taibei: Yunchen wenhua, 1987, p. 203.

with the Yellow Emperor and the chronology of ancient history
constructed by Sima Qian in support of this genealogy contributed
to the popularity of the idea that the Yellow Emperor was the
first ancestor of the Chinese 'race'.

There is a striking parallel in the ways in which the 'first
ancestor' of a lineage and the Yellow Emperor of the Chinese
race were conceived. Since the late Ming, it had become common
for different lineages with the same surname to 'join ancestors'
(*lianzong*) and establish fictive kinship ties through a famous historical figure.[52] To identify a fictive historical figure as the first
ancestor of a lineage became common practice in genealogical
writing in the Qing period. Each genealogy established a chronology and endowed the lineage with a historical background. In
a genealogy the entire descent group was traced back to the
first ancestor (*shizu*) and the scope of the lineage was defined
or delineated by all his descent lines.[53]

The entire Chinese population could be imagined as a collection
of lineages, since they all shared the same Han surnames. Like
the first ancestor of lineages, the Yellow Emperor came to be
hailed as the first ascendant of the Han lineage; members of the
Han race were represented as his sons and grandsons (*Huangdi
zisun*). In 1905 the revolutionary Song Jiaoren called himself 'one
descendant of the number ten surname of the Yellow Emperor'.[54]
In the preface he wrote for his planned 'History of the Invasion
by the Han Race-Lineage' (*Hanzu qinlüe shi*), he included all
the 450 million people living in China into the Han race-lineage.[55]

The idea of the Yellow Emperor as the 'first ancestor' of the
Chinese descent group was popularised in various revolutionary
journals. There is an illustration of the Yellow Emperor in the
collection of essays by revolutionaries entitled 'Spirit of the Yellow
Emperor' (*Huangdi hun*); he was given the title of 'First Ancestor
and National Founder of the Lineage-Race of the Middle Kingdom'
(*Zhongguo minzu kaiguo zhi shizu*). In the preface, the author
argued that the 'beginning of the branch [*pai*] of our race-lineage

---

[52] Gu Yanwu, *Rizhi lu* (Records of daily learning), Sibu beiyao edn.

[53] For a discussion of the debate over the scope of lineage as defined by the number of
generations of ancestors worshipped, see Chow, *Confucian ritualism*, chapter 4.

[54] Song Jiaoren, *Song Jiaoren ji* (Collected writings of Song Jiaoren), Beijing: Zhonghua
shuju, 1981, p. 2.

[55] Ibid., p. 3.

[*wu zhong*] can be traced back to the Yellow Emperor'. The author described himself as 'the purest yellow of the yellow progeny of the main core-line' (*Huangdi zisun zhi dipai Huang zhong huang*).[56] The redeployment of lineage terms such as *di pai* (branch of the core-line) and *shizu* (first ancestor) in a political discourse against the Manchus did not seem to be the result of a concerted effort on the part of the revolutionaries. Revolutionary ideas were disseminated not only in journals and books among urban educated people, they were spread through street talk, popular literature and drama.[57] Lineage terminology also abounded in propagandist literature. In Chen Tianhua's musical piece 'Courageous return' (*Meng huitou*), he used terms like 'founding patriarch' (*shizu gonggong*) and called the Chinese 'your sons and grandsons' (*ni de zisun*) or 'kin brothers' (*tongbao xiongdi*).[58]

Shifting the primordial tie of kinship and pseudo-kinship from the village level to a national level presented considerable difficulties. At the organisational level, the relatively parochial interests of localised lineages only served to divide rather than to integrate the entire population. But while there was almost no one from either camp who would appeal to the organisational strength of lineages for mobilisation, both the revolutionaries and reformists continued to redeploy lineage terminology in their debate about the new Chinese identity.

THE CHINESE AS A HAN 'RACE' AND A NATION

On 2 December 1906, addressing the supporters of the revolutionary course on the anniversary of the founding of the *Minbao* (People's Journal), the mouthpiece of the Tongmenghui, as 'my brothers of the Han race' and 'my 400 million brothers', Zhang Binglin read a eulogy of the Yellow Emperor, referring to him as 'our ancestor'. He concluded his speech by chanting: 'Long

[56] Luo Jialun (ed.), *Zhonghua minguo shiliao congbian* (Collectanea of historical documents of the Guomindang), Zhongguo Guomintang Zhongyang weiyuanhui, Taibei: Tangshi bianzuan weiyuanhui, 1968.

[57] Li Xiaoti, *Qingmo de xiaceng shehui qimeng yundong* (Lower class enlightenment in the late Qing period), Taibei: Institute of Modern History, Academia Sinica, 1992, pp. 125-34, 201-210.

[58] Quoted in Li, *Qingmo*, pp. 204-5.

live the *Minbao*! Long live the Han race!'[59]

Zhang Binglin put the finishing touch to the concept of 'Chinese people-state' (*Zhonghua minguo*) in an essay completed in 1907. Drawing upon his knowledge of Chinese philology, he pointed out that in one of the most respected dictionaries (the *Shuowen jiezi*), the 'people of the Middle Kingdom' (*Zhongguo ren*) were known as the Xia. He argued that the three terms Hua, Xia and Han denoted different aspects of the 'Chinese'. Hua referred to the land, while Xia and Han referred to the 'race'. By equating Xia and Han, Zhang was able to justify the term 'Han race' (*Hanzu*) and make it synonymous with the 'Chinese nation' (*Zhonghua minzu*). The term 'Chinese nation' therefore denoted both the 'racial-kinship' bond of the Chinese and their ties to the land. Zhang refuted the idea that the term *Zhonghua* only referred to an ethnic group sharing the same culture and that different races could become Han Chinese through accepting Chinese culture.[60] It should be noted that at the point when Zhang felt compelled to reject the reformists' culturalism, his 'racism' became more inflexible.

The creation of a racial identity excluding the Manchus was important because the Manchu rulers had promoted the idea that they and the Han were treated like members of the same family and the imperial court did not discriminate against the Han. For Zhang the Manchus' denial of the existence of any discrimination against the Han was a rhetorical device for perpetuating their oppression of the Han. It was precisely the political use of the denial of racial discrimination that compelled Zhang and the revolutionaries to expose the sustained discriminatory policy of the Manchus towards the Han. It was in opposition to the Manchus' oppression that he was determined to construct Han 'racism'; it was a weapon to delegitimise the Manchus. A new sense of identity as a race born of the same ancestor struggling to overthrow an alien Manchu race gained wider appeal in the second half of the first decade of the twentieth century.

---

[59] *Minbao* (People's journal), no. 10, pp. 81–82.

[60] Zhang Binglin, 'Zhonghua minguo jie' (Explaining *Zhonghua minguo*), *Xinmin congbao*, no. 15, repr. in Zhang and Wang, *Xinhai geming*, vol. 2, part 2, pp. 734–5.

The formation of the concept of a distinctive Han Chinese race originated in the political debate between reformists and revolutionaries in the first decade of the twentieth century. It drew conceptual components from indigenous as well as Western sources. The Manchu rulers, especially the Qianlong emperor, indirectly contributed to the formulation of the Han Chinese identity as they carefully and systematically constructed their own identity by compiling genealogies and maintained the Manchu language and customs. European notions of race could easily be grafted on to the indigenous kinship concept of *zu*. The peculiar term 'surname-race' (*zhongxing*) that Zhang Binglin chose to use as an alternative to 'race-lineage' (*zhongzu*) clearly reveals that the terms 'Han race-lineage' (*Hanzu*) and 'Chinese nation' (*Zhonghua minzu*) continued to connotate a patrilineal line of descent of a kinship group. The primordial meaning of *zu* continued to affect the way these terms were used and understood. The assumption that distinguishing surnames was a reliable method of tracing descent continued to influence the attempts of many scholars to study the Chinese as a race.

In the 1920s, the anthropologist Li Ji, in his quest to establish the purity of the Chinese race, also looked at surnames as an indication of blood-relationships. He also accepted the idea that the Han Chinese were the descendants of the Yellow Emperor.[61] The belief that the majority of inhabitants of China belong to the Han race is still taken for granted by most Chinese today.

Was Zhang Binglin a racist? (Benjamin Schwartz has called him a 'racialist'.[62]) There can be two answers to this question. As a political propagandist he was certainly a racist, deliberately constructing a Han racial identity and indulging in racist propaganda against the Manchu ruling class, but as an intellectual he was not. As Pamela Crossley has warned, his relationship with the Manchus has occasionally been oversimplified by historians.[63] When he spoke at the assembly celebrating the anniversary of the founding of the *Minbao* in 1906, he explained what he meant by 'nationalism' (*minzuzhuyi*): 'The most important point to know is that nationalism

---

[61] Dikötter, *Discourse of race*, p. 133.

[62] Benjamin Schwartz, *In search of wealth and power: Yen Fu and the West* Cambridge, MA: Harvard University Press, 1964, p. 184.

[63] P.K. Crossley, *Orphan warriors: Three generations and the end of the Qing world*, Princeton University Press, 1990, pp. 182-6.

does not mean the rejection of people of a different race. It means that no people of a different race are allowed to take away our government.'[64] In this sense Kauko Laitinen is correct to say that Zhang 'defined "races" not in terms of inherited physical and biological traits but in terms of history (i.e. in terms of power and culture): this was not racism in the modern sense of the word.'[65] Benedict Anderson has observed that racism and anti-semitism 'justify not so much foreign wars as domestic repression and domination'.[66] But for late Qing revolutionaries 'racism' was used against discrimination by the Manchus.

Finally, it is necessary to distance oneself from the rhetorical maze of the debate between the reformists and the revolutionaries, and return to 'current' idiomatic usage. Justification of discrimination can take many ideological forms. While the Manchus appropriated culturalism to justify their rule over the Han Chinese, they denied any crime of discrimination based on ethnicity. The persistent ethnic conflict between the Manchus and the Han Chinese exploded under unprecedented pressure from European encroachments. The reformists' appeal to a deep-rooted sense of culturalism in defence of the Manchu regime forced the revolutionaries to look for an ideological weapon that was powerful enough to overcome the strong tradition of culturalism. The introduction of European racial theories in the guise of scientific knowledge provided the timely coloration of modernity to an anti-Manchu racial ideology.

[64] *Minbao*, no. 10, pp. 83–4.

[65] Laitinen, *Chinese nationalism*, p. 94.

[66] Benedict Anderson, *Imagined communities*, London: Verso, 1983, p. 150.

YOUTAI

THE MYTH OF THE 'JEW' IN MODERN CHINA

Zhou Xun

While the prejudice against Jews has been regarded as 'a real and ongoing category in Western culture which is transmuted from age to age and from location to location', little attention has been paid to the myths of the 'Jew' and their impact in countries outside the West.[1] The present chapter draws on a wide variety of source material from the past two centuries to examine the images of the 'Jew' in China. However, what is of interest here is not the establishment of a boundary between the *real* and *fictional* aspects of these images. Rather, it is in the implications associated with the 'Jew' as a racialised Other who remains a distant mirror in the construction of the Self among various social groups in modern China.[2]

THE 'JEW' IN MODERN CHINA

In the same way as it is difficult to define the term 'Chinese' or 'Chineseness',[3] it is almost impossible to find a definition for the term 'Jew' or 'Jewishness'. As Sander Gilman rightly says,

[1] See Sander Gilman, *The Jew's body*, London and New York: Routledge, 1991, p. 5.

[2] This chapter is largely based on a Ph.D. dissertation currently being written under the supervision of Professor T.H. Barrett of the School of Oriental and African Studies (SOAS), University of London, and I thank him for his enormous help and encouragement over the years. I also thank Professor J. G. Feinberg of the United Medical and Dental Schools of Guy's and St Thomas' Hospitals, University of London, Ruth Herd of the University of Oxford and Lars Laamann of the British Library and SOAS, who read and commented on the present chapter. Finally, I am particularly grateful to Dr Frank Dikötter of SOAS, the editor of this volume; without his help, this chapter would not have been possible.

[3] For discussion, see the introduction to this volume by Frank Dikötter.

'It has been widely noted in the course of the twentieth century, from *fin-de-siècle* Vienna to Poland in the winter of 1990, that the label "Jew" could be applied to virtually anyone one wished to stigmatise whatever their religious, ethnic, or political identity or background.'[4] In China, definitions of the 'Jew' or 'Jewishness' are very complex. They are a symbol for money, deviousness and meanness; they can also represent poverty, trustworthiness and warmheartendness. It has religious as well as secular meanings. While it represents individualism, it also stands for a collective spirit. On the one hand it symbolises tradition, on the other hand it can equally invoke modernity. One day the 'Jew' is a stateless slave, another day the dominant power in the world. He is nationalist and at the same time cosmopolitan; he can be a filthy capitalist or an ardent communist, a committed revolutionary or a spineless loser. In other words, anything non-Chinese can be deemed Jewish, but anything Chinese is also Jewish; anything the Chinese need is Jewish, as is anything the Chinese despise.

By creating the 'Jew' as a homogeneous group, a constitutive outsider embodying all the negative as well as positive qualities which were feared or desired, various social groups in China were able to identify themselves as an integrated reference group – a homogeneous 'in-group', or in this case the 'Chinese'. These groups are able to project their own anxieties on to outsiders like the 'Jews'. The construction of the 'Jews' corresponds to a widespread fear of and need for an Other which can be found in many cultures and societies.[5]

THE EMERGENCE AND CONSTRUCTION OF THE 'JEW' AT THE TURN OF THE CENTURY (1895-1911)

Any attempt to determine when Chinese awareness of Jews as a different 'racial' group emerged would be arbitrary. The earliest record we have suggesting that Jews were considered different from the local Chinese is from the writings of the Jesuit missionary Matteo Ricci in 1605.[6] According to Ricci, the Jewish community

---

[4] Gilman, *The Jew's body*, p.6.

[5] For more readings on the subject of the Other, see Sander Gilman, *The Jewish self-hatred*, Baltimore, MD: John Hopkins University Press, 1986, pp. 1–21.

[6] Matteo Ricci, *Opere storiche del P. Matteo Ricci S.I.*, Macerata; Committato per le Onoranze Nazionali con prolegomeni note e tavole dal P. Pietro Tacchi-Venturi S.I., 2 vols, 1911-13,

in Kaifeng was referred to locally as the Blue Hat Muslims (*Lanmao Huihui*). It is evident that the term *Lanmao* was an outward mark which demarcated the Jews of Kaifeng from the local Chinese and Muslims. By contrast, *Huihui* in this context was a much more complex and perhaps more significant term, namely a Chinese term for Muslims which first appeared in the Yuan Dynasty (1279–1368) under Mongol rule. The nature of the term *Lanmao Huihui* indicates that in the sixteenth and seventeenth centuries, or perhaps earlier, the Kaifeng Jewish community was considered more closely related to the Muslims than to the local Chinese. However, by the middle of the nineteenth century these differences had become insignificant as the result of intermarriage and cultural assimilation. What was left to separate the so-called Jewish descendants in Kaifeng from other local Chinese was nothing more than fragments of Torah scrolls, prayer books, stone tablets and the faded memories of some members of the community.

Yet the fragmented nature of the Kaifeng community did not prevent some modernising élites in China at the turn of the century from constructing the 'Jew' as a racial group. For reformers like Liang Qichao (1873-1929) and Jiang Guanyun, the 'Jews' were an integral part of the new racial taxonomies they invented in order to represent the world as a collection of unequally endowed biological groups. Described as a 'historical race' (*you lishi de zhongzu*), the 'Jews' stood in symbolic contradistinction to the historical 'yellow race', as the reformers now referred to the Chinese. As early as 1903, Jiang Guanyun had already established the 'Jewish race' as a 'historical Caucasian race' descended from the Semites. The physical appearance of the 'Jewish race' (as well as other Semitic 'races') was imagined by Jiang to be characterised by an oval face, big eyes, thin lips and convex nose. In the following years, similar descriptions prevailed in representations of the 'Jew' in China.[7] In 1910, for instance, when Zhang Xiangwen, a historian and geographer, visited the assimilated 'Jewish' community in Kaifeng, he perpetuated these stereotypes by claiming that some of the 'Jewish' descendants had big noses

---

vol. 2, pp. 290-3.

[7] Jiang Guanyun, 'Zhongguo renzhong kao' (Inquiry into the Chinese race), *Xinmin congbao* (New people's journal), nos 40-1 (1903-4), pp. 4-5.

and deep eyes. He also claimed that one could still distinguish them by their 'Caucasian' physical features from genuine Chinese.[8]

Although these representations of the 'Jewish' race in China were actively constructed by Chinese intellectuals themselves, the language of anti-Semitism was appropriated from Western sources to reconfigure and legitimise indigenous racial discourse. The Christian missionaries in fact first introduced the image of the 'Jew' as the 'seed' of Abraham. According to many of their writings in Chinese, especially those of the Protestants since the mid-nineteenth century, people of the 'Jewish race', though dispersed throughout the world, were still bound together by a particular set of physical features:

> In London, New York, Paris, San Francisco and many other big cities, one can easily tell who is a Jew. [If one has a] look at the statue of Abraham, which was carved by an ancient Jew [or Jews] and was dug up a few years ago on the site of the ancient city of Nineveh, then [one] can immediately tell that the Jews of our time are the descendants of Abraham.[9]

From the mid-nineteenth century onwards, travel to the West also provided opportunities for Chinese intellectuals to encounter and appropriate the arguments of anti-Semitic discourse. In nineteenth-century Europe, evolutionary theories and racial anthropology provided anti-Semitic discourse with a pseudo-scientific legitimacy. At the same time, the 'Jew' also figured as a scapegoat in the socialist struggle against capitalism. The 'Jewish hatred' in medieval Europe, basically an expression of religious prejudice, shifted to struggles between the 'Aryan' race against the 'Semitic' race, the nationalists against the 'Jewish' outsiders, the socialists against the rich 'Jewish' capitalists. The 'Jew' was no longer portrayed only as the one who killed Christ or the leech who sucked the blood of the Christians: 'The perversity of the Jew's nature in betraying Christ over and over again throughout history becomes the biologically determined quality of the Jew which leads to the Jew's heartless role in the rise

[8] Zhang Xiangwen, 'Daliang fangbei ji' (A report on the visit to the stone tables in Kaifeng), *Nanyuan conggao* in *Contemporary Chinese Historical Documents Series,* no. 30, Wenhai shushe, vol. 1, n.d., p. 282.
[9] 'Lun Youtairen shanxun buyi benxing' (The unity and unchangeable character of the Jewish people), *Wanguo gongbao* (Globe magazine), 10: 306 (January, 1878).

of capitalism or communism.'[10] Thus, in the eyes of many anti-Semites in nineteenth-century Europe, the 'Jew' was 'born' to be a Rothschild dominating the world of finance and the stock markets, a Disraeli dominating the world of politics, or a revolutionary Marx fighting against established social order. Eventually the 'Jew' would take over the whole world and completely destroy the 'Aryan' culture so as to build a 'Jewish' empire on earth.[11]

However, in contrast to the attitudes of anti-Semites in Europe, Chinese intellectuals' envy of Jews was often mixed with curiosity and interest. Why should Jewish, not Chinese, culture dominate the world? Why should Judaism, not Confucianism, have been widely accepted as the guiding moral principle of human society? Why should a 'Jew', not a 'Chinese', be the richest man in the world? While such questions were asked, many modernising élites also attempted to prove that Chinese culture was still superior to the 'Jewish' culture. Thus it is not surprising to find that intellectuals such as Jiang Guanyun were very quick to translate the German assyriologist Friedrich Delitzsch's anti-Semitic work *Babel oder Bibel?* into Chinese.[12] Although Jiang himself was not exactly interested in either the so-called 'Biblical higher criticism' or anti-Semitism, Delitzsch's work served his purpose by demonstrating that the Mosaic law was not the world's oldest law code nor Hebrew culture the world's highest. Furthermore, Jiang remarked that the moral code of Confucius preceded Mosaic law.[13] On the other hand, Wang Tao (1828-97), an outstanding cultural intermediary who stood between tradition and modernity, was thrilled that an Eastern culture – Jewish culture or Judaism – should survive within Western culture. He used it as an example to prove to conservative scholars that they did not need to fear Western culture, because the Judaism which had survived and played an important role in the West had not managed very well at all in China. The assimilation of the Jewish community in China was powerful proof that Chinese culture was far superior

[10] Gilman, *The Jew's body*, p. 18.

[11] For a general study of anti-Semitism in nineteenth-century Europe, see Leon Poliakov, *The history of anti-Semitism*, Oxford University Press, 1965-75, 4 vols, vol. 4. For a more recent view, see Gilman, *The Jew's body* and *Jewish self-hatred*.

[12] It appeared as 'Shijie zuigu zhi fadian' (The oldest law code of the World), *Xinmin congbao*, 1901-3; see especially nos 33 and 43.

[13] Ibid.

to Jewish culture; therefore, it was still more superior to Western culture. Thus, according to Wang Tao, opening the door to the West would not destroy superior Chinese culture.[14]

The 'Jew' and money

In order to construct the 'Jews' as a 'race' with biologically specific features, Jiang Guanyun even traced the Western anti-Semitic image of the 'Jew' as financier back to its Semitic ancestry.[15] However, representations of the 'Jew' as a financier were not always perceived to be entirely negative. Xue Fucheng (1838-94), a diplomat who regarded the development of commercial industry as essential for China,[16] saw rich 'Jewish' financiers as a good illustration for his theory:

> England is one of the richest countries in the world, but the richest people in London are the Jews. Even the royal family of England cannot compete with the Jews. [...] Nowadays, no country dares to compete with the wealthy Jews; every country which wants large loans has to discuss it with the Jews, otherwise cannot be done. The Jews finally become the patrons for many national loans. No matter whether it is peace or war, prosperity or poverty, there is nothing on this earth including all the government secrets that the Jews do not know. They also have shares in every big bank in the world. Although one regards the English as good at commerce, they themselves admit that they cannot compete with the Jews. Thus the Jews are truly the most powerful people in the world.[17]

In other words, if China were as rich as the 'Jews', then it would be the most powerful nation in the world. Although China did not become rich, as Xue had wished, Chinese merchants overseas sometimes did. Ironically, the Chinese in Southeast Asia

---

[14] See Wang Tao, *Taoyuan chidu* (Essays of Wang Tao), version unknown, n.d., p. 86. For a further discussion of this point, see the first chapter of the present author's Ph.D. thesis, 'A History of the Chinese Understanding of Judaism'.

[15] Jiang Guanyun, 'Zhongguo renzhong kao', pp. 4-5.

[16] Xue Fucheng, *Chushi Ying Fa Yi Bi siguo riji* (Diaries of England, France, Italy and Belgium), Hunan: Yuelu shushe, 1985, pp. 82-3, 121-2, 132-3, 586. Also cf. the comments by Zhong Shuhe, ibid., pp. 33-9.

[17] Ibid., p. 793.

were sometimes disparaged early in the twentieth century as the 'Jews of the Orient'.[18]

The translation into Chinese of Charles Lamb's *Tales of Shakespeare* in 1904 was used to consolidate the image of the 'Jew' as a money-grabber still further. Among the reading public Shylock, the money-lender, became a stereotype of the 'Jew'. Furthermore, a number of historians even identified some commercial groups that had been engaged in money-lending in the Western regions of China in the past as Jews.[19]

The 'Jew' in 'racial' struggles

The dichotomy of Europeans into Aryan and Semitic 'races' inspired some Chinese abroad to manipulate the concept of 'Jews' as a useful weapon in their 'racial war' against the 'white race'. When Hong Jun, Xue Fucheng's contemporary and also a diplomat to Europe, was insulted by 'white' people of a Western church, he fought back by claiming that Jesus was a Jew with black hair and eyes like himself, therefore the 'whites' had no right to insult an Asian sharing descent with Jesus.[20] Shan Shili, one of the earliest Chinese female intellectuals who went to Europe, in her travel diary of 1910 passionately compared the anguish of the 'Jews' under the rule of the 'whites' with their freedom under the rule of the 'yellows' in Kaifeng. The division between 'Aryan' and 'Semitic' races was thus projected onto a more fundamental opposition between the 'white' and 'yellow' races. Shan even warned the Chinese that if they did not learn from the lessons of the 'Jewish race' they would not be able to win against the 'whites'.[21]

[18] Wachirawut (1910-25, son of Chulalongkorn of Siam), *The Jews of the Orient* (an anti-Chinese pamphlet), Siam, 1914, no other publication details. Cf. Benedict Anderson, *Imagined communities* (revised edn), London: Verso, 1992, pp. 100-1.

[19] Zhang Xingliang, 'Gudai Zhongguo yu Youtai zhi jiaotong' (Communications between China and Jews in antiquity) in *Zhongxi jiaotong shiliao huibian* (A collection of documents concerning communications between China and the West), Beiping: Furen University, 1930, vol. 4, pp. 4-20. See also Hong Jun, *Yuanshi yiwen zhengbu* (Supplement to the translation of the history of the Yuan dynasty), first completed and published in 1897, republished as part of *Guoxue jiben congshu* series, Shanghai: Shangwu yinshuguan, 2 vols, 1937, vol. 2, pp. 454-5. Tao Xisheng, 'Yuandai xiyu ji Youtairen de gaolidai yu toukou shoushuo' (The high-interest money lending and the poll-tax of the western regions of China in the Yuan dynasty and of the Jews), *Shihuo* (half monthly), 1, no. 7 (March 1935), pp. 54-5.

[20] Hong Jun, *Yuanshi*, p. 455.

[21] Shan Shili, *Guiqianji* (Travel in Europe), Changsha: Hunan renmin chubanshe, 1981, pp. 196-211.

The 'Jews' as a 'new people'

The myth of 'Jewish' power in the West had a great influence on Liang Qichao, one of the first reformers in the 1890s to propose a racialised world view. During his tour of North America, he pondered the question of the survival of the Chinese people. He saw the 'Jews' as an anti-image of the backwardness of the 'Chinese' and found them to be a perfect model for his call for a 'new people' (*xinmin*), or a collective nationalist spirit, which he believed to be essential to the progress and social well-being of China:

> Jews are the most powerful and influential group among the immigrants in America. I heard that four-tenths of the American banks and more than half the bankers in America are Jewish. [...] Jews completely control the local government of New York. No other group in the city can compete with their power. The situation is very similar in other big cities. [...] The reason that Jews can be so powerful is because they are very united. In this respect, no other races can compare with them. [...] In the modern era, Jews are the most famous people. For example, Disraeli, the former prime minister of England, was Jewish. [...] Schiff, the financial tycoon of New York, is Jewish. [...] And among all the famous people of the world as reported by New York's *Monthly Journal*, there were forty-eight Jews. [...] Alas! For thousands of years, Jews have been stateless. But they have survived as a race with enormous power, and they have also kept their own racial identity. By comparison, many other ancient peoples such as the Babylonians, Philistines, Greeks and Romans did not survive.[22]

Therefore, according to Liang, if the 'Chinese' race was going to survive, it must learn from the 'Jews' or, even better, become like the 'Jews' and control the world economy and global politics. Hence, the future of China was projected on to the myth of 'Jewish' power.

The 'stateless Jew'

With the rise of nationalism in China in the early twentieth

---

[22] Liang Qichao, 'Xindalu youji' (Travel diary of America), first published in *Xinmin congbao*, special supplement (1903), section 12, pp. 49-52.

century, some revolutionary thinkers represented the 'stateless Jew' as the imaginary prospect awaiting China. Articles on the pogroms in Russia began to appear in Chinese newspapers and journals after the Russo-Japanese war spread to the northeast of China in 1903. The Jewish problem, which was once completely un-known and uninteresting, now became of great relevance to Chinese nationalists. The lamentation of the 'stateless Jew' became a warning to the Chinese, and the 'Jewish race' was portrayed as an 'ugly race because they do not have a country',[23] which had deserved its inhuman treatment. While stirring up the fear of becoming like the 'stateless Jew', many Chinese nationalists reasoned: 'We are not like the Jews!' – their superiority was shown by the fact that they still had a country of their own. The argument went even further, with a strong anti-Jewish tone: the Jews deserved the awful situation in which they found themselves because they had no nationalist spirit or any sense of collective responsibility. They were portrayed as victims of materialism and individualism, whose love of money and personal happiness had finally got them into this terrible state. A huge loan to the Japanese by a Jewish financier in 1904 was seen by some Chinese as a bribe the 'Jews' had used to save themselves from the yoke of the Russians. The author of an article entitled 'The stateless Jews' made this negative comment: 'Because they are stateless even their money cannot save them.'[24] The writer's solution for the Chinese was to avoid emulating the 'Jews': if they loved money more than their country, the Chinese would end up stateless like the Jews. These nationalists further proclaimed that 'if [one] cannot protect one's country [*baoguo*], then one cannot preserve one's race [*baozhong*].'[25] Thus the 'Jews' were categorised as an 'inferior race' (*feizhong*).[26] In order to avoid being like the 'Jews' and to preserve the 'Chinese race', China had, before all else, to promote nationalism first.

[23] 'Eguo lüesha Youtairen' (The slaughter of the Jews in Russia), *Youxue yibian* (Study and translation), 9 (1903), p.93.

[24] 'Youtai yimin' (The stateless Jews), *Dongfang zazhi* (Eastern miscellany), 1, no. 4 (June 1904), p. 10.

[25] Ibid.

[26] 'Nuli yuexu' (On slaves), *Guomin riribao huibian* (National people's daily magazine), 4 (1904), p. 18. 'Eren lüesha Youtairen' (The slaughtering of the Jews by the Russians), *Jiangsu*, Tokyo, 4 (1903), p. 133.

REPRESENTATIONS OF THE 'JEW' IN THE EARLY REPUBLIC OF CHINA (1911-1930)

The 'Jew' as a 'nation'

With the fall of the Qing dynasty and the establishment of the Republic of China in 1911, racial nationalism was further encouraged by Sun Yatsen. In the eyes of Sun and his followers, nationalism was the sole generator of the rise and fall of any 'race'. Zionism was now perceived as the nationalist movement of the Jewish people, and it was thought that the nationalist spirit of Zionism is what held the 'Jewish race' together. While the so-called 'Jewish nationalist spirit' (*Youtai minzu jingshen*) became an inspiration for these Chinese nationalists,[27] the image of the 'ugly' and 'stateless Jew' evolved into one of a 'wonderful and historic nation'.[28] Just as they portrayed the so-called 'Han Chinese' as a pure biological entity, Sun and many of his contemporaries perceived the Jewish nation-race (*Youtai minzu*) as a homogeneous racial group characterised by common blood, language and culture. Since the 'Jews' were perceived as a nation with a common ancestor and a territory, Palestine was accepted by many Chinese nationalists as 'the national home of the Jewish people'.[29]

The 'Jews' as imperialists

Together with nationalism, the newly-founded Republic of China also provided the basis for growing anti-imperialism. The 'Jews' were sometimes portrayed as 'imperialists'. Chinese nationalists, like certain European nations, needed a scapegoat. Many of the articles on 'Jewish imperialism' were drawn from Japanese and Western sources. They followed the age-old anti-Semitic pattern by listing Jewish dominance in the world of finance, politics and the media, and conflated Freemasonry with Zionism, the Jewish plot to control the whole world. The 'Jews' were often

---

[27] Yin Qing, 'Minzu jingshen' (The national spirit), *Dongfang zazhi*, 16, no. 12 (Dec. 1919), p. 11. Also cf. Sun Yatsen, *Sanmin zhuyi* (The three people's principles), Shanghai: Shangwu shudian, 1927.

[28] See Sun Yatsen's letter to N.E.B. Ezra in 1920. A copy of this letter is now kept in the archives of the Hebrew University, Jerusalem.

[29] Discussed in detail in this author's Ph.D. thesis.

portrayed as the epitome of imperialism and the driving force
of evil in the capitalist world. In one article entitled 'The Jewish
empire',[30] the author declared: 'If one does not know the truth
about the Jews [Jewish imperialism], how could one say that
one understands the truth about the West [Western im-
perialism]?'[31]

By the end of the 1920s, the anti-imperialism campaign was
further intensified by Guomindang (GMD) members such as Dai
Jitao,[32] then the policy adviser for Chiang Kaishek and the GMD
government. Dai strongly believed that the main task of the GMD
should be to interpret and enforce Sun Yatsen's 'Three Principles
of the People'.[33] This meant securing China's international equality
and national liberty in order to fight against 'imperialism'. As
a result, Dai and his followers found the ideologies of French
nationalists such as Edouard Drumont and Charles Maurras, which
had strong anti-Semitic overtones, appealing and interesting.[34]
Zionism, which was portrayed by Drumont, Maurras and their
supporters as a destructive danger to France, thus became almost
comparable to the foreign danger, 'imperialism', which was feared
and fought against by these Chinese nationalists. Not only Zionism,
but also fascism, in its early years, was often conflated or equated
by these people with 'imperialism'. As with their misconceptions
about Zionism, they never really understood the nature of fascism.[35]
An article entitled 'Jews and Jewish ideology', translated from
a work by one of Maurras' supporters, appeared in 1929 side

[30] Qian Liu (transl.), 'Youtairen zhi diguo' (The Jewish empire), translated from Japanese, *Dongfang zazhi*, 8, no. 9 (Nov. 1911), pp.17-19.

[31] Ibid., p. 17.

[32] See Ke-wen Wang, 'The Kuomintang in transition: Ideology and factionalism in the "national revolution", 1924-1932', unpubl. Ph.D. thesis, University of Michigan, 1988.

[33] See Dai Jitao, *Guomin geming yu Zhongguo Guomindang* (The national revolution and the GMD of China), Shanghai: Dai Jitao's Office, 1925.

[34] Edouard Drumont was the president of La Jeunesse Nationale et Anti-Sémite and Charles Maurras was one of the founders of Action Française; both were prominent anti-Semitic organisations in France which arose in 1898 during the Dreyfus affair. See Leon Poliakov, *History of anti-Semitism*, vol. IV, part 1, section 2 and part 2, section 8.

[35] For a discussion of this question, see L.E. Eastman, 'Fascism in Guomindang China: The Blue Shirts', *The China Quarterly*, no. 49 (March 1972). Also cf. Maria Hsia Chang, *The Chinese Blue Shirt Society*, Institute of East Asia Studies, Berkeley: University of California, 1985; also W.F. Elkins, 'Fascism in China: The Blue Shirts Society', *Science and Society*, 33, no. 4 (1969), pp. 426-33.

by side with another article on the rise of fascism in Europe.[36]

THE 'JEWS' AND THE 'SCIENCE' OF RACE (1915-1949)

Although, as mentioned above, pseudo-scientific arguments in anti-Semitic discourse had reached China as early as the end of the last century, they were not widely explored till the New Cultural Movement in 1915. This movement emerged as a result of the demand for a new urban culture by the growing urban population. Many of the modernising élites, particularly the intellectuals (*zhishifenzi*) educated in Japan and the West, saw this as an opportunity to promote their newly-acquired 'Western' knowledge and to demolish the traditional Confucian heritage. Together with Western learning, the science of 'race' was introduced to a wider audience. However, the appropriation of the language of science was limited to the educated members of the reading public. While indigenous folk notions were revived through the selective use of new scientific vocabularies, elements of European anti-Semitic discourse were selectively introduced mainly to accommodate the ideas and anxieties of the intellectuals. For example, the circumcised penis, one of the most crucial marks of the Western image of the male 'Jew', was hardly mentioned by Chinese intellectuals, while they regarded the eagle-nose as the quintessential symbol of the 'money-loving Jew'. Blood, hair, colour, shape of face or nose and other phenotypical features were perceived by these intellectuals as indicating the racial distinctiveness of the 'Chinese' from the 'non-Chinese' and the more profound differences between 'superior' and 'inferior' races.

The 'Jew' as a superior race

If the 'Jewish' race could be classified as a branch of the 'white race', then, according to some intellectuals, it was also biologically 'superior', along with the 'yellow race' and in contrast with the

---

[36] Zhuochao, (transl.), 'Youtairen yu Youtaizhuyi' (The Jews and Jewishness), *Xin shengming* (New life), 2, no. 9 (1929). The original article was written in French by R. Lambelin, author of *Le règne d'Israel chez les Anglo-Saxons* (The reign of Israel over the Anglo-Saxons) and the French translator of *The protocols of the elders of Zion*. Also in the same issue, see Xiong Kangshen, 'Faxisidang de ducai zhengzhi' (The totalitarian politics of the fascists). *Xin Shengming* was one of the nationalist periodicals whose main purpose was to discuss and promote Sun Yatsen's 'Principles'.

inferior 'red', 'black' and 'brown' races. The image of the 'Jews' as a 'wonderful and historical nation' was further refined as a 'superior race' (*youxiu minzu*), and it was claimed that such superiority was manifested in the intellectual ability of the 'Jews'. Hu Shi, one of the leading figures of the New Culture Movement, also a celebrated scholar and philosopher of modern China, stereotyped the 'Jews' as an 'intellectual race' with impressive academic abilities and an adventurous spirit.[37] The need to create such a representation was obviously rooted in the anxiety over the backwardness of China and the belief, shared by many Chinese intellectuals of the New Culture Movement, that the intellectual class was the only hope for the reconstruction of their chaotic country. The reason why the 'Jews' were able to control world politics, world finance and the world in general was that the 'Jewish race', according to You Xiong, 'has intellectual gifts of quick understanding, rational thinking, good judgement, good organisation and fast action' and that they produced more superior lawyers, philosophers, thinkers, politicians, doctors, scientists, musicians and even chess players than any other race in the world.[38] Hence, in the same way that Liang Qichao had used the 'Jews' as an example in his call for a 'new people', intellectuals such as Yu Songhua also found in them a model for the restoration of the 'Chinese race':

> From antiquity to modern times, the Jewish race has produced many of the world's first-class geniuses. But in China, although a few [famous people] in history have attracted the admiration of the world, in modern times China has produced no talent able to compete internationally whether it be in academic, political or commercial life. How shameful we are when compared with the Jewish people, and what a disgrace to our ancestors.[39]

The contemporary backwardness of the 'Chinese' race, or more correctly the self-hatred and anxiety within these intellectuals them-

---

[37] Hu Shi, *Hu Shi koushu zizhuan* (An oral autobiography of Hu Shi), ed. by Tang Degang, Beijing: Wenhua chubanshe, 1989, p. 33.

[38] You Xiong, 'Youtai minzu zhi xianzhuang jiqi qianli' (The present situation of the Jewish race and its potential), *Dongfang zazhi*, 18, no. 12 (June 1921), p. 23.

[39] Yu Songhua, 'Youtairen yu Youtai fuxing yundong' (Jewish people and the Jewish renaissance movement), *Dongfang zazhi*, 24, no. 17 (Sept. 1927), p. 27.

selves, was explained as resulting from a lack of talent in China. However, this did not mean that the 'Chinese' race was inferior to the 'Jewish' race, since in the past China had also produced world-class geniuses. Another writer, Qian Zhixiu, was able to prove that although the 'Jewish' and the 'Chinese' races had very different characteristics, the latter shared all the advantages of the former, including intellectual ability. In conclusion, Qian proclaimed: 'the Chinese will be the Jews [world power] of the future' and 'China is the giant yet to be awakened.'[40]

The 'Jew' and eugenics

The pseudo-science of eugenics, or the myth of racial improvement through selective breeding, which became important in many countries in the 1920s and '30s, reached China at the turn of the century. Intermingled with traditional knowledge about selective breeding and 'prenatal education' (*taijiao*), it played a vital role in discussions of race among many Chinese intellectuals as well as revolutionaries. Since the New Culture Movement, it had been introduced to the reading public together with the science of 'race'. By the middle of the 1930s it had become a household word in China through the effort of the country's foremost eugenist Pan Guangdan (1898-1967),[41] who used the presumed superiority of the 'Jewish' race as an example of 'positive eugenics'.

According to Yu Songhua, a left-wing intellectual educated in Germany in the 1920s, the 'Jewish race' were eugenically the happiest race in the world because for generations they were constantly able to produce many of the world's best talents. Yu and many other intellectuals also compared Jewish civilisation with other great civilisations, such as those of Babylon, Greece, Rome, Spain and Turkey; while these had collapsed as a consequence of racial decrepitude, the Jews, though described as stateless, not only survived discrimination and persecutions for centuries, but also succeeded in maintaining the vitality of their

---

[40] Qian Zhixiu, 'Youtairen yu Zhongguoren' (The Jews and the Chinese), *Dongfang zazhi*, 8, no. 12 (June 1912), pp. 40-6.

[41] For a more detailed discussion of racial science and eugenics in Republican China, see Frank Dikötter, *The discourse of race in modern China*, London: Hurst, 1992, chapters 5 and 6.

race.[42] China, it was thought, had to tackle the issue of racial improvement and develop the ability to survive and progress like the 'Jewish' race.

Expanding on such a view, Pan Guangdan explained the 'Jewish' race's strong ability to survive as a consequence of their stock, strain, or breed (*xuetong*).[43] According to him, Yahweh was a family God and Judaism a tribal religion, hence worship of Yahweh and ancestor worship could not be separated. Pan therefore claimed that the 'Jewish' race emphasised transmission within the family, and 'it was regarded as the most unfortunate thing when one dies with no offspring to inherit the family name; in order to avoid such misfortune [...] the Jews have the tradition of marriage between widows and their brothers-in-law.'[44] Moreover, Pan praised the 'Jewish' race for its open attitude to sex. Hence, as Pan put it: 'At least in terms of members, the Jewish race will always survive.'[45] Pan also attributed the high quality of the Jewish race to good marriage traditions: 'These Talmudic traditions were the work of rabbis, the religious and intellectual leaders of the Jewish race; therefore, if a race has such outstanding people, then the standard of its marriage selection must be the highest. This is why the Jewish race has a very high IQ and it has produced many very intelligent people.'[46] Thus the 'Jewish' race became a positive testimony of Pan's concepts of eugenics, which underlined the inherent superiority of the intellectual class and exalted the family as the basic unit of the nation-race.

The 'Jew' as a product of racial discrimination

It would be an oversimplification to presume that all intellectuals in modern China articulated racial discourses in the same way. While many of them regarded the 'Jews' as one homogeneous

---

[42] Yu Songhua, 'Youtairen', pp. 25, 27; also cf. Chen Changheng and Zhou Jianren, *Jinhualun yu shanzhongxue* (Evolution and eugenics), Shanghai: Shangwu yinshuguan, 1925, 1st edn 1923, pp. 5-10.

[43] See Pan Guangdan, *Zhongguo zhi jiating wenti* (Problems of the Chinese family), Shanghai: Xinyue shudian, 1940, 1st edn 1928, pp. 316-18. Also, by the same author, 'Renwen xuanze – zongjiao zhi li' (Cultural selection –examples of religions), in *Yousheng yuanli* (Basic eugenics), *Guancha congshu*, Shanghai, 1939, first published in 1935 under the title *Zongjiao yu yousheng* (Religion and eugenics), Shanghai: Qingnian xiehui shuju, pp. 229-31.

[44] Pan Guangdan, *Yousheng yuanli*, p. 230.

[45] Ibid., p. 231.

[46] Ibid.

race, a few divergent voices such as He Ziheng and Wu Qinyou challenged such a view. In his article entitled 'The So-called Jewish People', He Ziheng used scientific methods and various statistics to undermine the idea of the 'Jewish race',[47] claiming that a large percentage of Jews in different countries did not have the so-called 'Semitic' nose, shape of head, deep dark eyes or black hair, and that 'no one can tell a Jew from an American or a European unless the Jews write the word "Jew" on their forehead.' He also dismissed the idea that all Jews shared 'common blood', merely pointing out that intermarriage between Jews and other 'races' had been common throughout history. He concluded that the 'Jews' were not a race but a product and victim of racial discrimination.[48]

But for many left-wing intellectuals of the 1930s, the representation of the 'Jews' as an oppressed people had a much more profound and symbolic implication in their struggle against the immediate enemy – the Japanese 'imperialists' – and their imagined outsider – the 'white' imperialists of the West. As Wu Qinyou put it: 'The significance of the Jewish people is not in whether they can be seen as a race or not, but in their common goal to unite together with all the oppressed people and to liberate the human race.'[49] The old dichotomy between the 'white' and 'yellow' race was reconstructed by merging the social notion of 'class' with the biological myth of 'race'. As the problem of 'race' was reconfigured into a question of 'class', the symbolic role of the 'Jew' was remodelled: 'the tears, blood and death of the Jewish people have awakened the oppressed Chinese.'[50] The oppressed 'Jews' had become the comrades of the oppressed 'Chinese' in their struggle against all oppressors.

---

[47] He Ziheng, 'Shijieshang you chuncuide minzu ma?' (Is there any pure race in the world?), *Xueshu jie* (The academic world), 1, no. 2 (Sept. 1943), pp. 12-6.

[48] Ibid., p. 16.

[49] Wu Qinyou, 'Youtai minzu wenti' (Problems regarding the Jewish race), *Xin Zhonghua zazhi* (New China miscellany), 4, no. 4 (Feb. 1936), p. 7.

[50] Li Zheng, 'Guanyu pai-You' (Regarding anti-Semitism), *Yibao zhoukan* (Translation weekly), 7 (Dec. 1938), p. 235.

ANTI-JEWISH POLICY IN JAPANESE-OCCUPIED CHINA (1937-1945)

Anti-Jewish policy was enforced by some of Japan's so-called 'Jewish experts' and the pro-Japanese parties in China after the Marco Polo Bridge incident on July 7, 1937. In the Japanese-occupied regions of China, a fair amount of anti-Semitic writings also began to appear.

In his recent book *Jews in the Japanese mind*, David Goodman has demonstrated that the Jewish myth had already appeared in Japan as early as the end of the last century.[51] However, the more immediate cause for the Japanese enforcement of an anti-Jewish policy in China was a pamphlet entitled *Der Kampf zwischen Juda und Japan* by Alfred Stoss, a retired German naval commander and an anti-Semite, which described the Jews as a dangerous threat to Japan, especially in China where the rich Jews in Shanghai were attempting to control Chiang Kaishek's nationalist party in order to fight the Japanese.[52] This work had obviously deepened Japan's concern with the 'mysterious Jew'. The influx of Jewish refugees from Nazi Germany into Shanghai since 1939 was also seen as a threat to Japanese control over the city.

To eliminate the purported 'Jewish threat' to the building of a 'Greater East Asia Co-prosperity Sphere', some of the Japanese 'Jewish experts' co-operated with President Wang Jingwei's pro-Japanese nationalist government and the Xinmin Hui (People's Renovation Society), a Japanese-controlled organisation based in Beijing which attempted to promote the 'Greater East Asia Co-Prosperity Sphere' ideology and to justify Japan's occupation in China.[53] Together they engaged in publishing anti-Semitic literature in China; their doing so may also have been an attempt to draw Chinese attention away from Japan's aggression. President

---

[51] David Goodman and Masanori Miyazawa, *Jews in the Japanese mind: The history and uses of a cultural stereotype*, New York: The Free Press, 1995; see also David Goodman's chapter in this book.

[52] *Youtai yu Riben zhi zhan* (The war between Jews and Japan), translated from Alfred Stoss's work in German entitled *Der Kampf zwischen Juda und Japan*, originally published in Munich in 1934. It was translated into Chinese and published by the Xinmin Hui after 1939.

[53] For a discussion on the Xinmin Hui see Akira Iriye, 'Towards a cultural order: The Hsin-min Hui (Xinmin Hui)' in A. Iriye (ed.), *The Chinese and the Japanese: Essays in political and cultural interactions*, Princeton University Press, 1980, pp. 254-74.

Wang Jingwei described the 'Jews' as the ancestors of all anarchists and communists:

> The Jews do not have a country of their own and therefore hate all nationalists; they lost their own culture and morality, so they detest all cultures and moralities; anarchism and communism are a product of this enmity.[54]

In early 1943, more than a year after Roosevelt – described as the 'puppet of the Jews' – declared war on Japan, the *Nanjing Republican Daily*, the official paper of Wang's puppet government, began to publish articles testifying to the 'Jewish danger' in China. An article entitled 'Jewish Imperialism in Shanghai' claimed:

> The modern history of the Jewish invasion of China began in 1832 when a group of Jews, headed by the Sassoon family and seconded by the East India Company, entered China to become involved in the opium trade. Soon these Jews, especially in Shanghai, built up an unshakable foundation in Chinese commercial business. However, they only engaged in illicit business and never brought any benefits to [Chinese] society; their names are associated with the opium trade, smuggling and the nefarious property business. They use their banks and similar organisations to obtain money by fraud, or they manipulate the stock market and use their lying skills to make huge profits [...]. A good example is provided by the Ravens of the American-Oriental Banking Corporation. Their actual leader is Starr, who has a Jewish father or mother and is a typical Jew. He first went to Japan in 1920 in the hope of making big money in the East, but because of the Japanese people's nationalist spirit and Japanese law, he was not able to exploit his innate skills and therefore came to Shanghai. After arriving in Shanghai, Starr got together with Raven. [...] He [Starr] opposes peace and supports Chongqing's [i.e. the GMD government's] terrorist activities, continuously trying to interfere in the harmony between China and Japan and create hatred between them and undo the achievements of the New Greater Asia Co-Prosperity Sphere.[55]

---

[54] *Nanjing minguo ribao* (Nanjing Republican Daily), Nanjing, 25 Feb. 1943.
[55] Ibid.

On March 15, 1943, after the Jewish refugees in Shanghai were forced into concentration camps, *Shanghai People's News,* a Japanese-controlled paper, began to publish articles to justify action. One article described these Jewish refugees as 'parasites':

> In the six years since they were kicked out of Europe and moved into Hongkou in Shanghai, they have clearly enjoyed a parasitic life here. [...] In recent years, in this happy land, the Jewish population has been multiplying like fleas. They use every chance to get their evil hands on this place. In the past, they controlled the commercial business and showed off on the stock market. Now they have even got their hands on the economic life in the slum areas. As long as they can make money, regardless of whether it is bad for the majority of citizens, they always try their best to get hold of it. This is the Jew's golden rule for survival.[56]

To justify the anti-Jewish policy further, the second half of the article stressed the evil characteristics of the 'Jews':

> Ordinarily the Jewish face looks miserable. The Jews hardly ever smile and, if they do, they are usually very bitter. However, when the Jews see money, their eyes suddenly open wide and a smile spreads across their faces. They can change their expression according to different circumstances and even the clowns in Beijing operas cannot imitate them. In business a Jew recognises only money, not people. As long as one pays money, he will do anything for it, even lose his dignity. [...] The Jews are always scheming and lying, and are indecent and avaricious pretenders. In their business, morality means nothing.[57]

Not only was the anti-Jewish policy in Germany justified by the evils of 'the Jews', but Japan's decision to follow that country's example was praised as a wise step forward:

> Although the Jews do not look very extraordinary from the outside, their ambitions are overwhelming. They are like

---

[56] 'Wuguo zhi min de lianpu: Youtairen zai Shanghai de jisheng quanmao' (The mask of the stateless people: The Jews' parasitic life in Shanghai), *Shanghai guomin xinwen* (Shanghai People's News), 15 March 1943.

[57] Ibid.

parasites – once they settle in a place, they reproduce wildly and suck everybody's blood. The European Jews are like this! The American Jews are like this! Now, the Jewish immigrants in China are also like this! That is why the Japanese army has to designate a restricted area [concentration camp] for the Jews. [...] The future settlement of the Jews in Shanghai must be dealt with urgently![58]

Although it is quite obvious that Japan attempted to project its sense of insecurity in occupied China on to the 'Jews' by constantly repeating the theme of 'Jewish imperialism', this certainly did not save that country from becoming the main target of a growing nationalist movement in China. In fact, the majority of Chinese at that time had never even heard the term 'Jew' and had no idea who they were. For most people in China the most immediate enemy was Japan. But it was also the case that before 1949, apart from a small number of intellectuals, nationalists and communists, hardly any Chinese were familiar with the term 'imperialist'. The closest approximation was *guizi,* which literally means 'devil' or 'devils'. However, while *guizi* has been used to refer to the Japanese, Americans, British and many others, it has never been used to refer to Jews.

OLD MYTHS AND NEW PHENOMENA, 1949-1995

With the official banishment of racial discourse by the Communist government after 1949, the myth of the 'Jew' seemed to lose its currency in China. However, the notion of 'race' did not disappear completely. For instance, Mao Zedong defined the nation as a distinct racial and cultural group, and it was in this way that Israel was seen in China to be the 'Jewish nation state': the old 'Jewish' race with its new country and new language. Like the left-wing intellectuals of the 1930s and '40s, Mao also conflated the notions of 'class' and 'race' into a vision of the struggle of the 'coloured people' against 'white imperialism'. China's political role in Afro-Asian solidarity from the 1960s onwards meant that the Jews in Israel, as the enemy of the oppressed Palestinians, could no longer be defined as oppressed people; they

[58] Ibid.

had now become 'the poisoned knife which the American imperialists have struck into the heart of Palestine'.[59]

After the death of Mao and the end of the Cultural Revolution
in 1976, the 'class' hatred between the 'Jewish' race in Israel
and the 'Chinese' people came to a close. However, the myth
of the 'Jew' in China did not cease to exist. On the contrary,
interest in the current state of Israel and the 'Jew' have reached
unprecedented levels since the 1980s. Professor Pan Guang, director
of the Centre of Israel and Judaic Studies in Shanghai, has commented that 'China's Jewish-Israel studies have reached a new
and exciting stage'.[60] However, the old myth of the 'Jew' continues
to distort the perceptions of many people in China. With the
appearance of a new market economy, particularly in cities like
Shanghai, the symbolic link between the 'Jew' and money has
emerged once again. While Shanghai eagerly welcomed 'Jewish'
investments from all over the world, Kaifeng, the city which
once had a small Jewish presence, went so far as to declare itself
a 'Jewish economic zone' in order to attract 'Jewish' money.[61]

China's recent interest in Jewish issues is not exclusively
economic. Especially since 1989, interest in Jewish studies is shown
by some intellectuals such as Zhang Shui to be a response to
efforts to reconfigure indigenous identities of race and nation.
As Zhang Shui has put it, 'In order to have a real deep understanding
of the vitality of Chinese culture, one must first study the interesting
anthropological fact that the Hebrew race, well known for its
immutability, was assimilated by the Han race and became Chinese-
Jewish descendants after entering China.'[62] The superiority of
the Han race and Chinese culture, it was claimed, seemed to
be manifested by the assimilation of the 'Jewish' race.

Such dubious studies are also encouraged in order to cover
up discrimination against so-called 'minority' groups. Thus, the
assimilation of the 'Jewish' community in China is portrayed by
scholars like Wu Zelin, a respected anthropologist, as demonstrating

[59] 'Mao Zedong sixiang shi Balesitan renmin de zhinan' (Mao Zedong's thought is the
compass for the Palestinian people), *Renmin ribao* (People's Daily), 16 May 1967, p. 5.

[60] Pan Guang, *The development of Jewish and Israel studies in China*, Occasional Papers of the
Harry S. Truman Research Institute, Hebrew University, Jerusalem, no. 2, 1992, p. 3.

[61] Li Li, 'The Jewish economic zone in Kaifeng', *Xianggang lianhebao* (United News [Hong
Kong]), 9 Jan. 1995.

[62] Zhang Shui, *Youtaijiao yu Zhongguo Kaifeng Youtairen* (Judaism and the Chinese Jews of
Kaifeng), Shanghai: Sanlian shudian, 1990, p. 1.

'the traditional magnanimity and tolerant spirit of the Chinese race, not only towards the Jewish people, but towards all other races. Therefore, [the Chinese race] always lives in harmony with all other races.' (In his youth, Wu himself described the 'Jews' as 'laughable, despicable, pitiable, admirable, enviable and hateful').[63] More recently, the so-called 'Jewish' descendants in Kaifeng have been given a monthly allowance by the Beijing authorities and freed from China's birth control policy.[64] The indications are that an entirely new 'Jewish' minority is about to be invented in mainland China.

[63] Wu Zelin, 'Preface' in Pan Guangdan, *Zhongguo jinle Youtairen de ruogan lishi wenti* (The Jews in China: A historical survey), Beijing: Beijing Daxue chubanshe, 1983, p. 11. Dikötter, *Discourse of Race*, p. 114.
[64] Li Li, 'The Jewish economic zone'.

MYTHS OF DESCENT, RACIAL NATIONALISM AND ETHNIC MINORITIES IN THE PEOPLE'S REPUBLIC OF CHINA

Barry Sautman

Although there is a long-standing myth that people in China form a homogeneous whole, referred to as the *Zhonghua minzu* ('Chinese nationality'),[1] 'racial' discourse is an extraordinarily sensitive issue. This sensitivity stems in part from immediate political concerns, such as the need to protect the claim that the issue of 'race' is dealt with more efficaciously in the PRC than in other states. For example, in 1988 the then-chief of the Chinese Communist Party (CCP), Zhao Ziyang, told a meeting on national unity that racial discrimination is common 'everywhere in the world except in China'.[2] Similarly, the head of the CCP in the Tibet Autonomous Region, Chen Kuiyuan, has pronounced that China's ethnic policies are more successful than those of other multi-ethnic societies.[3] While arguing that 'racial' problems are absent in its territory, the PRC government has called on the United Nations Commission on Human Rights to protect the

---

[1] See Sun Yatsen, *San min chu i; The three principles of the people*, Shanghai: Commercial Press, trans. by F. Price; ed. by L.T. Chen, 1927, reprinted, New York: DeCapo Press, 1975; Dru Gladney, 'Ethnic identity in China: The new politics of difference' in William Joseph (ed.), *China briefing*, Boulder: Westview Press, 1994, pp. 171-92.

[2] Andrew Roche, 'Chinese party chief says racism common everywhere but China', *Reuters*, 25 April 1988.

[3] Zhongguo guojia minwei (State Ethnic Affairs Commission of China), 'Development is the key for areas inhabited by minority nationalities – interviewing Chen Kuiyuan, Secretary of the Tibet Autonomous Region Chinese Communist Party Committee', *Renmin Ribao*, 10 Dec. 1993, p. 3, in British Broadcasting Corporation/Summary of World Broadcasts (*BBC/SWB*), 5 Jan. 1994.

rights of ethnic minorities elsewhere[4] and has denounced the rise
of racism and xenophobia in Europe and North America.[5]

Beyond the political implications of the claim that China has
solved all problems of 'race', sensitivity to the issue exists because
the myth of homogeneity postulates sharp biological and cultural
distinctions between people in China and most other peoples.
This myth is particularly manifest through a recent emphasis on
the purported common ancestry of China's different ethnic groups.
Several myths of origins focus on the common ancestry of the
Zhonghua minzu, in particular the myths of descent from the
dragon, from the Yellow Emperor and from Peking Man, all
of which contribute to the imaginary construction of China as
a homogeneous organic entity.

This essay analyses the promotion of biologised myths of descent
that underlie racial nationalism in the PRC. However, it argues
that racial nationalism in China serves mainly to reinforce the
prevalence of what is euphemistically called 'Great Han chauvinism'
(*da Hanzu zhuyi*). The construction of racial nationalism has
alienated important segments of ethnic minorities, undercuts the
effort to build Chinese state nationalism, and may ultimately jeop-
ardise the integrity of the state itself.

THE DRAGON AS PRIMAL ANCESTOR

From the mid-1980s onwards, the belated establishment of the
dragon as a totemic animal for all Chinese has been coupled
with the identification of 'Chineseness' as a set of physical characteristics. An attachment to the saurian symbol of Chinese
emperors is claimed as the common patrimony of all the people.
The Chinese are defined, in turn, in the words of Taiwan artist
Hou Dejian's popular song 'Descendants of the Dragon' (*Long
de chuanren*), by 'black eyes, black hair and yellow skin',[6] parameters
of Chineseness assigned not only by Hou, but by exiled 'democrats'
as well.[7]

[4] *Xinhua*, 'Envoy to UN conference on the "internal matter" of minorities protection', 14 Feb. 1995.

[5] *Xinhua*, 'Chinese delegate warns against new forms of racism', 6 Feb. 1995.

[6] James Tyson, 'Fiery symbol of Chinese culture comes into its own in the "Year of the Dragon"', *Christian Science Monitor*, 11 Jan. 1988, p. 7.

[7] See Berkeley Hudson, 'I asked myself whether I was wrong . . . . and whether Mao was

Morphological features, however, vary greatly and do not correspond to the stereotypes represented in 'Descendants of the Dragon'.[8] Moreover, despite claims by PRC writers that 'within the great family of the Chinese people, the Han and each minority group, almost without exception, are descendants of the dragon',[9] the dragon was never regarded as an ancestor symbol of all Han Chinese. Rather, it was considered to be the progenitor of ancient rulers only, such as Liu Bang, the Han dynasty is 'Great Ancestor' (*gaozu*), who claimed that his mother had conceived him after dreaming of a dragon. Indeed, from the Yuan dynasty onwards, common people were forbidden to associate themselves with the dragon in design and decoration.[10] The dragon symbol was reserved for the robes of the Emperor, princes and prime ministers, and a Dragon Flag was hoisted by the Qing dynasty only at the end of their reign, in imitation of foreign flags.[11]

The prohibition on the use of the dragon symbol by ordinary Chinese outlived dynastic China, and only since the 1970s have ordinary people begun to identify themselves with the dragon. For example, the preference for having a child during the Year of the Dragon, which recurs every twelve years in the lunar cycle, was not manifest before 1976 outside the PRC and before 1988 in mainland China. That preference 'is a new tradition of behaviour that the Chinese have only recently created'.[12]

To mark the fiftieth anniversary of the United Nations, the Chinese government presented a tripod decorated with fifty-six dragons, one for each officially-designated ethnic group in China, 'representing the Chinese nation as descendants of dragons'.[13] How-

---

wrong. I thought I was right. Chinese muckraker stirs up audience's opinions, memories', *Los Angeles Times*, 21 July 1988, p. 1; Ho Sheo Be, 'No core identity in Chinese culture', *Straits Times*, 8 May 1995, p. 9.

[8] James Shreeve, 'Erectus rising', *Discover*, 15, no. 9 (Sept. 1994), pp. 80-9.

[9] Zhang Ke, 'Gulaode Dongfang you yitiao long' (There was a dragon in the ancient east) in Zhang Ke (ed.), *Long* (Dragon), Guiyang: Guizhou renmin chubanshe, 1988, p. 3.

[10] Xu Naixiang *et al.* (eds), *Shuo long* (On the dragon), Beijing: Zijincheng chubanshe, 1987, pp. 4-19; Zhao Qiguang, 'Dragon: The symbol of China', *Oriental Art*, 38, (1991) pp. 71, 72-80.

[11] L. Newton Hayes, *The Chinese dragon*, Shanghai: Commercial Press, 1922, p. 62.

[12] Daniel Goodkind, 'Creating new traditions in modern Chinese populations: Aiming for birth in the year of the dragon', *Population and Development Review*, 17, no. 4 (Dec. 1991), p. 664.

[13] *Xinhua*, 'Bronze "century tripod" cast for United Nations', 6 Sept. 1995.

ever, myths of origins among China's ethnic minorities are not centred on the dragon, but include a variety of other animal progenitors, e.g. the wolf and the dog among Mongols;[14] the monkey among Tibetans;[15] the bear among Koreans, Ewenki and Oroqen;[16] the snake among the Gaoshan;[17] the cat among the Li;[18] and a dozen or more animals among Yi sub-ethnies.[19] Scholarly works about 'dragon culture' show that ethnic minorities have festivals and folktales in which dragons (and other animals) appear,[20] but none claims that any ethnic minority has a dragon totem.

Hou Dejian's song and its concept of common descent from a dragon have nonetheless taken on an official cast. The song has been praised for its patriotism,[21] performed on the popular New Year television programme,[22] and – despite Hou Dejian's expulsion from the PRC in 1989 – played in the background while a new Politburo Standing Committee was being introduced at the 14th CCP Congress.[23] The notion of the Chinese as descendants of the dragon, with forefathers who 'created five thousand years of China's brilliant civilisation', has even appeared in works that purport to provide a scientific account of human origins.[24]

---

[14] Francis Cleaves (ed.), *The secret history of the Mongols*, Cambridge, MA: Harvard University Press, 1982, p. 1.

[15] Bainqen, 'Bainqen further analyses causes and handling of Lhasa riots', Tibet Regional (Radio) Service in *BBC/SWB*, 12 Feb. 1988.

[16] Qin Guangguang, *Zhongguo shaoshu minzu zongjiao gailun* (Outline of Chinese ethnic minority religions), Beijing: Zhongyang Minzu Daxue chubanshe, 1988, pp. 9, 47, 55.

[17] Ma Yin, *China's minority nationalities*, Beijing: Foreign Language Press, 1989, p. 418.

[18] Qin, *Zhongguo shaoshu minzu*, p. 412.

[19] He Yuchua, 'Yizu de tuteng chongbai' (Totemic worship among the Yi ethnic group) in Song Enchang (ed.), *Zhongguo shaoshu minzu zongjia chubian* (First compilation of Chinese ethnic minority religions), Kunming: Yunnan renmin chubanshe, 1985, pp. 88-96.

[20] See Pang Jiang, *Ba qian nian Zhongguo long wenhua* (Eight thousand years of Chinese dragon culture), Beijing: Renmin ribao chubanshe, 1993, pp. 285-93; Ma Xiaoxing, *Long: Yizhong weiming de dongwu* (The dragon: A species of unexplained animal), Beijing: Huaxia chubanshe, 1995, pp. 104-5; Liu Zhixiong and Yang Jingcong, *Long yu Zhongguo wenhua* (The dragon and Chinese culture) Beijing: Renmin daxue chubanshe, 1992, p. 323.

[21] *Xinhua*, 'Northwest China Province Honours Yellow Emperor', 5 April 1980.

[22] *Xinhua*, 'Spring Festival TV Festival Focuses on National Unity', 24 Jan. 1984.

[23] Nicholas Kristof, 'Chinese shake up top party group', *New York Times*, 19 Oct. 1992, p. A1.

[24] See for instance Zhou Guoguang, *Ren zhi youlai* (The origins of man), Beijing: Zhongguo guoji changfan chubanshe, 1991, pp. 135-6.

THE YELLOW EMPEROR AS RACIAL FOUNDER

Coincident with the promotion of the myth of descent from the dragon, there has been a revival of the cult of the Yellow Emperor (Huang Di; purportedly born in 2704 BC). The status of this mythical emperor and founder of the first 'Chinese' state has been vigorously and officially elevated since the mid-1980s, and the cult was recently boosted further through the participation of CCP Politburo Standing Committee member Li Ruihuan in ceremonies honouring the 'first ancestor'.

The Yellow Emperor cult is centred on the notion that all Chinese are his descendants or, more properly, descendants of ancient rivals to the headship of state, the Yan (flame) emperor and Huang (yellow) emperor (*yan huang zi sun*). All Chinese, it is averred, 'are proud to be descendants of the Yellow Emperor'.[25] Proof of Chineseness through geneaological attestation of descent from the Yellow Emperor as 'father of the race' has a long history among Chinese families on the mainland and overseas.[26] There has also been a history of Chinese leaders invoking the image of the Yellow Emperor for nationalistic purposes. For example, Sun Yatsen, founder of the Republic of China, penned a sacrificial oration (*jiwen*) on the Yellow Emperor:

> China was founded 5,000 years ago,
> There the Yellow Emperor's name has been known since ancient times,
> He invented the compass-cart and suppressed the challenge of Chi You,
> Among the civilisations of the world, ours alone is the first.[27]

In 1937, to mark the establishment of the second United Front between the Guomindang and the CCP, both parties sent representatives to present sacrificial orations before the Yellow Emperor's tomb in Huangling county, Shaanxi province.[28] However, between 1949 and the 1980s veneration of the Yellow

[25] *Xinhua*, 'Hong Kong: Xinhua Hong Kong chief interviewed on Patten's proposals. Chinese diplomacy', 25 Jan. 1993.

[26] Lynn Pan, *Sons of the Yellow Emperor: A history of the Chinese diaspora*, Boston, MA: Little, Brown, 1990, pp. 10-11.

[27] Bai Ming and Li Yingke, *Huangdi yu huangdi ling* (The Yellow Emperor and his tomb), Xi'an: Xibei daxue chubanshe, 1990, p. 113.

[28] Ibid., p. 115.

Emperor was banned, while the tomb of Yan Di in Hunan province was severely damaged during the Cultural Revolution.[29] In the first thirty years of the PRC, not only were the Chinese no longer represented as the descendants of the Yellow Emperor and Yan Emperor, but the historical existence of these 'racial ancestors' was even doubted.[30] Indeed, scholars argued that these heroes merely symbolised gods, an argument well-supported by recent scholarship.[31] Until the mid-1980s, the Yellow Emperor and other rulers of his era were often portrayed unfavourably in works published in the PRC. One textbook noted that the function of early tribal state formations in the era of the putative Yellow Emperor was to protect the interests of noble tribal leaders by fighting other tribes and oppressing and exploiting slaves within them.[32]

However, in more recent years the state itself has taken steps to revive and reinforce the Yellow Emperor cult. His supposed tomb was declared by the State Administration of Museums and Archaeological Finds the 'number-one ancient tomb for protection by the state'.[33] Plans for its restoration were first mooted in 1987 and gradually expanded under provincial and then central government sponsorship.[34] While local ceremonies were conducted in the 1980s[35] and small-scale events are regularly staged for the benefit of non-mainland ethnic Chinese,[36] huge 'grand sacrificial rites' at the mausoleum on the occasion of the *Qingming* (Clear Brightness) remembrance festival are now increasingly attended

---

[29] Reuters, 'Chinese revive ancient imperial worship rite', 6 April 1993; *Xinhua*, 'Mausoleum of legendary founder of Chinese nation to reopen', 17 Feb. 1988.

[30] See Shang Yue, *Zhongguo lishi gangyao* (Outline of Chinese history), Beijing: Renmin chubanshe, 1954, pp. 4–5.

[31] Chang Kwang-chih, *Early Chinese civilization*, Cambridge, MA: Harvard Yenching Institute Monograph Series no. 23, 1976, p. 169; Zhao Jinliang, 'Shennong, Yandi he Huangdi kaobian' (Examination of the god of agriculture, Yandi and Huangdi), *Hunan Shifan Daxue shehui kexue xuebao* (Hunan Normal University Journal of Social Science), no. 2 (1995), pp. 171–92.

[32] Zhang Quanxi, *Zhongguo tongshi jianggao* (Lectures on the general history of China), Beijing: Beijing Daxue chubanshe, 1982, pp. 14–15.

[33] *Xinhua*, 'Mausoleum to be renovated next year', 11 Dec. 1991.

[34] *Xinhua*, 'Shaanxi restores Yellow Emperor's mausoleum', 5 March 1987; *Xinhua*, 'Magazine publishes emperor's tomb rebuilding plan', 13 March 1991.

[35] See e.g. *Xinhua*, 'Northwest China province honours Yellow Emperor', 4 April 1980; *Xinhua*, 'Qing Ming festival marked', 7 April 1981; *Xinhua*, 'Tomb of Yellow Emperor under repair', 27 July 1984.

[36] See e.g. *Xinhua*, 'Yanan tourism industry expanding', 12 Feb. 1995; *Xinhua*, 'Grand rite to be held at Yellow Emperor's mausoleum', 29 March 1995.

by senior officials and aimed at 'inspiring the national spirit'. In each succeeding year in the 1990s the celebrations have increased in size and been imbued with greater political prestige.[37]

In 1992 the *Qingming* rites for the Yellow Emperor were attended by some 1,000 'worshippers'.[38] In 1995, 5,000 representatives of different localities and organisations in China, with representatives of various overseas Chinese communities and 20,000 other participants, gathered at the mausoleum to pay homage after the renovation of the tomb had been completed at a cost of 4 million *yuan*.[39] A 'Yellow Emperor City' has been built in Hebei province, and Henan province has erected huge statues in the Yellow Emperor's honour. Hubei provincial officials have publicised that their territory was the home of Luozu, the Yellow Emperor's wife.[40]

The Yellow Emperor is extolled for early state leadership, his propagation of the 'Chinese race' through his twenty-five sons, and the assimilation into his Huaxia tribe of the peoples of the central plains.[41] He thus serves as a symbol of racial and state nationalism, an overlap reflected in the cult's official use: for example, Deng Xiaoping argued that the desire for the reunification of the mainland and Taiwan is innately 'rooted in the hearts of all descendants of the Yellow Emperor'.[42] A Chinese-American astronaut was acclaimed by PRC publications as 'the first descendant of the Yellow Emperor to travel in space'.[43] Overseas Chinese

[37] *Xinhua*, 'China: Memorial rite for Yellow Emperor', 5 April 1993; *Xinhua*, 'Scientist gives Hexian Ape-Man date', 7 April 1994; *Renmin Ribao*, 'Liang wan yu hai nei wai tongbao gongji huangdi ling' (Over twenty thousand compatriots from within and without the country pay public homage at the mausoleum of the Yellow Emperor), 6 April 1995, p. 1.

[38] *Xinhua*, 'Memorial ceremony for Yellow Emperor', 4 April 1992.

[39] *Renmin Ribao*, 'Liang wan yu hai nei wai tongbao gongji huangdi ling' (Over twenty thousand compatriots from within and without the country pay public homage at the mausoleum of the Yellow Emperor), 6 April 1995, p. 1.

[40] *Xinhua*, 'Henan to build statutes honouring mythical emperors', 22 April 1994; *Xinhua*, 'Birthplace of China's earliest empress discovered', 20 April 1995.

[41] Pan, *Sons of the Yellow Emperor*, p. 10; Ma Xinhua, '"Yan huang zisun" de chuanshuo shi zenmoyang chansheng de?' (How did the myth of 'descendants of the Yellow Emperor' come into being?) in Zhang Xiaoming (ed.), *Zhongguo lishi san bai ti* (Three hundred questions on Chinese history), Shanghai: Shanghai guji chubanshe, 1989, p. 25; Gao Zhanxiang *et al.* (eds), *Zhongguo wenhua da baike quanshu* (The great encyclopaedia of Chinese culture), 1, Changchun: Changchun chubanshe, 1994, pp. 664–5.

[42] *Xinhua*, 'Deng Xiaoping addresses national day ceremony', 1 Oct. 1984.

[43] Jim Mann, 'Reaction to shuttle loss a milestone for Chinese', *Los Angeles Times*, 7 Feb. 1986, p. 22.

scientists have been said to enjoy common interests that derive from their status as descendants of the Yellow Emperor.[44] All ethnic Chinese are thus supposed to be biologically attached to the Chinese state through their descent from the Yellow Emperor, and the Chinese state in turn takes cognisance of the bond among ethnic Chinese created by that common descent.

At times, the doctrine of descent from the Yellow Emperor is conflated with the myth of descent from the dragon,[45] as the leading writer on these ideas makes clear:

> Whoever is a descendant of the Yellow Emperor, no matter whether resident in the Chinese mainland or in Hong Kong, Macao, Taiwan or another part of the world, proudly recognises that the dragon is the symbol of China, that China is the land of the dragon and the Chinese people are the descendants of the dragon.[46]

Moreover, it has been asserted that the dragon and the Yellow Emperor are unifying symbols not only for Han Chinese but for all ethnic groups in China:

> The dragon and the phoenix are symbols of the descendants of the Yellow Emperor. Today their appearance is the result of a gradual evolution over thousands of years. They highly generalise the history of the formation and consolidation of Chinese ethnic groups. Their heads, eyes, scales, tails, claws, crowns, wings and feathers all exhibit signs of the totems of numerous tribes and abundantly manifest the integrative and attractive power of the blood and flesh relationship among Chinese ethnic groups.[47]

Yanhuang zisun refers to the Chinese nation, which is the world's most numerous and includes the Han, Man, Mongolian, Uighur, Hui, Tibetan, Yi, Miao, Yao, Bai, Zhuang, Tujia, Gaoshan and other ethnic groups, numbering more than fifty. [...] Because

[44] Ted Plakfer, 'Physicists bridge the gulf in relations', *South China Morning Post*, 7 Aug. 1995, p. 7.

[45] Li Xixing, *Huangdi ling yu long wenhua* (The Yellow Emperor and the culture of the dragon), Shanghai: Shanghai guji chubanshe, 1994.

[46] Zhang Ke, *Long*, p. 1.

[47] Wang Dayou, *Longfeng wenhua yuanliu* (Origins of dragon and phoenix culture), Beijing: Beijing gongyi meishu chubanshe, 1988, p. 1.

they all worship the emperors Yan and Huang, hence the name *yan huang zi sun*.[48]

It is well known, though not officially acknowledged, that the vast majority of Han Chinese regard only their own ethnic group, whether living in the PRC or elsewhere, as Chinese (*Zhongguo ren*) and hence descendants of the Yellow Emperor. Ethnic minorities who do not physically and culturally resemble the Han are not popularly viewed as authentically Chinese[49] or counted as fellow-descendants of the Yellow Emperor.

Intellectuals from ethnic minorities, including those who accept the parameters of state nationalism, contest the myth of the Yellow Emperor.[50] Some minority intellectuals may be part of ethnic groups that have their own myths of descent, for example from Chinggis Khan for Mongolians and the Chao Phaendin for the Dai.[51] Among the Uighurs or Tibetans, there is a consciousness of distinctive 'racial' and political histories[52] that precludes adherence to the Yellow Emperor myth.

With the resurrection of the ideal of a racially-based state,[53] through the myth of a Chinese people of the same 'race, blood and culture' – in the words of the dragon myth scholar He Xin[54] – myths of descent from the dragon and the Yellow Emperor are a basis for a racial nationalism that posits primal biological and cultural bonds among China's ethnic groups. These bonds, in turn, are thought to require a common adherence to state nationalism. Chinese are said not only to share a common ancestry but to also to derive from progenitors who, in distant eons long

---

[48] Ren Daobin *et al.* (eds), *Jianming Zhongguo gudai wenhua shi* (A concise dictionary of ancient Chinese cultural history), Beijing: Shumu wenxian chubanshe, 1990, pp. 2-3.

[49] Perry Link, 'China's "core" problem: ideology', *Daedelus*, 122, no. 2 (March 1993), p.195; Hsieh Shih-chung, 'On the dynamics of Tai/Dai-Lue ethnicity: An ethnohistorical analysis' in Stevan Harrell (ed.), *Cultural encounters on China's ethnic frontiers*, Seattle: University of Washington Press, 1994, pp. 315 fn. 13, 327.

[50] Cf. Wurling Borchigud, 'The impact of urban ethnic education of modern Mongolian ethnicity, 1949-1966' in Harrell, *Cultural encounters*, p. 279.

[51] Almaz Khan, 'Chinggis Khan: From imperial ancestor to ethnic hero' in Harrell, *Cultural encounters*, pp. 266-76; Hsieh Shih-chung, 'Tai/Dai-Lue ethnicity', pp. 303-7.

[52] Cf. Stevan Harrell, 'Introduction: Civilizing projects and the reaction to them' in Harrell, *Cultural encounters*, p. 33.

[53] See John Fitzgerald, 'The nationless state: The search for a nation in modern Chinese nationalism', *Australian Journal of Chinese Affairs*, no. 33 (Jan. 1995), pp. 84-90.

[54] 'Clouded Yellow', *Economist*, July 8, 1995, p. 31.

before the reign of the Yellow Emperor, separated themselves
out from non-East Asians and spread out from present-day southern
China to northeast Asia and beyond,[55] thus becoming what has
latterly been termed the 'core of the yellow race'.[56] Most renowned
among these putative progenitors is 'Peking Man'.

'PEKING MAN' AS CHINESE EVERYMAN

Chinese racial nationalism has also been promoted through the
popularisation of claims about 'Peking Man' (Beijing ren; sinanthropus
pekinensis) and other early hominids. Internationally, most
palaeoanthropologists advance an 'Out of Africa' or 'Garden of
Eden' hypothesis which postulates that homo erectus, the precursor
of homo sapiens, evolved in east Africa and spread out to Asia
as early as two million years ago. Much later – within the last
100,000 years – homo sapiens emerged, also in east Africa, and
replaced homo erectus throughout the Old World.

Most Chinese scholars reject this theory in favour of a polygenic
approach to human evolution.[57] They take the 'sinocentric' view
that the earliest humans did not originate in Africa but within
the borders of present-day China – according to the doyen of
Chinese archaeologists, Jia Lanpo, on the Qinghai-Tibet plateau[58]
or, in the view of other Chinese scholars, in present-day Guizhou
province.[59] After the discovery in 1995 of early anthropoid fossils
at Shanghuang, Jiangsu, the official Chinese media proclaimed
that 'simians, including the ancestors of humans, originated in
East Asia.'[60] It is asserted that the earliest progenitors of the Chinese
not only evolved from native Asian primates, such as ramapithecus,

---

[55] Fu Renyi, 'Dongbei diqu gurenlei huashi de faxian jiqi yiyi' (Discoveries of hominid fossils
in the northeast area and their significance), in Chen Guoqiang and Lin Jiahuang (eds), Dangdai
zhongguo renleixue (Contemporary Chinese anthropology) Shanghai: Sanlian shudian, 1991,
p. 155.

[56] See Frank Dikötter, 'Racial identities in China: Context and meaning', China Quarterly,
no. 138 (June 1994), pp. 411-12.

[57] Zhang Xingyong, Zhen Liang and Gao Feng, 'Zhongguo guyuan xinshu de jianli jiqi
renleixue yiyi' (The establishment of the genus of Chinese hominids and its anthropological
significance) in Chen Guoqiang and Lin Jiahuang, Renleixue, p. 170.

[58] Jia Lanpo, Early man in China, Beijing: Foreign Language Press, 1980, p. 3; Jia Lanpo and
Huang Weiwen, The story of Peking man: From archaeology to mystery, Beijing: Foreign Language
Press, 1990, pp. 240-4.

[59] Zhang Xingyong, 'Zhongguo guyuan', p. 159.

[60] Xinhua, 'Simians originate in Asia: Chinese scientists,' 14 Aug. 1995.

but became so detached from the development of humanity else-where that 'man developed independently in Asia' and different 'races' diverged at a very early date.[61] As early as several hundred thousand years ago, according to some official pronouncements, 'Chinese civilisation' appeared, emerging first in Inner Mongolia.[62]

Other scholars in China,[63] and a few elsewhere,[64] hold to a 'multi-regional evolution' or 'region continuity' model. This theory admits to an ultimately African ancestry for humanity, but argues that the Chinese are the product of one of several regionally distinct, parallel evolutions by already-differentiated ancestral popula-tions. In the Chinese case, descent is held to be from the most famous East Asian *homo erectus,* Peking Man, from whose remains, it is claimed, most information about *homo erectus* on a world scale is derived.[65] Separate evolution is said to have taken place in a context of regional morphological continuity through inbreeding and the early emergence of distinct 'Mongoloid' racial features.[66]

Typically 'Mongoloid' features are said to have already existed during the time of *homo erectus,* over one million years ago.[67] Internationally, however, the earliest date adduced for any 'Mongoloid' features among fossil remains found in China is in the late Pleistocene, among the early neo-anthropic *homo sapiens* who first emerged about 70,000 years ago.[68] Only some features of the key skull of the 'Upper Cave Man' (skull 101) found at Zhoukoudian, Hebei, and dated at about 16,900 years ago

[61] *Xinhua,* 'Complete fossil of Australopithecus found', 16 Nov. 1989; Wang Rukang, *Recent advances of Chinese paleoanthropology,* Hong Kong: University of Hong Kong Occasional Papers, 1982, p. 8.

[62] *Xinhua,* 'Inner Mongolia proved birthplace of Chinese civilization', 10 April 1989.

[63] Wu Rukang and Lin Shenglong, 'Peking Man', *Scientific American,* 248 (June 1983), pp. 86–94; Sun Yingmin and Li Youmo, *Zhongguo kaoguxue tonglun* (Introduction to Chinese archaeology), Kaifeng: Henan Daxue chubanshe, 1990, p. 52.

[64] Milford Wolpoff, 'Theories of modern human origins' in Gunter Brauer and Fred Smith (eds), *Continuity or replacement: Controversies in homo sapiens evolution,* Rotterdam: Balkema, 1992, pp. 25–64.

[65] Zhou Guoguang, *Ren zhi youlai* (The origins of man), Beijing: Zhongguo guoji changfan chubanshe, 1991, p. 128.

[66] Chris Jasper, 'Probing China's prehistory: The East–West clash over Asian origins', *Window* (Hong Kong), November 25, 1994, 34, pp. 32–7; Philip Habgood, 'The origin of anatomically modern humans in East Asia' in Brauer and Smith, *Continuity or replacement,* pp. 273–88.

[67] Zhou, *Ren zhi youlai,* pp. 132, 134.

[68] F.P. Lisowski, 'An overview of hominoid history and early humans in China', *Homo,* 33, no. 4 (1982), p. 254.

were deemed 'Mongoloid'.[69] Recently, scholars using multivariate statistical methods have compared the Zhoukoudian skull with recent 'Mongoloid' skulls and found no close affinities. They have concluded that 'a good insight into the racial structure of the Upper Paleolithic peoples [in China] is lacking'.[70]

The discovery of ancient human remains is consistently reported in the official Chinese media to support the theory of a separate evolution of the ancestors of the Chinese, the pre-historic existence of a Chinese nation and an 'East-West' duality dating back hundreds of thousands of years. For example, the discovery of a fossilised human skeleton, with 'typical Mongolian physical features' and dated at 28,000 years, in Lishui county, Hebei, in 1993 is said to 'cast doubt on popular views among anthropologists that the evolution of humans in East Asia stopped with *homo erectus* and that later *homo sapiens* migrated to Asia from Africa'.[71]

The same inference was drawn more strongly from a survey of the findings of Chinese archaeologists in recent decades. It is asserted that these have 'overthrown the conventional view that mankind originated in central and eastern Africa and later migrated to other areas of the world'.[72] The abundance of complete sets of 'ape man' fossils found in China is held to establish China's rank as 'one of the world's ancient nations'.[73] It is thereby implied that early hominids living in what is now China were already part of a Chinese nation; indeed, there has been discussion of the 'most ancient *Chinese* hominids' existing before Peking Man during the Pliocene and lower Pleistocene eras, i.e. between one and five million years ago.[74] The finding in Pan county, Guizhou, in 1994 of human remains and stone tools, dated at more than 320,000 years, is said to indicate 'cultural exchanges between the East and the West',[75] ruling out migration from outside East

---

[69] See William Howells, 'Origins of the Chinese people: Intrepretations of the recent evidence' in David Keightly (ed.), *The origins of Chinese civilization*, Berkeley: University of California Press, 1983, pp. 301-2.

[70] G.N. Van Vark and J. Dijkema, 'Some notes on the origin of the Chinese People', *Homo*, 41, no. 4 (1990), p. 147.

[71] *Xinhua*, 'Fossil of early human being found in Hebei', 10 Aug. 1993.

[72] *Xinhua*, 'Outlines complete evolutionary system in palaeoanthropology', 3 Feb. 1993.

[73] *Xinhua*, 'China has collected 279 complete sets of ape man fossils', 22 April 1994.

[74] Jia Lanpo and Ho Chuan Kun, 'Lumière nouvelle sur l'archéologie paléolithique chinoise', *L'Anthropologie*, 94, no. 4 (1990), pp. 851-60.

[75] *Xinhua*, 'Traces of ancient men found in Southwest China', 30 Nov. 1994.

Asia (i.e. from Africa) and implying that modern geographical notions had some salience for hominids.

Jia Lanpo has noted that 'every country tries to stretch out its own history' through the discovery of human fossil remains within its own territory. He sees Chinese scientists in a competition with foreigners working in Africa to show that China has more quasi-human fossils and the same stone tools aged millions of years as have been found in Africa.[76] In expressing these views, Jia not only implies that hominids living in territories now part of China were somehow 'Chinese', but also that one purpose of palaeoanthropology in China is to reinforce racial nationalism by showing the antiquity of the pedigree of the contemporary Chinese people.

Chinese scholars who enunciate less extreme sinocentric theories may prove to be closer to the prevalent views of scholars outside China. Another theory may even come to the fore, positing for instance that *homo erectus* evolved separately in Africa and Asia, but was replaced by the African-originated *sapiens*.[77] The point is, however, that in China, as in several other regions and countries,[78] archaeology is seen as a tool for the enhancement of nationalist sentiment. Archaeology is used by the state and its mass media to enhance nationalism through the propagation of 'the concepts of the long history, splendid cultural traditions, continuity and integration of the country'.[79] Many research designs are advanced with an eye to 'the relationships between archaeological resources and their socio-political implications for China's cur-

---

[76] Jia Lanpo, 'Gu renleixue yanjiu de yixie wenti' (A few questions of paleoanthropological research) in Chen Guoqiang and Lin Jiahuang (eds), *Renleixue yu xingyong: Renleixue yanjiu zhi si* (Anthropology and its applications: Anthropological research no. 4), Shanghai: Xuelin chubanshe, 1992, pp. 2-3.

[77] James Shreeve, 'Terms of estrangement: Race and science', *Discover*, 15, no. 11 (Nov. 1994), pp. 56-8.

[78] See Philip Kohl and Clare Fawcett, *Nationalism, politics and the practice of archaeology*, Cambridge University Press, forthcoming, 1996; Margarita, Andreu and T.C. Champion, *Nationalism and archaeology in Europe*, London: UCL Press, 1995; Michael Dietler, '"Our ancestors the Gauls": Archaeology, ethnic nationalism and the manipulation of Celtic identity in modern Europe', *American Anthropologist*, 96, no. 3, 1994, pp. 584-605; Philip Kohl, 'Nationalism, politics and the practice of archaeology in Soviet Transcaucasia', *Journal of European Archaeology*, 1, no. 2, 1993, pp. 181-9; Neil Silberman, *Between past and present: Archaeology, ideology and nationalism in the modern Middle East*, New York: Anchor Books, 1990.

[79] Chen Chun, 'Chinese archaeology and the West', *Archaeological Review from Cambridge*, 8, no. 1 (1989), p. 30.

rent social milieu'.[80] Thus, while internationally archaeologists consider that the first Chinese civilisation emerged in the Bronze Age, no earlier than 2200 BC,[81] leading PRC scholars have back-dated Chinese 'civilisation' by 1,000 years in order to show that it is at least as ancient as that of Mesopotamia and Egypt.[82]

Sinocentric views are a state-certified orthodoxy in China,[83] and the popular writings of Jia Lanpo have been officially commended for their role in patriotic education.[84] Peking Man, however, was not always emblematic of the Chinese everyman. Before the mid-1980s he was identified as the ancestor not of the Chinese, but of humanity as a whole:

> Humanity at the time [of Peking Man], in the face of extreme difficulties and working under bitter conditions, created early, primitive culture and propelled forward the history of human society.[85]

But since the mid-1980s, Chinese nationalist writers have waxed lyrical about the role of Peking Man in the racialised construction of the Chinese nation:

> Peking Man, together with Lan Tian ape-man in the central plain and Yuanmo ape-man in the south, are the glorious representatives of the primeval ancestors of the Chinese nation [*Zhonghua minzu*]. Amid hardships and difficulties they founded the illustrious ancient culture of the Chinese nation.[86]

The views of this 'uniquely Chinese school of archaeology'[87] accord with claims for the propinquity of Chinese ethnic groups

[80] John W. Olsen, 'The practice of archaeology in China today', *Antiquity*, 61 (1987), p. 287.

[81] Chang Kwang-chih, 'Ancient China and its anthropological significance', *Symbols* (spring/fall 1984), p. 2.

[82] Lothar von Falkenhausen, 'On the historiographical orientation of Chinese archaeology', *Antiquity*, 67, p. 844.

[83] See Paul Erickson, 'The story of Peking man: From archaeology to mystery. Book review', *Science*, 2500, no. 4986 (1990), p. 1456; Jasper, 'China's prehistory', pp. 32-7.

[84] *Xinhua*, 'Popular history readers commended', 14 June 1984.

[85] Zhang Quanxi, *Zhongguo tongshi jianggao* (Lectures on the general history of China), Beijing: Beijing Daxue chubanshe, 1982, p.4.

[86] Lu Jianshong, 'Beijingren shi zenmoyang faxian de? Ta you naxie juyou de wenhua tezheng?' (How was Peking man discovered? What are its cultural characteristics?) in Zhang Xiaoming, *Zhongguo lishi*, p. 23.

[87] *Xinhua*, 'Decade of archeological achievement', 17 May 1989; An Zhimin, 'Chinese Archaeology: Past and present', *Archaeological Review from Cambridge*, 8, no. 1 (1989), p. 16.

and a biological division between Chinese and non-Chinese. To be sure, the sinocentric view admits exceptions to a strict distinction between Chinese and non-Chinese, but only for proximate peoples who might enhance the status of an imagined 'racial' Greater China.[88] Thus it is claimed that the 'Hexian ape-man' discovered in Anhui province is part of the 'evolution of China's ancient forebears and the forebears of the whole of East Asia'.[89] It is also asserted that the ancestors of the Japanese may have originated in what is today the Guangxi Zhuang Autonomous Region,[90] but it is notable that no claims are made for a familial relationship with the less 'prestigious' peoples of the Asia-Pacific region, even though, for example, human biologists have adduced through mitochondrial DNA studies that the likely origin of the Polynesians is in southern China.[91]

THE GREAT WALL AS ETHNIC MINORITY PROJECT

The myth of a biological distinctiveness within PRC national discourse purports to convince ethnic minorities of their primordial and hence unambiguous positioning within the ambit of a Chinese nation. In purpose these myths can be classed with the recent promotion of another important emblem of Chineseness, namely the Great Wall. Although the Great Wall has been much studied as a symbol of cultural nationalism, it also has a function as an inclusive symbol of racial nationalism. As Andrew Waldron has demonstrated, it constitutes a variety of discontinuous and often modest barriers constructed in different eras. Throughout most of Chinese history it was portrayed negatively, as 'a symbol not of national greatness but rather of dynastic evil'.[92] It has only taken root as a ubiquitous popular emblem since the 1970s, and in particular since the rise to power of Deng Xiaoping in 1978.

[88] Cf. Stephen Uhalley, '"Greater China": The context of a term', *Positions*, 2, no. 2 (fall 1994), p. 283.

[89] *Xinhua*, 'Scientist given Hexian Ape-man date', 6 April 1994.

[90] *Xinhua*, 'Japanese may have originated in southwest China', 30 Nov. 1994.

[91] R.J. Trent *et al.*, 'Beta-globin gene haplotypes in Polynesians are predominantly southern Chinese in type', *Human Heredity*, 40 (1990), pp. 285-9.

[92] Andrew Waldron, 'Representing China: The Great Wall and cultural nationalism in the twentieth century' in Harumi Befu (ed.), *Cultural nationalism in East Asia*, Berkeley: Institute of East Asian Studies, University of California, 1993, p. 40; Andrew Waldron, *The Great Wall of China: From history to myth*, Cambridge University Press, 1990, pp. 214-19.

The Great Wall became increasingly a national symbol after 1984, when Deng urged its restoration. Then in the late 1980s its promotion as an emblem of China accelerated with photo exhibitions, dance presentations, a television series etc.[93] It has been termed by Luo Zhewen, a leading scholar and member of the Chinese People's Political Consultative Conference member, 'an embodiment of the spirit and force of the Chinese nation';[94] he has noted that the walls were built to ward off horse-borne invaders from the north, northwest and northeast[95] and used in conflicts with peoples who are now regarded as ethnic minorities. He has nevertheless also written that

> [S]ince China is a state of many nationalities, many rulers of minority nationality groups eventually achieved the exalted position of Emperor of China. After the Qin (217-210 BC) there were only three dynasties ruled by emperors of Chinese nationality that carried out substantial work on the Wall: the Han, Sui and the Ming. Many more of the minority nationality-led dynasties (namely Northern and Eastern Wei, Northern Qi, Northern Zhou, Liao and Jin) worked on the Wall. Thus the Great Wall is the joint achievement of all of China's minority nationalities.[96]

In essence, Luo Zhewen and other writers have turned the Great Wall into a symbol of multi-ethnicity. Its representation has shifted from being a 'defence for the rulers of different Chinese nationalities' to an achievement of ethnic minorities in China.[97] However, to argue that it was a multi-ethnic project is rather like characterising Germany's *Festung Europa* of 1940-4 as a pan-European endeavour. Although it is not directly a myth of common descent, the emphasis on the participation of ethnic minorities

---

[93] See *Xinhua*, 'Great Wall reappears on stage and TV screen', 30 Nov. 1987; *Xinhua*, 'Photo exhibition features Great Wall', 9 Dec. 1987.

[94] *Xinhua*, 'Studies on Great Wall increased', 22 June 1995.

[95] Ibid.; Luo Zhewen, 'The Great Wall' in Yu Jin (ed.), *The Great Wall*, Beijing: Cultural Relics Publishing House, 1980, p. 2; *Xinhua*, 'Album on Great Wall comes off press', August 28, 1980. See also Thomas Barfield, *The perilous frontier: Nomadic empires and China*, Oxford: Basil Blackwell, 1989, pp. 16-17, 32.

[96] Luo Zhewen, 'The Great Wall in history' in Daniel Schwartz, *The Great Wall of China*, London: Thames and Hudson, 1990, p. 220. See also Luo Zhewen *et al.* (eds), *Wan li changcheng*, Beijing: Zhongguo jianzhu gongye chubanshe, 1994, pp. 334-7.

[97] Luo Zhewen, *The Great Wall*, p. 5.

in the construction of what is now the principal symbol of the Chinese nation is intended to show that the minorities have always been ethnically Chinese. Like the Han, they expended blood and treasure to defend and expand the power of the Chinese state, something they surely would not have done had they not already been part of the *Zhonghua minzu*.

The ethnic minorities in the north of China are well aware that the Great Wall was mainly directed at solving political and military conflicts between nomadic peoples and the Chinese state. The portrayal of the Great Wall as partly a minority project is further evidence of the breadth of the current effort to construct an inclusive meta-myth of racial nationalism that lends legitimacy to the Chinese state.

RACIAL NATIONALISM AND THE TIBETAN EXAMPLE

Attitudes toward ethnic minorities in China are ambivalent, although official discourse often stresses their common ancestry. This is the case with Tibetans. As part of its effort to combat Tibetan separatism and underpin contemporary Han-Tibetan political relations, the Chinese state has pressed the idea that the two peoples are part of a common 'race'.

On the other hand, Tibetan leaders in exile have long claimed that the Han and Tibetans are politically and culturally unrelated and that Chinese policy was designed 'to wipe out the entire Tibetan race'.[98] In recent years they have also emphasised that Tibetans and Han Chinese are 'racially' distinct. For example, the Dalai Lama has stated:

> Recent scientific studies of archaeological findings have revealed that the Tibetans and Chinese have been two distinct peoples since the dawn of human civilisation. There are clear evidences that the genesis of civilisations in China, Tibet and India are different. Based on this, the distinct existence of the Tibetan race is clear.[99]

[98] Jonathan Landay, 'Tibetan exiles shaken by Lhasa violence', United Press International, 10 Oct. 1987; Press Trust of India, 'China encouraging terrorism against India says Dalai Lama's representative', in *BBC/SWB*, 23 Oct. 1993.

[99] Dalai Lama, 'The importance of Indian initiative on Tibet', *Tibetan Bulletin* (July-August 1993), p. 1.

However, available evidence, based on genetic markers, indicates that there is great diversity among the Han and the minority populations, so much so that geneticists believe that it is 'difficult to make valid comparisons of the Chinese as a group with other ethnic groups'.[100] Both Han and Tibetans are genetically heterogeneous and overlapping.[101] The two peoples are thus neither 'racially' alike nor 'racially' distinct. PRC sources have nevertheless joined battle with their political enemies on this ground and use the same 'racial' concepts to make a variety of claims of a biological identity of Han and Tibetans. The thesis that Tibetans are descendants of Peking Man, propounded by a palaeontologist at the Chinese Academy of Sciences, was publicised in the spring of 1989,[102] perhaps not coincidentally, soon after large-scale disturbances in Lhasa. Archaeological evidence has been said to show that the early historical Tibetan and Yellow River Chinese cultures were identical.[103] It has been claimed that Tibetans are not only part of the Chinese state but also 'part of the Chinese nation' through descent from ancient 'Chinese immigrants' from Gansu and Qinghai provinces.[104]

The eminent anthropologist and Vice Chairman of the National People's Congress Standing Committee, Fei Xiaotong, has stated: 'Both Han and Tibetan people are from the same origin – the Qiang – which was one of the most powerful nationalities in ancient China.'[105] However, both in ancient times[106] and in the contemporary era[107] the Qiang have been considered an ethnic group distinct from both Han and Tibetans. There have also been assertions of literal 'ties of blood' through alleged 'genetic similarities between the Tibetans and Han'. This

---

[100] H.W. Goedde *et al.* (eds), 'Population genetic studies in three Chinese minorities', *American Journal of Physical Anthropology* (1984), p. 283.

[101] Chen Kuang-ho, 'Genetic findings and mongoloid population migration in China', *Bulletin of the Institute of Ethnology*, no. 73 (spring 1992), pp. 223, 228.

[102] *Xinhua*, 'Tibetans are descendants of Peking man: Anthropologist', 13 April 1989.

[103] *Xinhua*, 'Stone age ruins shed light on Tibet's history', 19 Oct. 1990.

[104] *Ta Kung Pao*, 'China's study negates the theory of Tibetans coming from abroad', *Foreign Broadcast Information System (FBIS)*, 11 Dec. 1989, p. 32.

[105] Tammy Tam, 'CPPCC member says most Tibetans live in poverty', *Hong Kong Standard*, FBIS-CHI-88-223, November 18, 1988, pp. 39-40; see also E.G. Pulleybank, 'The Chinese and their neighbors in prehistoric and early historic times' in David Keightley (ed.), *The origins of Chinese civilization*, Berkeley: University of California, 1983, p. 423.

[106] See for instance Zhang Weiwen and Zeng Qingnan, *In search of China's minorities*, Beijing: New World Press, 1993, p. 144.

[107] Ma Yin, *China's minority nationalities*, pp. 228-31.

putative genetic connection is alleged to contrast with sharp differences between the leukocytic antigen of the white blood cells
of Tibetans and the antigen of the white blood cells of neighbouring
Nepalese and Indians.[108]

The Chinese state has attempted since the late 1980s to include
Tibetans within the myth of homogeneity, and the idea of Han
Chinese and Tibetans having a common ancestry implicitly places
the two ethnic groups on the same level. Indeed, there is fulsome
official praise of the innate talents of Tibetans. Chen Kuiyuan
has remarked that in developing a market economy, 'Tibetans
do not lag behind others in intelligence,'[109] and another official
in Tibet praised the 'remarkable intelligence' displayed by Tibetans
in renovating the Potala palace.[110]

The inclusive racial nationalist stance, however, comes up against
widespread Han conceptions of Tibetan inferiority, which are
particularly focused on the question of intelligence. For political
reasons, such conceptions are absent from PRC publications, but
it is not unusual to find Han disparagement of ethnic minorities
recorded by Westerners and non-PRC Han Chinese who visit
China's minority areas, speak with people from various walks
of life, and hear unabashed derogatory comments.[111] These comments are especially strong when the subject is the intelligence
of Tibetans.[112] This 'ingrained prejudice and local negative opinion
towards minorities' is inevitably noted by the minorities themselves.
Prejudice and evolutionary notions derived from the nineteenth-century
anthropologist Lewis Morgan and from Friedrich Engels of the progres-
sions of peoples through stages from 'primitive' to 'advanced' are
mutually reinforcing ideological obstacles to the success of racial
nationalism and the state nationalist project it is intended to legitimise.[113]

---

[108] *Remin Ribao*, 'Zangzu shi Zhonghua minzu yi bufen' (Tibetans are part of the Chinese
nation), 28 Dec. 1989, p. 3.

[109] *Tibet People Broadcasting Station*, November 21, 1994, 'Chen Kuiyuan on how separatism
affects Tibet's prosperity', in *BBC/SWB*, 26 Nov. 1994.

[110] *Xinhua*, 'Potala palace group hear praise for renovation project', 10 Aug. 1994.

[111] See for instance Hsieh Shih-chung, 'Tai/Dai-Lue ethnicity'.

[112] See Pierre-Antoine Donnet, *Tibet: Survival in question*, London: Zed Books, 1994, p. 171;
Elizabeth Grinspoon, 'Tibet: Chinese are reweaving the region's social fabric', *Los Angeles
Times*, 14 June 1994, p. 6; Lena Sun, 'Ethnic animosities reborn as Chinese traders flood
Tibet', *Washington Post*, 15 Sept. 1994, pp. A27; Catriona Bass, *Inside the treasure house*,
London: Gallancz, 1990.

[113] See Stevan Harrell, 'Linguistics and hegemony in China', *International Journal of the Sociology*

Often mytho-historical imaginings have underpinned efforts to
convince peoples that a putative common lineage biologically
mandates their support for state's racial nationalist agenda and
thus for the state itself. To that end, state leaders in a variety
of political systems have often insisted that scholars reinterpret
history to conform to the racial nationalist mould. Referring to
the place of scholars in this process in Nazi Germany, Heinrich
Himmler stated:

> The one and only thing that matters to us, and the thing
> these people are paid for by the State, is to have ideas of
> history that strengthen our people in their necessary national
> pride. In all this troublesome business we are only interested
> in one thing – to project into the dim and distant past the
> picture of our nation as we envisage it for the future.[114]

Myths of descent have been so central to state constructions
of racial nationalism that scholars of the day have become influential
through arguments, ranging from the tendentious to the ludicrous,
that incorporate 'prestigious' individuals and peoples of the past
into racially-based meta-histories. As Stephen Asma has detailed
in a discussion of 'noumenal racism', Chinese culture was attributed
by a prominent mid-nineteenth-century American writer to the
'Caucasian blood' of Confucius and other renowned Chinese
thinkers. Twentieth-century German archaeologists claimed the
ancient Greeks as migrants from northern Europe, and 'Western'
scholarship has a long history of reinterpreting cultured Egyptians
of antiquity as 'white'.[115]

Myths of descent and, more generally, the politicisation of
pre-history and history are all the more important when racial
nationalism is used to force-pace the construction of an overarching
ethnicity taking in majority and minority ethnic groups.[116] That
this agenda is inclusive does not necessarily mean that it is benign.
As Etienne Balibar has observed about 'race', the 'inclusive' can

of Language, 103 (1993), pp. 111-12.

[114] Quoted in Bettina Arnold, 'The past as propaganda', *Archaeology*, 45, no. 4 (July 1992),
pp. 30-7.

[115] Stephen Asma, 'Metaphors of race: Theoretical presuppositions behind racism', *American
Philosophical Quarterly*, 32, no. 1 (Jan. 1995), pp. 13-29.

[116] See Clare Fawcett, 'The politics of assimilation in Japanese archaeology', *Archaeological
Review from Cambridge*, 5, no. 1 (1986), pp. 43-57.

also be the oppressive.[117] Apart from questions of their historicity, the myths of descent now promoted in China substitute Han-based imaginings for the autochtonous understandings of ethnic minorities of their origins and histories. How useful these myths are as tools for sustaining state nationalism among ethnic minority peoples is therefore highly questionable.

For the people of China as a whole, myths of descent aimed at bolstering racial nationalism, by emphasising the supposed Chinese biological distinctiveness, draw a scientifically false wall of separation between Chinese and other peoples. Myths of descent aimed at promoting racial nationalism are not only a-scientific, but are also politically perilous. The use of nationalism in the service of modernising, authoritarian and nationalist states to reconstruct an artificial overarching ethnicity has produced a series of tragedies that span the twentieth century.[118]

The question is not so much whether the common ranks of Chinese citizens (the *lao bai xing*) will adhere to and act upon racial nationalism, as whether racial nationalism is likely to permeate the 'dominant class' and serve as a basis for its coherence long into the future.[119] Elites of other states, for instance those of the ex-Yugoslavian lands, found that making nationalism, based on similarly dubious historical claims central to their 'nation-building' project, led to ethnic rivalry among leaders in which the most virulent ultra-nationalists emerged successful.[120] The events that followed were untoward but predictable. Myths of descent, as building blocks of racial nationalism, may thus have political consequences far beyond those anticipated by their promoters. We should closely observe how these myths are further developed in China.

---

[117] Etienne Balibar, 'Racism and nationalism' in Etienne Balibar and Immanuel Wallerstein (eds), *Race, nation, class: Ambiguous identities*, London: Verso, 1991, p. 39.

[118] Alain Touraine, *Critique of modernity*, Oxford: Blackwell, 1995, p. 165.

[119] See Stephen Hill, 'Britain: The dominant ideology thesis after a decade' in Nicholas Abercrombie *et al.* (eds), *Dominant ideologies*, London: Unwin Hyman, 1990, p. 2.

[120] V.P. Gagnon, 'Ethnic nationalism and international conflict: The case of Serbia', *International Security*, 19, no. 3 (winter 1994-5), pp. 130-66.

Part II. JAPAN

THE INVENTION OF IDENTITY
RACE AND NATION IN PRE-WAR JAPAN

Michael Weiner

Where a nation is assumed to possess a set of unique characteristics which make it a nation and distinguish it from other populations, these same characteristics may be used as 'racial' boundary markers.[1] In these circumstances, rather than existing as independent categories, 'race' and nation may come together ideologically.[2] The extent to which in Japan such assumptions inform the national agenda rather than a narrow nationalist one has been discussed many times in recent years.[3]

The assumptions which underpin claims to national exclusivity have also been, and remain, a cardinal feature of the class of literature associated with the *nihonjinron*, or Japaneseness; a discourse of difference, which sets forth the unique capabilities of the Japanese and the distinctive features of their culture. Although voluminous, this literature has also lacked a clear conceptual distinction between cultural and 'racial' categories. A single term, *minzoku*, is regularly used as a synonym for the Japanese 'race', ethnie and nation.[4]

[1] This chapter is a revised version of an article which first appeared in *Ethnic and Racial Studies* (18.3, July 1995). Gratitude is also due to the anonymous readers for their critical suggestions and to the Japan Foundation Endowment Committee which generously supported the initial research.

[2] David Goldberg, *Racist culture*, Oxford: Blackwell, 1994, p. 79; Ōnuma Yasuaki, *Tanitsu minzoku shakai no shinwa 'o' koete* (Beyond the myth of the homogeneous society), Tokyo: Toshindo, 1986, p. 69; Harada Tomohiko *et al.* (eds), *Kōza sabetsu to jinken* [4] (On discrimination and human rights), Tokyo: Yūzankaku, 1985, pp. 201-2 and 208-14.

[3] See, for example, Yamanaka Keiko, 'New immigration policy and unskilled foreign workers in Japan', *Pacific Review*, 66, no. 1 (1993), p. 73; Shimada Haruo, *Japan's "Guest Workers": Issues and public policies*, University of Tokyo Press, 1994, p. 47; *Sankei Shinbun*, 19 Dec. 1990; *Nikkei Weekly*, 14 June 1993.

[4] Yoshino Kosaku, *Cultural nationalism in Japan*, London: Routledge, 1992, p. 25.

Within the literature both 'race' and 'culture' have also been treated as phenomena that occur naturally, further reinforcing their credibility as factors that explain social relationships.[5] This conflation of biological and cultural determinants is by no means confined to the present or earlier post-war period but has its origins before 1945.

In light of the above, this chapter has three objectives: to evaluate the claim that the modern Japanese state has evolved as an expression of the specific characteristics of a homogeneous people; to trace the relationship between ideologies of 'race' and nation in the construction of a modern Japanese identity; and to identify those elements which have historically informed perceptions of the excluded Other against whom this identity has been produced and reproduced.

The argument advanced here is that historically social structures and attitudes in Japan have been imbued with 'racial' meaning, and that these meanings are themselves fluid, dynamic and contingent. That is to say, both 'racial' meanings and 'racialised' identities are historically specific, and can only be understood in relation to other factors – economic and political – and the international environment within which they emerged and have since been transformed. Rather than displacing a sense of 'nationness', the ideological space connoted by 'race' has intersected with that of nation.

A second concern here is to identify the various strands of 'racialised' discourse which developed, and the processes by which European imperialist perspectives on 'race' were adopted in Japan. Although the state is presented here as the primary focus of ideological articulation and struggle, areas of contestation and confrontation have been, and remain, diverse. The marginalised groups referred to here are not cast in the role of passive participants. As elsewhere, the minorities in modern Japan have resisted the imposition of 'racialised' identities, and the exploitation which these identities countenanced.[6]

---

[5] Michael Weiner, 'Discourses of race, nation and empire in pre-1945 Japan', *Ethnic and Racial Studies*, 18, no. 3 (1995).

[6] Ian Neary, *Political protest and social control in pre-war Japan: The origins of Buraku liberation*, Atlantic Highlands, NJ: Humanities Press, 1989, pp. 50-74; Susan Pharr, *Losing face: Status politics in Japan*, Berkeley: University of California Press, 1990, pp. 75-89; Michael Weiner, *Race and migration in imperial Japan*, London: Routledge, 1994, pp. 154-86.

To appreciate how racialised ideologies have transformed attitudes to Self and Other, it is necessary to distinguish between two terms: *jinshu* and *minzoku*. For example, the Japanese *Encyclopedia of the Social Sciences* enumerates skin colour, physical stature, hair texture, cranial form, nose shape and blood type as the defining criteria of *jinshu* (race).[7] In contrast, the term *minzoku* is commonly rendered as equivalent to 'ethnicity' or 'ethnos'.[8] Suzuki Jiro has noted in this context that the possession of fixed physical characteristics is not a necessary element of a *minzoku*.[9]

Although this distinction seems clear enough, the literature of both the pre- and post-war periods is full of contradictory evidence. As noted at the outset, the term *minzoku* has come to denote both cultural and physiological determinants.[10] In the Japanese edition of Ruth Benedict's *Race: Science and Politics*, *minzoku* is preferred to *jinshu*, while the *Encyclopedia of the Social Sciences* contains a definition of *minzoku* which allows for factors of consanguinity to be included.[11] An even more explicit overlap is contained in the 1930 edition of the same encyclopedia, where *minzoku* is defined as having three essential components: common blood, a shared culture and collective consciousness.[12]

The conflation of cultural and 'racial' criteria by which *minzoku* could be identified has taken various forms. In a 1938 publication entitled *The New Japanism and the Buddhist View on Nationality*, Takakusu Junjiro argued that a dominant Yamato or stem 'race' existed, which had assimilated various pre-historic racial groupings. This 'culture of the Japanese blood', Takakusu concluded, had subsequently been preserved through the 'virtuous rule of succeeding emperors'.[13] A parallel discourse of 'consanguineous unity' is contained in an English-language *History of Japan*, published

[7] *Shakai kagaku daijiten*, Tokyo: Kagoshima shuppankai, 1968, vol. 11, pp. 27-8.

[8] Yasuda Hiroshi, 'Kindai Nihon ni okeru "minzoku" kannen no keisei' (Formation of 'racial' consciousness in modern Japan), *Shisō to Gendai*, no. 31 (1992, p. 62.)

[9] Cullen T. Hayashida, 'Identity, race and the blood ideology of Japan', unpublished Ph.D. dissertation, University of Washington, 1976, p. 14.

[10] Yasuda, 'Kindai Nihon', p. 62; Yun Kwan-cha, 'Minzoku no gensō to satesu' (The fantasy and failure of *minzoku*), *Shiso* (Dec. 1993), p. 16.

[11] *Shakai kagaku daijiten*, Tokyo: Kagoshima shuppankai, 1968, vol. 17, p. 366.

[12] *Shakai kagaku daijiten*, Tokyo: Shakai shisōsha, 1930, p. 587.

[13] Hayashida, 'Identity', p. 29.

through a Japanese government tourist agency in 1939.[14] The putative relationship between blood and culture is made more explicit in Kada Tetsuji's *Jinshu minzoku sensō* (*Jinshu, minzoku, war*), published in 1940. These three terms are treated independently, but in the text the biological basis of *minzoku* is never in doubt. The origins of *minzoku* lie in the distinctive *jinshuteki* (racial) and *seishinteki* (spiritual) qualities of a people; listing among the specific properties of a *minzoku* – common blood, culture, language, customs and religion. Kada concludes: 'We cannot consider *minzoku* without taking into account its relation to blood.'[15]

In fact, throughout the 1920s and early 1930s, numerous publications appeared which argued a biological or genetic basis for the distinctiveness and superiority of the Japanese people. For example, a 1930 edition of the populist journal *Nihonshugi* (*Japanism*) carried an article in which the unique qualities of the Japanese nation were identified as a manifestation of what the author, Ihei Setsuzo, termed *ketsuzokushugi* (the ideology of the blood family).[16] A parallel argument can be found in Hozumi Nobushige's *Ancestor Worship and Japanese Law* (1901).[17] In Hozumi's view, Japanese society had always had three primary elements (the Imperial family, the regional clan and the family unit), each forming a discrete though inter-related consanguineous community.[18]

The precise historical moment when *minzoku* displaced *jinshu* in social science is difficult to determine, but the process was well under way by the late 1920s, and completed during the

---

[14] John Dower, *War without mercy: Race and power in the Pacific War*, New York: Pantheon, 1986, p. 222.

[15] Kada Tetsuji, *Jinshu, minzoku, sensō* (*Jinshu, minzoku* and war), Tokyo: Keio shobō, 1940, pp. 70-1.

[16] Hayashida, 'Identity', p. 82.

[17] Though less well known than his brother Hozumi Yatsuka, a specialist in constitutional law who later assisted Yamagata Aritomo draft his famous attack on the perils of socialism, Hozumi Nobushige was a respected legal scholar in his own right. Having spent the years 1876-80 in England, Nobushige returned to Japan where he became one of the principal commentators on the theories of Herbert Spencer. See I. Kikuchi, 'Hozumi Nobushige to shakai ken' (Hozumi Nobushige and social rights), *Nihon Gakushi-in Kiyo*, 30, no. 1, March 1972, pp. 24-5. *Ancestor worship and Japanese law* was written on his return from a second visit to England in 1899.

[18] Ito Mikiharu, *Kazoku kokka kan no jinruigaku* (Anthropology of family state consciousness), Tokyo: Minerva shobō, 1982, pp. 31-2.

Pacific war. According to Dower, *minzoku* were perceived as 'organic collectivities that transcended their individual members and gave rise to distinctive national characters, representing *in toto* a fluid conjunction of blood, culture, history and political form.'[19] Culture had, in effect, been transformed into a pseudo-biological property of communal life. Moreover, both terms had already come to have a functional equivalence as concepts which made any distinction irrelevant. It has been argued elsewhere that if culture is regarded as manifesting a primordial or innate essence, reliance on cultural or ethnic criteria in distinguishing between peoples works in the same way as biological determinism.[20] The important distinction is not between cultural or physiological characteristics, but between the ways in which these criteria are signified and acted upon. The historical processes through which groups or nations evolve have been based on these assumed innate qualities – either cultural or biological – and subsequently located within specific material and power relations.

The Imagined Community of Nation

The categories of inclusion and exclusion on which the Japanese of the Tokugawa period (1603-1867) relied to distinguish themselves from other groups of people did not assume a 'racialised' form. Likewise, although there is evidence of xenophobia in Tokugawa law, as in the exclusion edicts against Christian missionaries, there is little to suggest that the inequality it assumed was 'racially' based. The *yabanjin* (barbarian) was viewed as inferior, but this reflected cultural or political considerations. Indeed, it was not until the Japanese encountered the European enslavement of Africans that negative images of 'blacks' began to emerge. But, as Leupp has argued, Tokugawa accounts of barbarian behaviour were not informed by the colour stigma alone:

> The term *kuronbo* applied to black people was of course derogatory, but so were the terms applied to the white Westerners. Myths about black people were invidious, but so were the myths about the Dutch. It was said, for example,

---

[19] Dower, *War without mercy*, p. 267.

[20] Robert Miles, *Racism after 'race relations'*, London: Routledge, 1993, p. 101.

that they had no heels, or urinated, like dogs, when raising one leg.[21]

The development of national consciousness in post-1868 Japan was itself contingent on a series of articulations and re-articulations following the Meiji Restoration of 1868. In due course the political, economic and social rupture which the restoration signified would be re-defined as a historical continuity, with links to an ancient past. The language and imagery of nationalism, in erecting a set of new symbolic boundaries around Japan, also suggested that the nation was a naturally occurring or primordial community of which the citizenry had always been a part.[22] The naturalisation of culture, of which these processes formed an integral part, re-cast the meaning of 'Japaneseness' in powerful images of the purity and homogeneity of the nation, the family and the Japanese way of life. The nation was conceived as an extended family, with the Emperor as semi-divine father to the national community and head of state. The imagined community thus received its ultimate sanctification at the sacred level, in Shinto, while reverence for the Emperor as *minzoku no ōsa* (head of the people) and loyalty and obedience to the state were given equivalent status.

However, new ways of viewing the world did not emerge unchallenged in a vacuum. Just as Meiji industrialisation depended on the existence of well-established market relations and the importation of Western technology, Japanese ideologues drew inspiration for their construction of a national identity both from the West and through the appropriation and manipulation of indigenous myths. The search for a usable past engaged the resources of academics, educators, journalists, politicians and government officials. Their interests and concerns often intersected; politicians were frequent contributors to newspapers, while academics were called on to advise on matters of public policy and education. Although there was no master theme to which they all subscribed, their efforts would also assist in the dissemination of 'racial' knowledge and the production of 'Otherness'.

Throughout the final decades of the nineteenth century, in particular, statesmen, bureaucrats and unofficial publicists alike

---

[21] Gary P. Leupp, 'Images of black people in late mediaeval Japan and early modern Japan', *Japan Forum*, 7, no. 1 (1995), p. 6.

[22] Yasuda, 'Kindai Nihon', p. 63.

were occupied in attempts to establish the criteria for 'Japaneseness'. It was recognised that the muscular nationalism of the imperial powers would have to be met by an equally assertive Japanese nationalism if sovereignty were to be preserved.[23] The contours of this identity, which invoked powerful images of communal solidarity and exclusivity, were further refined through the lens of scientific 'racism' embodied in the writings of Haeckel, Lamarck and Spencer.[24] The diffusion of social Darwinism, in particular, would provide scientific legitimacy both for the laws of the market place and for the notion that social and political development was a manifestation of the aggressive interplay of natural forces.[25] For Shiga Shigetaka and other intellectuals associated with the newspaper *Nihon* and the journal *Nihonjin,* the nation was increasingly identified with *minzoku* – a term first popularised by Shiga in the late 1880s. In common with other terms like *kokusui* (national essence) and *kokuminshugi* (civic nationalism), *minzoku* was a critical element in the development of a popular nationalism which arose partly in response to what was regarded as the excessive Westernisation of the previous decades. As articulated by Shiga and his contemporary Kuga Katsunan, *minzoku* manifested the unique characteristics (historical, geographical and cultural) of the nation.[26] This sense of nation was later appropriated by constitutional scholars like Hozumi Yatsuka, for whom the *kokutai* (national polity) was identified with the imperial line and the network of beliefs sustaining it – principally ancestor worship.[27] In common with Inoue Tetsujirō, Kato Hiroyuki and other family state theoreticians, Hozumi argued that the Japanese *minzoku* was the manifestation of common ancestry rather than shared culture.

---

[23] Kenneth B. Pyle, *The new generation in Meiji Japan,* Stanford University Press, 1969, p. 75.

[24] Shimao Eikoh, 'Darwinism in Japan', *Annals of Science,* no. 38, (1981), pp. 93–102; Sharon H. Nolte, *Liberalism in modern Japan,* Berkeley: University of California Press, 1987, p. 44; Marius B. Jansen, 'Japanese imperialism: Late Meiji perspectives' in Ramon H. Myers and Mark R. Peattie (eds), *The Japanese colonial empire, 1895-1945,* Princeton University Press, 1984, p. 66.

[25] Carol Gluck, *Japan's modern myths,* Princeton University Press, 1985, p. 209; Michael Weiner, *The origins of the Korean community in Japan, 1910-1923,* Atlantic Highlands, NJ: Humanities Press, 1989, pp. 14–22.

[26] Kuga Katsunan, 'Kokumin teki no kannen' (Citizen's consciousness), 1889, cited in Nishida Taketoshi and Uete Michiari (eds), *Kuga Katsunan zenshū,* Tokyo: Misuzu shobō, 1969, vol. 2, pp. 7–8.

[27] Hozumi Yatsuka, *Kasei oyobi kokutai* (The family system and the national polity), 1892, cited in Yun, 'Minzoku', p. 16.

A parallel line of argument was pursued by Ueda Kazutoshi in *Kokugo to Kokka to,* published in 1894. In this seminal piece, Ueda emphasised that the Japanese polity had been, and would continue to be, sustained by the Japanese 'race', and argued that the Japanese language itself was a manifestation of the inherited qualities of its people.[28] Like his contemporary Fukuzawa Yukichi, Kato Hiroyuki's early advocacy of the 'natural rights' of man would later be replaced by a firm commitment to Darwinian theories of social evolution.[29] In 1905, Kato provided a Darwinian analysis of the current struggle between Japan and Russia for hegemony in East Asia. A Japanese victory, he concluded, was inevitable due to the superiority of a homogeneous polity which had been thoroughly integrated within the emperor system.[30]

To their credit, other intellectuals were prepared to contest the assumptions underpinning belief in Japanese exceptionalism. For example, Onishi Iwao challenged the existence of a Yamato 'race', descended from a common ancestor.[31] Another critic of the Spencerian interpretation of social development and inter-national relations was Tanaka Odo, who rejected the 'mystical patriotism and national self-worship surrounding the Russo-Japanese war' as impediments to Japan's development as a modern industrial state. In a study of Fukuzawa Yukichi, Tanaka challenged the existence of a uniquely Japanese polity (*kokutai*), replacing it with a constantly evolving sense of nationality (*kokuminsei*). Writing in 1915, Tanaka advanced this argument a stage further in suggesting that co-existence with other nationalities and respect for them were the criteria on which the Japanese *kokuminsei* should be judged. It was a stance which defended the right of all peoples to maintain their political and cultural autonomy, and contested the ideological basis of imperial expansion.[32]

Although intellectuals and journalists performed an important

---

[28] Yun 'Minzoku', p. 16.

[29] Kato Hiroyuki, 'Kokutai shinron' (New treatise on the national polity), 1875, in *Meiji bunka zenshū*, Tokyo: Nihon hyoron shinsha, 1955, vol. 2, pp. 111–12. See also Irokawa Daikichi, *The culture of the Meiji period* (edited and translated by Marius Jansen), Princeton University Press, 1986, p. 253.

[30] Kawamura Nozomu, 'Sociology and sociology in the interwar period' in J. Thomas Rimmer (ed.), *Culture and identity: Japanese intellectuals during the interwar years*, Princeton University Press, 1990, p. 67.

[31] Yasuda, 'Kindai Nihon', pp. 81–2.

[32] Nolte, *Liberalism*, pp. 44, 51–2, 145–6.

role as channels of legitimation, the idea of nationalism was nurtured primarily through the institutions of the state. By about 1910, state-inspired nationalism had penetrated all strata of society and offered the Japanese people an easily accessible explanation of their social, political and economic position, both domestically and internationally. It was a nationalist ideology whose central motif was that of the *kazoku kokka* (family state), itself the product of a re-working of the concepts of citizen and nation in accordance with myths of common ancestry.[33] The existence of a Yamato *minzoku* sharing a common ancestry, history and culture had become as canonical and 'natural' to the Japanese as it was to their contemporaries in England. While the physical and historical evidence of migrations to the Japanese islands was not denied, the migrations were deemed to be of such antiquity that they had long since formed a single 'race' and culture.[34]

In defining the Japanese nation as a collective personality, characterised by uniformity and homogeneity, the family state was itself conceived as a reflection of the inherited qualities and capacities of its people. The immutable characteristics which distinguished the Yamato *minzoku* provided, what Balibar has termed, 'a historical backbone ... a concentration of qualities that belong "exclusively" to the nationals: it is in the race of "its children" that the nation can contemplate its true identity at its purest. Consequently, it is to the race that the nation must cleave.'[35]

The articulation of an ideology in which the categories of 'race' and nation so clearly overlapped was not unique to Japan. This reification of the nation as an organic entity had clear parallels in contemporary Europe where the conceptualisation of nations as 'naturally occurring groups identified by cultural *differentiae*' implied that the 'symbols of "nation" were themselves grounded in race'.[36] Given that Japan was consciously modelling its behaviour in other spheres of activity on its European and North American contemporaries, it is hardly surprising that Japanese 'racial' thought

---

[33] Irokawa, *Culture of the Meiji period*, p. 283.

[34] Representative of this school of thought was Kida Sadakichi's *Nihon minzoku no kōsei* (Characteristics of the Japanese *minzoku*), published in 1938; cited in Yun, 'Minzoku', p. 27.

[35] Étienne Balibar, 'Racisme et nationalisme' in Étienne Balibar and Immanuel Wallerstein (eds), *Race, nation, classe*, Paris: Éditions de la Découverte, 1988, cited in David Theo Goldberg (ed.), *Anatomy of racism*, Minneapolis: University of Minnesota Press, 1990, p. 284.

[36] Miles, *Racism*, p. 62. See also Paul G. Lauren, *Power and prejudice: The politics and diplomacy of racial discrimination*, Boulder, CO: Westview Press, 1988, p. 40.

drew much of its inspiration from the most advanced Western nations and developed in response to it. In the context of late nineteenth-century imperial expansion, the new Japanese national identity interacted with and was further refined through contact with the scientific 'racism' of the West.

SOCIAL DARWINISM IN JAPAN

The agents through which social Darwinism entered Japan in the late nineteenth century were extremely diverse. It is, however, possible to identify two distinct, though mutually reinforcing, sources of Darwinist inspiration: the role of foreign academics employed by the Meiji state, and the direct experience of Japanese diplomats and scholars while posted abroad.

It was from the vantage point of Tokyo Imperial University, where they held professorial appointments, that a number of foreign academics introduced an entire generation of Japanese scholars to the scientific disciplines of anthropology and linguistics, as well as the pseudo-science of social Darwinism. Darwinian theories of natural selection were first introduced by Edward Morse, a founder member of the Tokyo Anthropological Society and first Professor of Zoology at Tokyo Imperial University, in a series of lectures on evolutionary theory given in 1877. A Japanese edition of Thomas Huxley's *Lectures on the Origin of Species* appeared two years later, while the publication of Morse's 1877 Tokyo lectures in 1881 brought Darwin's theories to an even larger audience.[37] The evolutionary theories of both Haeckel and Lamarck were also available to Japanese intellectuals, although neither achieved the immense popularity of Herbert Spencer. A Japanese translation of Spencer's evolutionary theory first appeared in 1884, and some thirty translations of his works had appeared by the turn of the century. The provision of a classificatory grid which located the Japanese within a hierarchy of 'race' and offered a scientifically reasoned yet easily accessible explanation for both the complexities of a modern society and national survival found a receptive audience among academics, journalists and politicians alike.

The dissemination of social Darwinism was also encouraged

[37] Shimao, 'Darwinism', pp. 93-102.

by early Japanese encounters with the various 'racisms' prevalent in the United States and the European colonies. These extend from a mission to the United States in 1860 to the Iwakura mission of 1871-3. In addition to the official reports, which were unavailable to the public, individual envoys and their attendants published personal accounts, often in diary form. For example, Yanagawa Kenzaburo, a member of the 1860 mission, seems to have uncritically absorbed the prejudices of his American hosts; his reference to the inherent stupidity and inferiority of blacks is paralleled by comparisons between blacks and the *Eta* outcasts drawn by Kimura Tetsuya.[38] Far more expansive was Kume Kunitake, later professor of history at Tokyo University, and one of two official secretaries who accompanied the Iwakura mission to Europe and the United States a decade later, whose two-volume account of the mission was first published in 1878 with the title *Tokumei zenken taishi Beiō kairan jikki* (A true account of the tour in America and Europe of the special embassy). In this and later publications Kume wrote at length of the origins and distinctive characteristics of the various peoples encountered by the mission.[39] His assessment of the industrial and military achievements of the Western powers included the following on the 'racial' origins of the British:

> The people of Britain are descended from two *shu* (races), the Celts and the Goths, and are divided into four *shu* (nations) – the English, Welsh, Scots and Irish – each possessing different languages and *fūzoku* (customs). The Celtic *jinshu* (race) were the original inhabitants of the country, but from about the year 450 AD Angles and Saxons gradually occupied the lowlands of England. The original inhabitants withdrew to the mountains of Scotland and Wales and the island of Ireland. The invaders from Germany were of the Gothic *shu* [race] and are referred to as the Anglo-Saxon *shu*. Later invasions by the Danes and the Normans took place, with all occupying the country of England. This was the origin of the English *jinshu* [race].[40]

[38] Leupp, 'Images', p. 7.

[39] I am indebted to my colleague, G.H. Healey, for bringing this source to my attention, and for making his notes available.

[40] Kume Kunitake, *Tokumei zenken taishi Beiō kairan jikki*, Tokyo: Iwanami shoten, 1985, vol. 2, p. 38 (hereafter *Jikki*).

In contrast to the British, whose inherent industriousness Kume regarded as the basis of their country's wealth and power, Spain's decline as a world power had come about through the indolence of its people:

> The people of Britain are unable to be idle for even a moment. The Spaniard makes a profession of sleeping all day, but a sole of an Englishmen's foot never rests on the ground. In Spain, as a consequence, merely to reduce the length of one's siesta is sufficient to gain a reputation for hard work.[41]

In these passages, Kume relies exclusively on the same character (*shu*) which appears in *jinshu* to describe various populations. Rather than signifying physiological differences, *jinshu* is defined in terms of cultural attributes. But an earlier passage in which Kume uses the character *shu* to describe the condition of the 'Indian' population of North America contains references to both physiological and cultural characteristics. Like Kimura a decade earlier, Kume also draws a direct physiological comparison between certain American 'Indians' and the *senmin* (literally lowly people) of Japan, a category which during the Tokugawa period incorporated the *Eta* and *Hinin* outcast groups:

> The American *dojin* [aboriginals] are known generally as 'Indians'. [...] Their physiognomy is like that often encountered among the *senmin* in Japan; swarthy skin, large nose, thick lips and high cheekbones. Their clothes are cast-offs which they beg from the ordinary citizens. They are incapable of learning a fixed mode of life.[42]

Kume's memoirs, *Kyūjunen kaikoroku* (A record of my ninety years), published in 1935, manifests the same conflation of cultural and 'racial' determinants. A section detailing the Iwakura mission's passage through the American Mid-West and California contains numerous references to relations between the Caucasian settler and native Americans. In the following, he comments on the fate of weaker 'races' when they come into contact with the more aggressive whites:

> The assertion by those who comment on the rise and fall

[41] *Jikki*, vol. 2, p. 39.
[42] *Jikki*, vol. 1, pp. 132-5.

of *jinshu* that the blond white-skinned *shuzoku* (race) will flourish while the Indians, Ainu *et al.* will become extinct is no exaggeration.[43]

Further evidence of the impact of social Darwinism on Japanese racial discourse can be found in a 1883 publication, *Nihon jinshu kairyōron* (Improvement of the Japanese race), in which the author, Takahashi Yoshio, advocated intermarriage with Westerners as the preferred means of enhancing the inferior physical and intellectual capacities of the Japanese.[44] Four years later, views identical to these were expressed by Kato Hiroyuki in a short piece entitled *Nihon jinshu kairyō no ben* (A justification for the improvement of the Japanese race).[45] The then prime minister, Ito Hirobumi, sought a second opinion from Herbert Spencer, who subsequently advised against interbreeding with Europeans on the grounds that hybridisation between disparate 'races' would, as in Latin America, produce disastrous consequences for both.[46]

Though of a later date, the social-Darwinist imprint could also be found in the pseudo-scientific disciplines of eugenics and serology embraced by a number of scholars during the interwar years. In their search for the unique origins of the Japanese 'race', Furuhata Tanemoto and Furukawa Takeji, for example, attempted to establish a deterministic link between blood type and social characteristics on the basis of fieldwork among the Ainu of Hokkaidō and the aboriginal population of Taiwan. Their claim for a definitive relationship between blood-type and temperament were widely publicised in such respected journals as *Hanzaigaku Zasshi* (Journal of Criminology) and *Minzoku Eisei* (Race Hygiene).

The impact of 'racial' as well as related theories of geographical or climatic determinism was also evident in contemporary textbooks, in which national achievement was cast in terms of the inherent capacities of its people or other natural factors. The work of Thomas Buckle, whose *History of Civilisation in England* was widely admired in Japan, represented a prime example of

[43] Kume Kunitake, *Kyūjunen kaikoroku* (A record of my ninety years), Osaka: Waseda Daigaku shuppanbu, 1935, vol. 2, p. 238.

[44] Ishii Ryoichi, *Population pressure and economic life in Japan*, Chicago University Press, 1937, pp. 38-9.

[45] Yun, 'Minzoku', p. 15.

[46] Nancy Stepan, *The idea of race in science: Great Britain 1800-1960*, London: Macmillan, 1982, p. 105.

this latter school of thought.[47] Along with history, geography – and, through it, knowledge of the outside world – formed an integral part of the national curriculum in Meiji schools. Early texts like Fukuzawa Yukichi's *Sekai kunizukushi* (World geography [1869]), of which more than a million copies were sold, grouped countries into an evolutionary hierarchy of barbarian, semi-civilised and civilised. Japan was cast as a country in transition from semi-civilised to civilised status. Although all civilised states were European in character, not all European nations were civilised. Echoing the views of Kume Kunitake, Fukuzawa wrote of Spain as a nation whose decline as a world power had come about as a result of inherent character deficiencies in its people. Scholarly enthusiasm for and interest in deterministic theories of social evolution also ensured that the assumed relationship between geography and *kokka ishiki* (national consciousness) featured prominently in secondary school textbooks. As a frequent contributor to school textbooks, Tsuboi Shogoro, professor of Anthropology at Tokyo Imperial University and a former student of Edward Morse, was typical of scholars who brought social Darwinism to a wider audience.

Increased ministerial control over textbook content in the years following the Imperial Rescript on Education (1890) did little to dampen enthusiasm for deterministic theories of social evolution. On the contrary, 'racial' differences between and within individual nations featured even more prominently. In that part of the *Bankoku chiri shoho* (Geography for beginners) which charts relations between the native American and Caucasian populations of the United States, the destitution of the former is portrayed as a consequence of their 'primitive and simple nature'.[48]

The social-Darwinian vocabulary thus provided an analytical framework which, as elsewhere, would be employed to justify wars of imperial expansion, while stifling complaints of social injustice and inequality within Japan. Within the context of the late nineteenth century and the early twentieth, characterised by both the social and economic upheavals associated with rapid

[47] Stefan Tanaka, *Japan's Orient: Rendering pasts into history*, Berkeley: University of California Press, 1993, pp. 39-40.

[48] Takeuchi Keiichi, 'How Japan learned about the outside world: The views of other countries incorporated in Japanese school textbooks, 1868-1986', *Hitotsubashi Journal of Social Studies*, vol. 19 (1987), p. 9.

industrialisation within Japan and the gradual acquisition of colonial
territories, national success was increasingly perceived as a manifestation of *seizon kyōsō* (struggle for survival) and *yūshō reppai* (survival
of the fittest).[49] This sense of national pride itself depended almost
entirely on how well Japan measured up against its most potent
rivals, and how far these accomplishments were recognised internationally. Everything else was relegated to the background,
with the indigenous populations of Hokkaidō, Taiwan and Korea
classified as stagnant, degenerate and incapable of appreciating
the resources they possessed.

Paradoxically, perhaps, it was also in the area of international
relations, particularly between Japan and the other imperial powers,
that a 'two-tiered' and, at least on the surface, contradictory conception of 'race' was articulated.[50] It was a conceptualisation which,
on the one hand, was predicated on a conflict between the white
and yellow 'races',[51] while on the other it assumed distinct and
immutable differences in intellectual and cultural capacities between
the Yamato *minzoku* and those of China and Korea. This allowed
Japanese ideologues to conceive of the world's population as com-
prising three 'races', along the lines set out by Arthur de Gobineau
and other European 'racial' theorists. Within this framework, the
Japanese were identified as belonging to the same 'racial' stock
as Koreans and Chinese. This did not, however, preclude the
existence of a further definition, which identified 'race' with
nation; a definition which, in equally deterministic terms, distinguished members of the Yamato *minzoku* from Chinese or
Koreans.

THE EXCLUDED OTHER

The production of theories of inclusion and exclusion was not
limited to those who lived beyond the spatial confines of Japan.
Social and economic relations within Japan were also commonly
viewed through a parallel, deterministic framework of the survival
of the fittest. These 'racisms' of the interior affected not only

[49] Gluck, *Japan's modern myths*, p. 209.
[50] Shimazu Naoko, 'The Japanese attempt to secure racial equality in 1919', *Japan Forum*, 1,
no. 1 (April 1989), p. 93.
[51] Oyama Azusa (ed.), *Yamagata Aritomo ikensho* (Memoranda of Yamagata Aritomo),
Tokyo: Hara shobō, 1966, p. 341.

traditional outsider populations, but the urban and rural poor in general. In each case, particular groups were identified not only by their poverty, but by certain assumed physical or cultural characteristics which set them apart.

In late nineteenth- and early twentieth-century Japan, *kasō shakai* (lower-class society) was excluded from mainstream society by virtue of both economic position and what were adjudged innate moral deficiencies. Although such groups were also referred to as *tennō no sekishi* (children of the emperor), evoking images of a seamless family state, they existed mostly beyond the pale of normal society. As with the adventures of *Bōken Dankichi*, referred to below, early accounts of the urban poor read like 'adventure stories in faraway lands'. That such reports were often compiled by officials engaged in the task of civilising the savage interior was itself significant, since it depended on the prior identification and exclusion of certain groups within the boundaries of the state. The urban slum was represented in contemporary newspapers and journals as the symbolic opposite of *bunmei* (civilisation). In contrast to the modern and civilised city, of which it was undeniably a part, the urban slum of the Meiji period was presented as a world existing somehow beyond civilisation; its inhabitants were depicted as the descendants of 'remote foreign races' on whom images of both *yaban* (savagery) and *ikai* (barbarism) were projected. In a classic 1897 study of Osaka slum-dwellers, for example, the area is described as a different world; inhabited by 'countless deaf, crippled, limbless and pygmies, all wrapped up in worst rags, wriggling like worms with griefs filling the air.'[52]

Such contemporary accounts are broadly comparable to those applied to the peasantry, whose 'peculiar physiognomy' made them readily identifiable.[53] In Mayama Seika's *Minami koizumi mura*, published several years after the Russo-Japanese war, peasant life was depicted as one of unspeakable misery, and the peasantry likened to 'insects that crawl on the ground.'[54] The author found

[52] Chubachi Masayoshi and Taira Koji, 'Poverty in modern Japan: Perceptions and realities' in Hugh Patrick (ed.), *Japanese industrialization and its social consequences*, Berkeley: University of California Press, 1976, pp. 391–437.

[53] Mikiso Hane, *Peasants, rebels and outcasts: The underside of modern Japan*, New York: Pantheon, 1982, pp. 34–5.

[54] Irokawa, *Culture of the Meiji period*, pp. 223 and 244.

it impossible to accept that 'the blood flowing in those miserable
peasants also flows in my body'. The former outcasts, too, despite
formal emancipation in 1871, were described by officials in Mie
prefecture thirty years later as a 'race' apart; ruthless, cruel and
lacking in any moral sense.[55] In all cases parallels can be drawn
across time, to the negative images of commoner and peasant
held by the samurai élites of the Tokugawa period, and across
space to the imagery employed against the 'lower orders' in the
industrialising nation states of late nineteenth- and early twentieth-century Europe and North America.

The Meiji period also witnessed the establishment of a colonial
order in Hokkaidō. Employing institutional and administrative
mechanisms very similar to those later deployed in Korea and
Taiwan, the Meiji state moved to exploit the island's strategic
and economic potential. In a process repeated elsewhere in the
empire, the Ainu were constructed as a primitive and 'racially'
immature population in a discourse which justified the colonial
project and made it inevitable. The colonial relationship with
the Ainu, and their categorisation as primitive savages, also provided
an initial context in which images of indigenous inferiority could
be contrasted with those of a modern, civilised Japan.

The maturation of a Japanese national identity thus found its
fullest expression in the context of the political, economic and
social processes which developed under colonial rule in Hokkaidō,
Korea and Taiwan. If a strongly collectivistic nationalism allowed
the Japanese to partake of a vibrant and assertive identity, the
existence of empire confirmed not only Japan's status as a truly
civilised nation but their own manifest superiority *vis-à-vis* the
peoples of East Asia. If industrial and technological achievements
were the indices of civilisation and enlightenment, then a lack
of material development could be regarded as scientific evidence
of inferior status. It was this very lack of both a martial spirit
and the institutions of modern industry which persuaded many
in Japan that the peoples of East Asia could only achieve a civilised
state through exposure to the work habits and martial values
which had produced a powerful Japan.[56] The first official history
of Hokkaidō, edited by the prominent Ainu scholar, Kōno

[55] Hane, *Peasants, rebels,* p. 146.
[56] *Jiji Shimpo,* 13 Aug. 1885, in Keio Gijuku (ed.) *Fukuzawa Yukichi zenshū* (The collected
works of Fukuzawa Yukichi), Tokyo: Keio gijuku, 1964, vol. 10, p. 381.

Tsunekichi, in 1918, confirmed that responsibility for the colonisation of Hokkaidō had fallen to the Japanese because 'no other
superior race was in contact with the *Ezo*'.

When the process of colonial acquisition began, first as a means
of acquiring economic privilege and later through territorial control,
it was justified in Tokyo as it had been in Europe. For some,
like Fukuda Tokuzo, the clear correlation between economic
development and the inherent and differing capacities of human
societies made Japanese expansion inevitable. Writing in 1902,
Fukuda argued that the transformation of Korea from a pre-
industrial to a modern capitalist society could only be accomplished
through Japanese intervention.[57] Imperial expansion was, in effect,
a redemptive mission to which the Japanese, by virtue of the
superiority of their *minzoku*, would have to resign themselves.

This perspective, founded upon the assumed inability of native
populations to manage their own affairs, reaffirmed a sense of
national solidarity and 'racial' superiority among the Japanese
people, regardless of what class they occupied at home. The sub-
division of the human species, which these assumptions affirmed,
also imposed a set of obligations on Japan as the colonising power.
These included not only raising colonial peoples to a level commensurate with their 'natural' abilities, but preserving the essential
and superior qualities of the Japanese 'race'. For some like Tokutomi
Sohō, imperial expansion was not merely an expression of Japan's
distinctive 'national essence' and the equally unique *kokuminsei*
(characteristics of its people), but the best available means of ensuring
the survival of the Japanese 'race'. His application of the laws
of natural survival in the arena of international relations also bears
comparison with a contemporary European publicist like Jules
Harmand.[58] Using terms remarkably similar to those of Tokutomi,
Harmand argued that 'conquest' was but a 'manifestation of the
law of struggle for existence' to which France was unavoidably
committed 'not merely by nature which condemns us to perish
or conquer, but also by our civilisation'.[59]

[57] Hatada Takashi, *Nihonjin no Chōsen kan* (The Japanese image of Korea), Tokyo: Keiso
Shobō, 1972, pp. 34-5; Yamabe Kentaro, *Nikkan heigo shōshi* (A short history of the
annexation of Korea), Tokyo: Iwanami shoten, 1978, p. 242.

[58] Jansen, 'Japanese imperialism', p. 66.

[59] Raymond F. Betts, *The false dawn: European imperialism in the nineteenth century*,
Minneapolis: University of Minnesota Press, 1975, pp. 12-13.

The marginalisation of subordinate populations, either as colonial subjects or as migrant labour drawn to the metropolitan core, was interpreted almost exclusively within the complementary discourses of 'race' and nation. Kawamura Minato has argued in this context that by the late 1920s 'mass orientalism', in which images of colonial and other inferior populations were contrasted with Japanese modernity and civilisation, had become an integral part of popular commonsense discourse. Imagery of this type was a regular feature in both novels and children's comic strips, the most popular of which was Shimada Keizo's *Bōken Dankichi* (Dankichi the Adventurer), which serialised the South Seas adventures of a Tintin-like protagonist. Second only to *Bōken Dankichi* were tales of the aptly-named common soldier, *Nora-kura* (Black Mutt), in which the (Chinese) enemy were regularly depicted as pigs.[60]

Core ideas of progress and civilisation, of which social scientific discourse formed an important part, further assisted in the ordering of popular knowledge of the excluded Other. An extremely popular vehicle for the celebration of modernity, civilisation and, subsequently, imperial expansion were the *hakurankai* (national expositions). In addition to Japanese participation in a number of international expositions held in Europe and the United States, the Meiji government hosted a similar series of expositions in Tokyo and Osaka between 1877 and 1903 as showcases of industrialisation and progress. Modelled on the first international exposition held in the Crystal Palace in 1851, Japanese variants were held in 1877, 1881, 1890, 1895 and 1903. Designed by the respected anthropologist, Tsuboi Shōgorō, the *Jinruikan* (Hall of Mankind) was intended as the centrepiece of the Fifth Industrial Exposition held in Osaka in 1903. Tsuboi's plan to exhibit the 'races' of the world in their 'natural' settings encountered vigorous opposition from Chinese, Koreans and Ryukyuans who objected to representations of their cultures as frozen in the past. The stark imagery of a primitive Asia, in contrast to a modern, civilised Japan, was however preserved in other exhibits detailing the lives of Ainu, Taiwanese aboriginals and Malays. The popular discourse

---

[60] Kawamura Minato, 'Taishū Orientarizumu to Ajia ninshiki' (Mass Orientalism and the perception of Asia) in Kawamura Minato (ed.), *Kindai Nihon to shokuminchi: Bunka no naka no shokuminchi* (Modern Japan and its colonies: Colonies in popular culture), vol. 7, Iwanami shoten, 1993, p. 119; Hane, *Peasants, rebels*, p. 75.

of the primitive Other was also sustained by the imagery of the Japanese civilising mission. Representations of this type were evident at both the *Takushoku Hakurankai* (Colonial Exposition) of 1912 and at the Natural History Museum in Sapporo. The latter contained life-size waxwork reproductions depicting the Japanese 'exploration' of Hokkaidō in 1870. The 'new' history of Hokkaidō, cast in images of a redemptive Japanese project and tethered to invidious stereotypes of racial infantilism and primitivism, was there for all to see.[61]

The set of meanings which the expositions and museum exhibitions of this type attached to the populations of outlying territories fused popular and socially scientific understandings of the Other within a dominant discourse of 'race'. By providing detailed and scientifically verified information about the 'racial' character, behaviour and habits of the Other, the social sciences offered both a further justification for paternalistic control and an archival resource on which colonial administrators could draw. Within the colonial context itself, 'racialised' discourses informed both policy formulation and administrative practice. Inequality was attributed to differences in national or 'racial' characteristics; differences which marked some peoples as unfit to survive in the struggle for existence. As such, their exclusion from the national community was adjudged natural and inevitable. Writing in 1918, Hiraoka Sadataro, the former governor of Karfuto, drew on the diverse threads of 'racial' knowledge in defining the Ainu as 'unadapted members of humanity...who have nothing to contribute to its well-being'. He further warned his readers that 'the introduction of Ainu blood into that of the Japanese will violate the movement to preserve our *kokusui*' (national essence).[62]

Even liberal-minded theorists like Nitobe Inazo and Takekoshi Yosaburo reasoned that, given the immense gulf separating the Japanese from their colonial subjects, it might be centuries before the latter could be raised to a level commensurate with civilisation.[63] Nitobe's assessment of the 'hairy Ainu' as a stone-age people

---

[61] Richard Siddle, 'Racialisation and resistance: The evolution of Ainu-Wajin relations in modern Japan', unpubl. Ph.D. dissertation, University of Sheffield, 1995, pp. 198-201.

[62] Ibid, pp. 184-5.

[63] Takekoshi Yosaburo, 'Japan's colonial policy' in *Oriental Review*, 3, no. 2 (1912), pp. 102-3; Mark R. Peattie, 'Japanese attitudes toward colonialism, 1895-1945' in Myers and Peattie, *Japanese colonial empire*, p. 94.

doomed to extinction also bears comparison with his earlier account of the Korean people, written in 1909:

> The very physiognomy and life-style of these people are so bland, unsophisticated and primitive that they belong not to the twentieth or the tenth – or indeed to the first century. They belong to a prehistoric age. [...] The Korean habits of life are the habits of death. They are closing the lease of their ethnic existence.[64]

The colonial project would therefore respect the laws of social evolution while enabling the Japanese to fulfil the obligations imposed by 'racial' superiority and cultural maturity. This dominant-subordinate structure was further reinforced by the traditional Confucian concept of *taigi mibun* (proper place), which locked the peoples of the empire into a fixed set of power relationships. This in turn not only assisted in the construction of colonial populations as 'racially' and culturally immature, but provided a gloss of tradition to the most extreme forms of political oppression and labour exploitation.

Paradoxically the same discourse of empire which reified assumed 'racial' differences between coloniser and colonised also presupposed the ultimate assimilation of the latter by the former. In acknowledging shared cultural and, in certain instances, 'racial' origins, some colonial theorists argued in favour of a common 'racial' destiny for the peoples of East Asia. But prewar assimilation policies demanded nothing less than complete abandonment of an independent Ainu, Taiwanese or Korean identity and its replacement by Japanese forms of behaviour. Nor did the objectives of assimilation necessarily extend to the eventual provision of equal citizenship rights. Instead, assimilation was perceived as a process which would enable colonial peoples to assume their natural and proper place in a 'racially' defined hierarchy of dependent states within the empire.[65] The outcome, it was assumed, would be a new colonial identity retaining certain aspects of indigenous culture, while sharing a sense of community and purpose with

---

[64] Nitobe Inazo, *Thoughts and essays*, Tokyo: Teibi Publishing Company, 1909, pp. 214 and 216.

[65] Takeda Yukio, 'Naichi zaijū hantōjin mondai' (The problem of peninsulars [Koreans] residing in Japan), *Shakai Seisaku Jiho*, no. 213 (1938), p. 121.

the Japanese.[66] The state could thus project the colonial enterprise as familial and as an expression of the natural social order. Moreover, by fulfilling its civilising mission in Asia, a role thrust upon Japan by virtue of the dynamic qualities of its own people, the continued purity and vitality of the Japanese race would also be ensured.

---

[66] Dower, *War without mercy*, pp. 274 and 281.

'SAME LANGUAGE, SAME RACE'
THE DILEMMA OF *KANBUN* IN MODERN JAPAN

Kazuki Sato

As Japan entered the Meiji period (1868-1912), *kanbun* (Chinese classics and classical writing), which had formed the basis for Tokugawa (1603-1868) education, became a compulsory part of the new school curriculum.[1] The problem, however, was that while *kanbun* continued to be taught in the schools, the road to modernity signalled a change in Japan's reverence for China as a cultural mentor. For most Japanese, whose feelings for China were coloured by an ambivalence which ranged from respect to contempt, support for *kanbun* began to waver.

The special relationship which Japan and China were said to have shared from ancient times was dictated by the intellectually sophisticated level of China's culture whether in art, calligraphy, literature or Confucianism. Moreover, it was a relationship existing only between intellectuals.[2] From the 1870s, however, the Japanese public at large regarded the Chinese as aliens, just as they did other foreigners. Indeed, their first actual encounters in their daily life with Chinese people, as opposed to Chinese thought, followed the signing of the Sino-Japanese Amity Treaty (*Nisshin shūkō jōki*) in 1871. On the popular level, both the gap between Japan and China's willingness to modernise and the general uneasiness the Japanese experienced with people unfamiliar to themselves were instrumental in molding an image of the Chinese as ethnically inferior.

[1] See R. P. Dore, *Education in Tokugawa Japan*, Berkeley and Los Angeles: University of California Press, 1965, especially chap. 4.

[2] Donald Keene, *Landscapes and portraits: Appreciations of Japanese culture*, Tokyo: Kōdansha, 1972, pp. 259-62.

In the light of the promotion of the early Meiji Westernisation programme, it became an important factor to draw attention to the spiritual significance of Japan's cultural identity. Turning to China, with which Japan shared a rich historical and cultural heritage, was invaluable in achieving that aim. For example, from the 1890s, elementary school children all over Japan memorised the Imperial Rescript on Education (*Kyōiku chokugo*), which was infused with Confucian morality. The addition of *kanbun* to the curriculum in the middle school years assured an even higher level of Chinese education. Even a sense of racial identity was interpreted within a framework of opposition between 'Caucasians' and 'Asians', in which Chinese were regarded as next of kin. Alignment with the Chinese rather than with Westerners was justified not so much in terms of physical similarities, but more as a result of the close geographical and historical links thought to exist between the two countries. The term coined by intellectuals which best expressed that community of interests was *dōbun dōshu*, 'same language, same race', stressing the shared ethnic and intellectual heritage of Japan and China while emphasising the differences between East and West. *Dōbun dōshu* was seen as a way of promoting emotional bonds with China and of enhancing the significance of *kanbun* study.

From the 1890s onwards, the ambivalent attitudes towards China began to spread, and nationalistic sentiment gained adherents. Things Chinese came to be repositioned alongside things Western, as both were identified as foreign in nature. As the desire for expansion into China became more widespread, Japan distanced itself from China rather than being on the receiving end and seeking China's sympathy and understanding. It was for Japan to seize the initiative and maintain a position of leadership *vis-à-vis* people who were now considered to be different.

These developments did not mean that *kanbun* or reliance on the notion of *dōbun dōshu* disappeared. Until 1945, *kanbun* remained an obligatory subject for middle-school students; just as *dōbun dōshu* previously symbolised the 'good will' that 'officially' expressed the Japanese position towards China. However, as the significance of the intellectual heritage and presumed common origin of Japan and China lost its original meaning and the Japanese cast aside their psychological debt to China, *kanbun* and *dōbun dōshu* were reconfigured to accommodate a new perspective. This chapter addresses the Japanese attempt to construct a racial identity by tracing the shifts within the debate over *kanbun* and *dōbun dōshu* on both the intellectual and popular levels from the 1870s till the inter-war period, placing these debates within the social and historical context of Japanese imperialist aims in China.

THE ILLUSION OF *DŌSHU*: THE CHINESE AS A DIFFERENT RACE

Of the different interest groups embroiled in the controversies over Japan's diplomatic policies in China in the late nineteenth century, those who emphasised the closeness which was thought to bind the two countries inextricably used the term *dōbun dōshu*. In spite of their insistence that 'We are both Orientals and share a common language, customs and similar temperament', such statements had little credibility in a society where most citizens had embraced the state's quest for Westernisation.[3]

   Dōbun dōshu ran counter to these interests in two ways. First, if Japan and China did in fact share a common heritage, then China too deserved the epithet of 'uncivilised'. Even advocates of *dōbun dōshu* conceded that 'Since Japan took the first step and embarked on a programme which extolled the benefits of civilisation and enlightenment (*bunmei kaika*), the Japanese have denigrated the Chinese in order to win the approbation of the West. China's respect, once essential to Japan's well-being, is a vestige of the past.'[4] Secondly, the argument that a country's diplomatic policies could be determined by historical ties or blood relations, as implied by *dōbun dōshu,* was considered to be irrational. In other words, the scope of the bonds which united one country to another should be decided purely according to the standard of 'civilisation' a country had attained. A scholar writing in 1884 remarked disdainfully: 'Expressing an affinity for people who are physically alike and an aversion for those unlike us in appearance, without taking into consideration intellectual qualities or the good

---

[3] *Tokyo nichinichi shinbun* (The Tokyo daily newspaper), 28 Nov. 1875, in Shibahara Takuji, Igai Takaaki and Ikeda Masahiro (eds), *Taigaikan: Nihon kindai shisō taikei* (A view from abroad: Modern Japanese intellectual history series), vol. 12, Tokyo: Iwanami shoten, 1988, p. 259.

[4] Ibid., p. 259.

of the state, smacks of the barbaric.'[5]

As early as the 1920s, the opinion that the Sino-Japanese war marked a turning point in the Japanese attitude toward China from one of respect and intimacy to one of disdain and scorn was increasingly heard. Recent research has continued to support that view.[6] Hashikawa Bunzō, one of the few scholars to question its validity, thought that until the eve of the Sino-Japanese war Japan still remained culturally and emotionally dependent on China.[7] On the other hand some Japanese, such as a former feudal lord from central Japan who hoped to curry favour with the Chinese, wrote flowery, self-effacing statements praising the Chinese for their superior ways: 'Your calligraphy is superb, and your prose is beyond reproach. Even if hundreds of thousands of Japanese monkeys [like myself] tried to imitate you, we could never reach the heights of the venerable Chinese with the queue.'[8] However, such statements were limited in number and generally only appeared several years before the war. When hostilities actually erupted, such flagrant self-denigration by the Japanese was no longer in vogue. One reason was that after Japan's 'exclusion' policy officially ended in 1853, a small number of working-class Chinese, hitherto an unknown entity in Japan, entered the country and took up residence in concessions reserved for foreigners. Unlike the Chinese literati, who were revered for their classical training, these people earned their livelihood as traders, merchants, unskilled labourers and even domestics. Moreover, the image they conveyed was not concomitant with a people from a country revered for its sophisticated culture.

The *Yomiuri* newspaper carried a piece in 1876 recounting an incident which involved a Chinese worker, dubbed 'Mr Pigtail' by the press. While hawking his goods, he had collided with a buckwheat noodle delivery man. Forced to make good on

---

[5] *Jiyū shinbun* (The free press), 28-30 Aug. 1884, in *Taigaikan: Nihon kindai shisō taikei*, vol. 12, pp. 290-1.

[6] Iguchi Kazuki, 'Nihonjin no kokusai seijikan' (A Japanese view of international politics) in Iguchi Kazuki (ed.), *Kindai Nihon no kiseki: Nisshin-Nichiro senso* (Trends in modern Japanese history: The Sino-Japanese and Russo-Japanese wars), vol. 3, Tokyo: Yoshikawa kōbunkan, 1994, pp. 232-3.

[7] Hashikawa Bunzō, *Jungyaku no shisō: Datsu'a ron igo* (Loyalty and treason: In the aftermath of 'On leaving Asia'), Tokyo: Keisō shobō, 1973, p. 366.

[8] Sanetō Keishū (tr. and ed.), *Ōkōchi bunsho* (Ōkōchi documents), Tokyo: Heibonsha, Tōyō bunko, 1964, p. 43.

the overturned noodles, he declared: 'Since I had to pay all of 6 sen to cover the cost of the noodles, they belong to me.' He then scooped up the noodles which were strewn about on the dirty road, wrapped them in a towel, and continued on his rounds.[9] Such articles, together with rumours spread by word of mouth, helped to create a new representation of the Chinese as poor, dirty and penny-pinching. By 1894 this image had already become common in the minds of the Japanese public at large.

Nevertheless, negotiations on the issue of the unequal treaties, a thorn in Japan's side since the late 1850s, depended in part on Japan's willingness to allow foreigners to reside outside the concessions in areas of their own choosing. For Japanese citizens, who were accustomed to maintaining a certain social distance from foreigners, the possibility of becoming members of a diverse community was filled with fear and uncertainty. The question of mixed residence not only forced the public to come to terms with the issue that different people lived in close proximity, but was also instrumental in forming the modern notions of race and identity. The trauma which this debate triggered, moreover, was not directed towards Westerners, who were a historically and culturally unknown quantity, but against the Chinese.

For the average Japanese at that time, the only Chinese they had contact with were the men and women who made their homes in the concessions located in capital cities and ports like Nagasaki and Yokohama. Because their social status overlapped with that of the Japanese working class, they aroused feelings of rivalry and jealousy among their Japanese counterparts. Chinese merchants, for example, were described on the one hand as 'persevering and industrious,' and on the other as 'greedy and quick to make money'. Those performing unskilled tasks were portrayed as 'people who do not seem to mind being harnessed like cows or horses and put to work'.[10] Because it was assumed that the Japanese exhibited none of these negative qualities, competing with the Chinese for jobs on similar terms was deemed impossible.

[9] *Yomiuri shinbun* (Yomiuri newspaper), 26 May 1876, quoted in Miyatake Gaikotsu, *Meiji kibun* (Gossip in Meiji), Tokyo: Hankyōdō, 1925, reprinted in Yazawa Eiichi and Yoshino Takao (eds), *Miyatake Gaikotsu zenshū* (Complete works of Miyatake Gaikotsu), vol. 1, Tokyo: Kawade shobō shinsha, 1986, p. 218.

[10] Editorial, 'Shinajin no naichi zakkyo o ronzu' (A discussion on mixed residency and the Chinese), *Nihonjin* (The Japanese), no. 35 (Nov. 1889), reprint, Tokyo: Nihon tosho sentā, 1983, vol. 2, pp. 297-8. (Page citations are to the reprinted edition.)

Even after the more than twenty-year-long debate over mixed residence reached a conclusion in 1899 and foreigners were permitted to live freely in Japan, the Chinese continued to be singled out and were prohibited from working as unskilled labourers.[11]

That is not to say that the Japanese passively resigned themselves to the presence of Chinese residents. Positive qualities like the business acumen and diligence exhibited by Chinese residents were regarded as legitimate cause for suspicion and reason enough to be vigilant towards them. When the novelist Tsubouchi Shōyō (1859-1935) published a futuristic allegory in 1886, detailing the social conditions that would exist in a Japan overridden by foreigners, public interest soared. Tsubouchi's predictions fuelled the fears of many Japanese: 'By nature Chinese workers are a sneaky bunch and their avarice knows no bounds. No matter how small the profit may be, they're determined to take on all the work they can. Whether the Chinese are engaged as day labourers, perform odd jobs or pull rickshaws, they rush out to try and grab any available job. The Japanese will surely be overpowered.'[12]

Nevertheless, the issue involved more than competition with Chinese commercial skills and friction over employment opportunities. Chinese residents were not seen to be members of a privileged class and were said to lack the cultivation that was expected from a highly sophisticated culture. Some Japanese went so far as to attribute their 'cunning' and 'avarice' to their indigent backgrounds. In their minds, nothing but misfortune could be gained from the entry into Japanese society of this class of Chinese. The following discussion which was found in Tsubouchi's allegory was a re-enactment of an interview that occurred between Tsubouchi and Prime Minister Ōkuma Shigenobu (1838-1922). It expressed the sentiments harboured by many Japanese.

[11] Chinese were prohibited from engaging in farming, fishing, mining, construction, manufacturing, and working as 'coolies', at the same time as mixed residence was approved. They were permitted, however, to work as domestics. See Takita Sachiko, '"Tan'itsu minzoku kokka" shinwa no datsu shinwaka' (Beyond the myth of the single nation state) in Kajita Takamichi (ed.), *Kokusai shakaigaku: Kokka o koeru genshō o dōtoraeru ka* (International sociology: How to interpret trends related to the transcension of national boundaries), Nagoya: Nagoya daigaku shuppankai, 1992, p. 295. For a discussion in English of mixed residence, see Carol Gluck, *Japan's modern myths: Ideology in the late Meiji period*, Princeton University Press, 1985, pp. 136-7.

[12] Tsubouchi Shōyō often used the pen name Harunoya Oboro during the 1880s. Harunoya Oboro, *Naichi zakkyo: Mirai no yume* (Mixed residence: A dream for the future), 1886, reprint, Tokyo: Fukunaga shoten, 1926, p. 194.

Politician: Don't you think Hibikiyama [a *sumō* wrestler] is getting stronger these days?

Prime Minister: Yes, but he plays dirty ... the same way Chinese merchants conduct business.

Politician: ... Talking about the Chinese, did you hear the news about the opium cache? ...

Prime Minister: ... These Chinese have abominable customs. More important, they're influencing Japanese morals. Just look at what has happened in [Japanese] working-class neighbourhoods. In the past six or seven years, Japanese standards of morality have gone way downhill.

Politician: ... We're going to have to adopt the same kind of exclusion policy that the Americans did, and do it fast. Spiritually, they [Chinese] are debasing our morals. Socially, they are ruining our economy.

Prime Minister: Dealing with these Chinese is as bothersome as contending with fleas or buzzing mosquitoes on a summer evening. Spiritually and economically the Chinese have laid siege to our country. It's as if they caught us by surprise in our sleep and sucked our blood like fleas or mosquitoes.[13]

In fact, the exclusion of Chinese immigrants first started in the United States. The influx of cheap Chinese labour into California in the 1860s led to a series of anti-Chinese demonstrations in the following decade aimed at banning Chinese labourers from entering the country. By the 1900s, prejudice was no longer limited to the Chinese, but directed against the Japanese as well. A more inclusive immigration act which banned all Asians received Congressional approval in 1924.[14] Under the circumstances, Japanese sympathies should have rested with the Chinese, certainly at the time when Tsubouchi Shōyō was writing. Instead, the Japanese chose to side with the Americans. In a situation of economic conflict, they assumed that the real or imagined behaviour exhibited by Chinese residents was the natural result of specific cultural and racial 'characteristics'. It has been observed that

[13] Ibid., pp. 136-7.

[14] On the psychology behind America's exclusion of Chinese immigrants, see Sean Dennis Cashman, *America in the guilded age: From the death of Lincoln to the rise of Theodore Roosevelt*, New York University Press, 1984, pp. 113-14. For further discussion on America's exclusionary policies, see Warren I. Cohen, *America's response to China: A history of Sino-American relations*, New York: Columbia University Press, 1990, pp. 30-1.

this process is typical of the formation of racial identities.[15] In other words, for Japanese in this period, similarities in physical appearance did not elicit feelings of camaraderie or create harmonious ties between the two peoples. As the discourse over mixed residence intensified, the argument ceased to be based primarily on cultural distinctions, and came to include biological differences separating the Chinese from the Japanese.

Miyake Setsurei (1860-1945), editor of the nationalistic magazine *Nihonjin* (The Japanese) and representative of the type of modernising intellectuals who were active at that time, first couched his prejudices in cultural terms when he spoke in 1889 of the evils which would befall a Japan teeming with Chinese residents. 'They are a vulgar people who know no shame, have no manners or moral standards. They are uneducated ignoramuses. Once they start descending on us, their numbers will multiply and they will continue spreading out. The myriad of evil habits they transmit will corrupt our way of life.' However, Miyake's warning was not founded solely on cultural preconceptions. Racial prejudice was also apparent in his choice of words. 'If the descendants of these inferior Chinese people increase in Japan, some members of the Yamato race will definitely inherit their genes. Alas, the make-up of our people will undergo a complete change. Our purity of purpose and the loyal spirit of our men, which took over two thousand years to come into existence, will collapse in an instant.'[16]

In another article which appeared in the 1889 issue of *Nihonjin,* the author claimed: 'Our ancestors passed through Mesopotamia, Arabia, Egypt and India. Descendants of the Caucasoids, they traveled across the ocean and immigrated to our land.'[17] In 1890, yet another article went so far as to show that 'the progenitors of Japan were Japanese and could never have been Chinese.'[18] The writer stressed that even if the Japanese resembled the Chinese

[15] See John Rex, 'The role of class analysis in the study of race relations: A Weberian perspective' in John Rex and David Mason (eds), *Theories of race and ethnic relations*, Cambridge University Press, 1988, pp. 72-4.

[16] Editorial, 'Shinajin no naichi zakkyo o ronzu', *Nihonjin*, no. 35 (Nov. 1889), vol. 2, p. 299 (page citation is to the reprint edition).

[17] 'Nihonjin no hakujin ni taisuru chii' (The Japanese position on Caucasians), *Nihonjin*, no. 28 (June 1889), vol. 2, p. 698 (page citation is to the reprint edition).

[18] 'Nihonjin no shiso wa Nihonjin nari' (The Japanese origin is Japanese), *Nihonjin,* no. 58 (Nov. 1890), vol. 4, p. 638 (page citation is to the reprint edition).

physically, they were racially different. By arguing that the Japanese shared a common origin with Caucasians and not with the Chinese, the question of Japan's racial identity was thrown further into confusion, making it difficult to attach any meaning to the notion of *dōbun dōshu*.

DŌBUN COMES UNDER ATTACK: KANBUN VERSUS KOKUGO

From the late nineteenth century onwards, *kanbun* apologists like the writer and journalist Morita Shiken (1861-97) lamented the fact that the work performed by scholars of classical Chinese had been reduced to carrying out a few formalised and perfunctory tasks. Erudite scholars, he argued, spent their days writing epitaphs for tombstones, eulogies for monuments, epigraphs for books, and compiling travelogues and biographical accounts of famous people.[19] Morita contended that the Chinese classics, which were written in *kanbun* and formed the basis for Confucian studies, had to be preserved; reading the texts in the original was essential for inculcating into the Japanese the proper standard of ethics characteristic of Confucianism. Moreover, because *kanbun* served as a tool for mastering the precise meanings of Chinese characters and idiomatic expressions, it was impossible to write sophisticated Japanese prose without a thorough grounding in the fine grammatical points and stylistic elements of *kanbun*. In the narrow sense, the use of the term *dōbun* connoted a common language, but in a broader sense it implied a cultural commonality based on shared values. In other words, language and morality were seen to be conterminous with cultural identity. The two roles which Morita attributed to *kanbun* both fitted the concept of *dōbun dōshu*.

With the rise of nationalism in Japan in the late 1880s, however, most Japanese sought to establish an independent identity that would distance themselves from China, rather than searching for ways which emphasised the shared cultural heritage of both countries. Not only the concept of *dōshu*, with its emphasis on

[19] Morita Shiken, 'Wagakuni ni okeru kangaku no genzai oyobi mirai' (The present and future of Chinese studies in Japan) in Katō Shūichi and Maeda Ai (eds), *Buntai: Nihon kindai shisō taikei* (Literary styles: Modern Japanese thought series), vol. 16, Tokyo: Iwanami shoten, 1989, pp. 35-8.

the sameness of 'race', but also *dōbun,* or same language, found itself in an increasingly unfriendly environment. Some Japanese language professors at Tokyo Imperial University advised that all references to Chinese should be eliminated from the Japanese written language. One highly respected Japanese language professor at the Imperial University, Ueda Kazutoshi (1867–1937), who returned to Japan from a research trip to Germany just at the time Japan was defeating China in the Sino-Japanese war, aired his dissatisfaction with the situation in a public speech:

> In today's society, unless you are proficient in Chinese, you are not qualified to write an imperial rescript, let alone any formal documents. Moreover, you have absolutely no hope of securing a good position in society. [...] As long as you can write in *kanbun,* the prose is considered correct. If you write in the vernacular, you are labelled a fool for using vulgar, colloquial language. Unfortunately, supporters of modern Japanese are hard to find these days. [...] Since the beginning of history, Japan has never come under China's yoke, and now our army and navy are winning victory after victory. Even though the Chinese people must pay obeisance before the Japanese flag, what a tragedy to think that our national language still remains governed by *kanbun.*[20]

The disapproval of Japan's cultural dependence on China resulted not only from the influence of *kanbun* on the Japanese language, but also from Japan's reliance on Confucian ethics. Loyalty and filial piety, both basic tenets of Confucianism and the foundation on which the Imperial Rescript on Education (1890) rested, became a cause for dissent behind the scenes. Yoshikawa Akimasa (1841–1920), a former Minister of Education and one of the authors of the Rescript, admitted twenty years later that when word got out about the contents of the Rescript, he anticipated a barrage of criticism against a doctrine steeped in Confucian ethics but passing as the moral backbone of the Japanese people.[21] The promul-

---

[20] Ueda Kazutoshi, 'Kokugo kenkyū ni tsuite' (Research on the national language), 1894, in *Meiji bungaku zenshū* (Collected works on Meiji literature), vol. 44, Tokyo: Chikuma shobō, 1968, pp. 114-15. For Ueda's role in the development of the national language (*kokugo*), see Fujii Sadakazu, 'Kokubungaku no tanjō' (The birth of a national literature), *Shisō*, no. 845 (Nov. 1994), Tokyo: Iwanami shoten, p. 58.

[21] Yoshikawa Akimasa, 'Kyōiku chokugo gokashi jijō' (Circumstances surrounding the Imperial Rescript on Education), *Kyōiku jiron* (Education chronicle), no. 6 (July, 1912),

gation of the Rescript called into question the meaning of 'traditional' values, rekindling the old Edo controversy voiced by nativist scholars like Motoori Norinaga (1730-1801), who debated Japan's position in relation to China.[22] When Ueda Kazutoshi was named to head a prestigious committee within the Ministry of Education in 1898, it was evident that the call for a culturally independent Japan had come to reflect the official stand. As a result, the continuation of *kanbun* in schools met with further difficulties.

The first official plan to drop *kanbun* from the middle school curriculum was published in 1900 by the Ministry of Education.[23] In 1918, Ueda's colleague at the Imperial University, Haga Yaichi (1867-1927) asserted:

> Everyone already knows that standard Japanese is syntactically influenced by *kanbun,* and includes a great deal of vocabulary extrapolated from *kanbun,* but why persist in continuing with this practice? We must rid ourselves of the vestiges of that perverse period when the Japanese language was overpowered by *kanbun.* Even what we teach our children is essentially a code of ethics that came from China. When I think of it from the perspective of our national education policy, I realise how serious the situation has become.[24]

In 1921 the Minister of Education, Nakahashi Tokugorō (1864-1934), remarked, 'Isn't it enough that elements of *kanbun* are already in our Japanese language texts? Why do we need to devote special class time to *kanbun*?'[25] Nakahashi, too, agreed that *kanbun* had to go.

In spite of the resolution handed down by the Ministry of Education in 1900, followed by an outpouring of sentiment in

---

reprinted in *Kyōiku chokugo kanpatsu kankei shiryōshū* (Documents on the promulgation of the Imperial Rescript on Education), vol. 1, Tokyo: Kokumin seishin bunka kenkyūjo, 1939, p. 460.

[22] Gluck, *Japan's modern myths,* p. 125.

[23] *Shibun rokujūnen* (Sixty years of Chinese studies), Shibunkai (ed.), Tokyo: Shibunkai, 1929, p. 290.

[24] Haga Yaichi, 'Chūgakkō ni okeru kanbun o haishi seyo' (Abolish Chinese classics from the middle-school curriculum), *Kokugo kyōiku* (National language education), vol. 3, no. 9 (1918), reprinted in *Kokugo kyōikushi shiryō* (Documents on the history of national language education), vol. 5, Tokyo: Tokyo hōrei shuppan, 1981, pp. 174-5.

[25] *Yomiuri shinbun,* Jan. 16, 1921.

favour of the demise of *kanbun,* the Ministry failed to execute its plan. The main reason was that for almost twenty years *kanbun* apologists, like the members of the Shibunkai movement founded in 1918, were so strident in their opposition that they were able to override even a decision taken by someone of Nakahashi's stature. The Shibunkai, composed of teachers of *kanbun* at the university and lower school levels, together with conservative politicians, published a monthly magazine, *Shibun,* extolling the benefits of Confucianism and *kanbun.*[26] Anxious to win political support for their cause, they exerted pressure on powerful members of the Diet. As a result of their efforts, resolutions advocating further advancement of *kanbun* in schools won formal approval in the Diet for three consecutive years, beginning in 1921. Not only was the Ministry of Education forced to shelve its original proposal, but in 1923 the government went a step further and awarded a large sum of money to the Great Eastern Cultural Association (Daitō bunka kai) to establish the College of Great Eastern Culture (Daitō bunka gakuin) devoted solely to Chinese classical studies.

However, winning recognition for *kanbun* in the Diet and among some government leaders did not assure the support of intellectuals or society at large. The *Yomiuri* newspaper chided the *kanbun* apologists: 'In this day and age no one cares about what Confucius said except bald, old men who do a lot of non-sensical raving about *kanbun.*'[27] A 1924 editorial in the *Tokyo asahi* newspaper was critical of the government's decision to sub-sidise the College of Great Eastern Culture, pointing to more worthwhile undertakings: 'What a ridiculous waste of money for the government to provide financial assistance for *kanbun.*'[28] Obviously, this did not amount to a full vindication for *kanbun*'s defenders. Their defence of the advantages of the linguistic and moral training to be gained from studying *kanbun,* supported by the use of the *dōbun dōshu* myth, was already losing ground. Since the Japanese were increasingly aware of an identifiable, unified Japanese language quite distinct from Chinese, studying

[26] *Shibun rokujūnen,* pp. 316-22. See also Martin Collcutt, 'The legacy of Confucianism in Japan' in Gilbert Rozman (ed.), *The East Asian region,* Princeton University Press, 1991, pp. 151-2.

[27] *Yomiuri shinbun,* 8 July 1923.

[28] *Tokyo asahi shinbun* (Tokyo asahi newspaper), 20 Nov. 1924.

kanbun, which depended exclusively on the use of Chinese characters, became a laborious task for students. Although classes in moral training (*shūshin*) were also compulsory and equally stressed Confucian morality, the *shūshin* texts were written in plain Japanese and taught ethics through heroic accounts of historical Japanese figures or topics directly related to everyday life in Japan. In contrast, *kanbun* texts taught Confucianism on the basis of esoteric Chinese classics which had little relevance to students' lives. One middle-school student complained: 'Why do we have to slave over obtuse texts to learn about moral issues that are obvious to any dumb-bell?'[29] A Diet member, commenting on the status of *kanbun* teachers in schools, declared: 'Those *kanbun* teachers who specialise in Confucian studies ought to admit that at school, they are ranked at the bottom of the hierarchy and regarded by colleagues and students alike as passé.'[30] Not only the Ministry of Education, but a large segment of society had come to find *kanbun* a fruitless endeavour. *Kanbun* apologists were no longer in a position to stress Japan's linguistic and moral obligations to China. A new *raison d'être* was needed.

A NEW LIFE FOR *DŌBUN DŌSHU*

Although neither the public's perception of China nor the country's educational policy harmonised with *dōbun dōshu,* it once again attracted attention after the Russo-Japanese war in 1905. Used repeatedly from the 1870s by Japanese politicians and journalists, *kanbun*'s defenders now saw this as a perfect device for stressing the presumed immutable differences between 'East' and 'West'. They increasingly racialised different identities into an opposition between 'white' and 'yellow'. For example, during the First World War, elder statesman Yamagata Aritomo (1838–1922) advised: 'Rivalry between the white and yellow races will probably intensify. The way to maintain independence as a nation and assure that the white race treats us as equals is for Japan and China, who share the same language and skin colour, to break down the barriers separating our two countries and to create a

---

[29] Gotō Asatarō, 'Kanbunka ni kyōmi arashimeyo' (Creating an interest in the study of Chinese classics), *Shibun,* vol. 11, no. 2 (1928), pp. 1–2.

[30] 'Kangaku shinkō ni kansuru kengian' (Diet resolution on the promotion of Chinese studies), *Shibun,* vol. 5, no. 2 (1923), p. 6.

solid front.'[31] In fact, the myth of *dōbun dōshu* was more than a mere nationalist appeal to defend the 'yellow race' from the 'white race.' As Japan moved into the twentieth century, it became a convenient ploy used to rationalise Japan's entry into China and its right to exercise control over China's internal affairs. On the one hand, *dōbun dōshu* was a persuasive ideology which united Japan and China against the West. On the other hand, it created an inseparable gulf between Japan and China. Japan, moreover, hardly considered China its equal. Even Konoe Atsumaro (1863-1904), who lectured on *dōbun dōshu* more than ten years before Yamagata Aritomo, remarked: 'The Chinese have a tendency not to be systematic in the way they work. They would benefit from having the opportunity to work with the Japanese. The Japanese must assume the dominant position in order to "educate" and "lead" the Chinese in the right direction.'[32] As expansionist policies gave rise to a sense of economic, military, cultural and biological uniqueness, Japan expended much energy defining itself as a superior race. The literary critic Sugiyama Heisuke (1895-1946) confirmed these feelings when he wrote in 1938: 'When the Japanese moved into China, it was natural that they thought of their own interests first and not those of the Chinese.' He went on to say: 'Japanese are not only superior to Chinese on the battlefield, but they are also one rank ahead of them in brain power.'[33]

The more pride the Japanese took in their own presumed uniqueness, the more the portrayal of the Chinese as a strange, different and inferior race spread among the general public. First, the very idea of *dōshu*, or same race, was already contested on a popular level, as illustrated in the controversy over anthropological exhibitions. Protests voiced by Chinese exchange students over the

[31] Yamagata Aritomo, 'Ikensho' (My opinion), (1915), quoted in Ban'no Junji, *Meiji: Shisō no jitsuzō* (Meiji: The reality of thought), Tokyo: Sōbunsha, 1977, p. 133.

[32] Konoe Atsumaro, 'Hiroshima enzetsu: Tōa dōbunkai no mokuteki' (Speech delivered in Hiroshma: The aims of the East Asian common language association), (1900) in Tōa bunka kenkyūjo (ed.), Tōa dōbunkaishi (The history of the East Asian common language association), Tokyo: Kazankai, 1988, p. 184. Konoe shared similar views on 'solidarity' with Arao Sei, an important force behind the founding of Konoe's Tōa dōbunkai. See Douglas R. Reynolds, 'Training young China hands: Tōa dōbun shoin and its precursors, 1886-1945' in Peter Duus, Ramon H. Myers and Mark R. Peattie (eds), *The Japanese informal empire in China, 1895-1937*, Princeton University Press, 1989, pp. 222-3.

[33] Sugiyama Heisuke, *Shina to Shinajin to Nihon* (China, Chinese and Japan), Tokyo: Kaizōsha, 1938, p. 24.

Osaka Exhibition (1903) were successful in the first decade of the century.[34] But by the 1910s, popular support and even enthusiasm for public displays which focused on imagined racial and cultural differences enabled organisers of exhibitions to ignore such Chinese protests. For example, one Chinese student wrote an impassioned and irate letter which was published in a Chinese newspaper after he returned home. It included these words: 'Japanese museums only like to display models which depict uncivilised Chinese customs that are a carry-over from ancient times. These exhibitions prove that the Japanese are resorting to psychological means to make fools out of the Chinese.'[35] This student resented the fact that Japan represented China as a country frozen in time. He also established a connection between racism and imperialism. Portraying the Chinese as uncivilised people merely served Japan's ambition to colonise China.[36] However, the letter had virtually no impact.

Secondly, in contrast to the unpopular *kanbun* texts, various books written by old China-hands about the 'strange' lifestyle and customs of that 'mysterious' country beyond the sea came to enjoy a wide readership on a popular level, in the same way that the anthropology exhibitions attracted attention. Gotō Asatarō (1881-1945), one of Japan's foremost China-hands, published thirty-one such books from 1927 to 1932 describing in detail the opium addiction, drinking habits and toilet manners of the Chinese.[37]

---

[34] *Zhejiangchao*, no. 2 (1903), p. 134. Also see Yan Ansheng, *Nihon ryūgaku seishinshi: Kindai Chūgoku chishikijin no kiseki* (An intellectual history of Chinese students in Japan: Trends among modern Chinese intellectuals), Tokyo: Iwanami shoten, 1991, pp. 99-102, and Paula Harrell, *Sowing the seeds of change: Chinese students, Japanese teachers, 1895-1905*, Stanford University Press, 1992, pp. 127-8. The official name for the Osaka Exhibition was Naikoku kangyō hakurankai.

[35] Excerpts from this letter were later printed on 31 May 1919, *Osaka asahi shinbun* (Osaka asahi newspaper) and reprinted in Kyoto daigaku jinbun kagaku kenkyūjo (ed.), *Nihon shinbun Go-Shi hōdō shiryō shūsei* (A collection of documents in Japanese newspapers on the May Fourth Movement), Kyoto: Kyoto daigaku jinbun kagaku kenkyūjo, 1983, p. 82.

[36] For a discussion of the relationship between colonialism and cultural discrimination based on the anthropological viewpoint, see Kawamura Minato, 'Taishū Orientarizumu to Ajia ninshiki' (Mass Orientalism and the perception of Asia) in Ōe Shinobu *et al.* (eds), *Kindai Nihon to shokuminchi* (Modern Japan and its colonies), vol. 7, Tokyo: Iwanami shoten, 1993, pp. 126-32.

[37] See Mitsuishi Zenkichi, 'Gotō Asatarō to Inoue Kōbai' in Takeuchi Yoshimi and Hashikawa Bunzō (eds), *Kindai Nihon to Chūgoku* (Modern Japan and China), vol. 2, Tokyo: Asahi shinbunsha, 1974, pp. 27-45.

These efforts to separate Japan culturally from China entailed a more critical view of *kanbun* among many Japanese. The world of Chinese classics and the 'real' China were considered two separate and unrelated realms. Indeed, this distancing was central to Japan's imperialist aims. In stressing the differences between the two countries, Gotō habitually remarked: 'If Japan thinks one way, you can be sure that China will think another way.'[38] In a similar vein, the increasingly nationalistic journalist Tokutomi Iichirō (Sohō) (1863-1957) remarked: 'One cannot surmise what the Chinese are really like from the ideals they uphold [in their ancient texts]. If you want to understand their true nature, it would be better not to examine their moral philosophy. The best approach is to do the opposite of what Confucius said.'[39] The politician Hara Sōbei, in his book on the Chinese 'national character' (*kokuminsei*) published in 1932, made the critical observation that the Chinese were such a conspicuously cruel people by nature that 'Now I understand the reason Confucius repeatedly stressed benevolence and philanthropy.'[40] The fact that an anti-Confucian movement flared up among intellectuals in 1915 during the New Culture Movement was thought to attest further the importance of this line of thinking.

Fully recognising that a different strategy was needed, the *kanbun* apologists changed their arguments. Rather than clinging to the myth of *dōbun dōshu*, they turned their attention to what one *kanbun* scholar called 'the essential differences separating the Japanese and Chinese peoples'.[41] They began to represent the Japanese, and not the Chinese, as the true embodiment of Confucianism, explaining that Confucianism had taken root in Japan rather than China by virtue of the country's superior history and cultural traditions. Pointing to the warrior ethic (*bushidō*), they claimed: 'Japan's warrior ethic epitomises the way in which Confucianism was revitalised in Japan.'[42] Moreover, they insisted

---

[38] Gotō Asatarō, 'Shinajin no shosai ni deiri shite' (Frequent visits to the studies of Chinese intellectuals), *Shibun*, vol. 8, no. 4 (1926), p. 35.

[39] Tokutomi Iichirō, *Shina yūki* (A China travelogue), Tokyo: Minyūsha, 1918, p. 524.

[40] Hara Sōbei, *Shina shinri no kaibō* (Analysing the Chinese mind), Tokyo: Tokyo shobō, 1932, p. 63.

[41] Wakamiya Unosuke, 'Minzokusei sai no kenkyū' (A study of the differences in national character) *Daitō bunka*, vol. 3, no. 3 (1926), Tokyo: Daitō bunka gakuin, p. 15.

[42] Wakamiya Unosuke, 'Daitō bunka no katsuryoku sei' (The vitality of the great Eastern culture), *Daitō bunka*, vol. 3, no. 1 (1926), p. 15.

that as their country could claim an unbroken line of emperors, 'Only Japan fits the Confucian ideal.'[43] Much later, similar sentiments were expressed in the opening section of *The Cardinal Principles of the National Entity*, a nationalist tract prepared by the Ministry of Education, which further strengthened the view of the country's divine origins and uniqueness. Although it stated that Eastern culture had entered Japan from India and China, it insisted that Confucianism, like Shintoism, could only be embodied within the pure Japanese spirit.[44]

By the 1920s, *kanbun* ceased to be studied from the vantage point of a foreign culture. Instead, it was incorporated as part of Japan's superior moral and cultural 'traditions'. The term *dōbun dōshu*, used since the Meiji period by many intellectuals who believed that Japan and China shared the same intellectual heritage, lived on, but its emphasis shifted to become a very useful ideology. First, it promoted the notion of a Confucian tradition binding Japan and China together against the West. Secondly, within this imagined tradition, it established a clear hierarchy, giving Japan the moral and spiritual right to lead the Chinese militarily, politically and culturally. However, the idea of solidarity that *dōbun dōshu* originally conveyed stood in contradiction to this hierarchical construct. The social and literary critic Takeuchi Yoshimi (1910-77), well-known for his intellectually astute observations of modern Sino-Japanese relations, vociferously objected to *dōbun dōshu*'s function in the 1930s, a decade marked by the rapid growth of fascism. Takeuchi accused members of the academic community of misrepresenting and sullying the term *dōbun dōshu* in a calculated effort to cooperate with imperial Japan's China policy, even though it was evident that the Japanese felt totally divorced from China and things Chinese. He summarised his opposition when he said: 'I (or perhaps it's better to say we) despise this term known as *dōbun dōshu*. For me, it stands for something tainted and full of impurities. Not only am I unable to use it myself, but if I hear others using it, I lose respect

---

[43] Shionoya On, 'Kōshi to waga kokutai' (Confucius and our national polity), *Shibun*, vol. 8, no. 5 (1926), p. 3. Uno Tetsuto, Shionoya's colleague, expressed similar sentiments about China and Japan during a visit to China in 1906. See Joshua A. Fogel, *The cultural dimension of Sino-Japanese relations*, Armonk, NY: M.E. Sharpe, 1995, pp. 113-4.

[44] *Kokutai no hongi* (Monbushō, 1937), p. 1. Translated as 'Cardinal principles of the national entity of Japan' by John Owen Gauntlett in Robert King Hall (ed.), *Kokutai no hongi: Cardinal principles of the national entity*, Cambridge, MA: Harvard University Press, 1949.

for them as educators and look on them contemptuously as flawed human beings.'[45]

In fact, *dōbun dōshu* had already come to reflect the vision conveyed by a term like the Greater East Asia Co-Prosperity Sphere (*Dai-Tōa Kyōeiken*), namely, the expulsion of Western powers from Asia and the establishment of a Japanese hegemony. Even the atrocities committed against people in China, beginning with the Manchurian Incident in 1931 and continuing into the 1940s, were justified psychologically on the basis of a Japanese cultural ascendancy.

As early as the 1870s, the idea of a distinctive Japanese national identity was intricately linked to imagining differences from people in China. In order for the Japanese to form their own national identity, the construction of the Chinese as a racially different people was crucial to that purpose. Even before the Sino-Japanese war, when the Japanese came into direct contact with the Chinese, the first recorded discussions centred around dissimilarities in appearance and later came to address differences in genealogy and the genetic factors determining their behaviour. By the twentieth century, although the debates about the presumed biological differences between Japanese and Chinese continued, the most vocal arguments were based on culture. These debates generally stressed the purity of the Japanese 'race' and subsequently gave rise to a new way of thinking associated with *dōbun dōshu*. In the case of the Japanese and Chinese, for example during the Second World War, the invocation of cultural differences was more powerful and eventually more destructive than the use of biologising arguments in mobilising total war with China. From the mid- to the late nineteenth century, *kanbun* was considered to be a detriment in the construction of Japanese nationalism. By the early twentieth century, however, cultural communalities ironically came to be used as a barometer for measuring Japan's racial superiority.

---

[45] Takeuchi Yoshimi, 'Dōbun dōshu' (Same language, same race), *Chūgoku*, no. 7 (1963), Takeuchi Yoshimi, *Takeuchi Yoshimi zenshū* (Complete works of Takeuchi Yoshimi), vol. 10, Tokyo: Chikuma shobō, 1981, pp. 32-3.

THE AINU AND THE
DISCOURSE OF 'RACE'

Richard Siddle

Racialised expression, through which social differences between human collectivities have come to be regarded as 'natural' and inevitable, is a constituent feature of modernity.[1] As Miles has argued, whenever racialised discourse serves 'to differentiate, to exclude and to dominate', then it can be described as racism.[2] This insight leads us away from the reification of 'race' and racism towards the study of historically specific racisms, articulated by groups located within specific constellations of material and power relations. Consequently, although racism is usually considered a Western phenomenon, instances can also be identified in East Asia. This chapter examines the racialisation of the Ainu, the indigenous people of northern Japan who were dispossessed and marginalised by the Japanese colonisation of Hokkaidō, a process which began in earnest in 1869.

The subordination of the Ainu under a colonial order, and their dispossession as the land and resources they controlled were unilaterally appropriated in the name of 'development' by the Japanese state, took place during the early stages of Japan's transition to modernity. During this period Japan was heavily dependent on the new knowledge introduced from the West, then at the zenith of its own imperial glory. As the precarious situation of the Ainu began to attract Japanese public attention from the 1890s, the notions of 'race' and nation were gaining increasing currency as intellectuals debated Japanese identity and the nature of the

---

[1] See D.T. Goldberg, *Racist culture: Philosophy and the politics of meaning*, Oxford: Blackwell, 1993, for an extended discussion of this.

[2] R. Miles, *Racism after 'race relations'*, London and New York: Routledge, 1993, p. 44.

state, and devoted considerable energy to the establishment of
a 'sense of nation'. By the early twentieth century, these categories
had become effectively identical for many Japanese in the common-sense perception of the consanguineous *Yamato minzoku*,
or 'Japanese race', that developed in the context of the ideological
drive to establish the Emperor as the head of the family-state.[3]
The destitution and marginalisation of the Ainu that resulted from
the colonisation and economic development of Hokkaidō after
1868 were interpreted almost exclusively within the confines of
these complementary discourses. Inequality was attributed to innate
and immutable inferiority that marked the Ainu as among the
unfit in the 'struggle for survival'. Besides providing an explanation,
notions of 'race' also justified relations of domination and the
further exclusion of the Ainu from participation in the economic
and political life of the nation. Racialised understanding operated
at all levels of society, informing both the policies of the colonial
administration and the attitudes of Japanese immigrants in their
day-to-day interactions with Ainu. Colonial relations with the
Ainu thus provided an important initial context in which notions
of 'native' inferiority and Japanese modernity were articulated
and gained acceptance among the general public as common-sense.

This chapter aims to show how the Ainu were enmeshed
within the 'racial' discourse of the time, and how the images
that developed shaped specific policy measures and furthered their
subordination to the state. The discussion focuses on three groups
of people associated with state authority who were primarily concerned with the Ainu; scholars, officials and educators. Finally,
there is a brief consideration of how stereotypes of Ainu 'racial'
inferiority were propagated and reproduced among the public
at large.

THE GROWTH OF AINU STUDIES

Ainu studies originated and developed during the late nineteenth
century when Japan was an eager student of the scientific knowledge
of the West. The presence of a so-called 'primitive' people, under
control and easily accessible, contributed greatly to the development

---

[3] For a general discussion of the overlap between 'race' and nation see Miles, *Racism after
'race relations'*, pp. 53–79. For Japan, see M. Weiner, *Race and migration in Imperial Japan*,
London and New York: Routledge, 1994, pp. 7–37, and this volume.

and formation of the disciplines of anthropology, archaeology and linguistics in Japan.[4] Since the scientific paradigms of most human and infant social sciences in those early days were overwhelmingly influenced by ideas of evolution, obsessed with hierarchical classification and the explanation of 'natural' difference between primitive and civilised societies, the Ainu were tailormade material for research by both Western visitors and their Japanese students. As Japan became more confident and began seeking acceptance as a civilised country, and later, as a Great Power, the Ainu, in the guise of a primitive Other, served also as a yardstick against which the civilisation and progress of Japan could be measured.

While Japanese travellers, officials and explorers had produced accounts of the Ainu during the Tokugawa period (1600-1868), even those most sympathetic to the Ainu had viewed them through Confucian-inspired images of civilised and barbarian. For the majority of Japanese merchants and migrant workers in pre-modern Hokkaidō negative stereotypes of the barbarian Ainu emphasised their inhuman origins and habits and their bizarre and filthy appearance.[5] Many of the European travellers and explorers in the eighteenth and early nineteenth centuries, on the other hand, had been favourably impressed by the Ainu they encountered, deeming them 'noble and hardy full-grown men as opposed to their effeminate Japanese rulers', but also courteous and gentle; an ideal personification of the noble savage.[6] Later Western visitors, however, generally took a more negative view. For these men and women, the Ainu fitted into the hierarchical classification of humanity on its lowest rungs as a race of primitive savages.

Certain themes and images run consistently through their writings. The Ainu were incapable of progress: 'After a century of contact with the Japanese, they have learned no arts, adopted

---

[4] For a general overview of the development of Ainu studies, see S. Takakura, *Ainu seisaku shi: Shinpan* (A history of Ainu policy: New edition), Tokyo: Sanichi shobō, 1972, pp. 534-40; Ainu Bunka Hozon Taisaku Kyōgikai (ed.), *Ainu minzoku shi* (Ainu ethnology), Tokyo: Daiichihōki shuppan, 1970, pp. 26-62; H. Fujimoto, *Ainugaku e no ayumi* (Steps towards Ainu studies), Sapporo: Hokkaidō shuppan kikaku sentā, 1983.

[5] Premodern stereotypes of the Ainu are discussed in R. Siddle, 'The Ainu: Construction of an image' in J. Maher and G. Macdonald (eds), *Diversity in Japanese culture and language*, London: Kegan Paul International, 1995, pp. 74-84.

[6] J. Kreiner, 'European images of the Ainu and Ainu studies in Europe' in J. Kreiner (ed.), *European studies on Ainu language and culture*, Munich: Iudicium Verlag, 1993, pp. 33-4.

no improvements' (Hitchcock); 'so little have they profited from the opportunities offered to them during the last thousand or two thousand years, that there is no longer room for them in the world' (Chamberlain). As savages, they lived in the present, incapable of higher thought: 'Like the monkeys, the Ainu cannot concentrate their attention, and they are easily wearied' (Landor); 'low unlettered savages without moral courage, lazy, and strongly given to drunkenness' (Morse). Those Ainu of mixed ancestry were often described in pejorative terms; for Landor the 'half-breeds' were 'malformed, ill-natured, and often idiotic', or 'ill-tempered, lazy, and vindictive'. Chamberlain warned future visitors to Hokkaidō that 'the comparatively smooth half-breeds usually speak Aino, dress Aino fashion, and are accounted to be Ainos', thus misleading those seeking the real savage. As for hairiness, most accepted this as an Ainu characteristic, although Bird thought reports on this 'much exaggerated', while Landor, for his part, encouraged such exaggeration with sketches of extremely furry Ainu. There was general agreement that the Ainu were doomed to extinction: 'the race is rapidly dying out, destroyed by consumption, lunacy, and poverty of blood' (Landor); 'descending to that vast tomb of conquered and unknown races which has opened to receive so many before them' (Bird). For Chamberlain, 'the existence of this race has been as aimless, as fruitless, as is the perpetual dashing of the breakers on the shore of Horobetsu'. A few observers also picked up some of the earlier stereotypes widely held by Japanese. Morse remarked that the Ainu 'do not have any knowledge of the simplest arithmetic', and Bird also mentioned that the Ainu 'have no method of computing time, and do not know their own ages'.[7] Finally, for those tempted by visions of 'noble savagery', Hitchcock gave the following warning in his description of the Ainu:

---

[7] R. Hitchcock, 'The Ainos of Yezo, Japan' in *Annual report of the Board of Regents of the Smithsonian Institution, showing the operations, expenditures and condition of the Institution for the year ending June 30 1890. Report of the U.S. National Museum*, Washington: Smithsonian, 1891, p. 443; I. Bird, *Unbeaten tracks in Japan: An account of travels in the interior including visits to the aborigines of Yezo and the shrine of Nikko*, Rutland, VT, and Tokyo: Tuttle, 1973, pp. 231, 307, 280; A.H.S. Landor, *Alone with the hairy Ainu. Or, 3,800 miles on a pack saddle in Yezo and a cruise to the Kurile islands*, London: John Murray, 1893, pp. 271, 269, 274, 295-6; B.H. Chamberlain, *The language, mythology, and geographical nomenclature of Japan, viewed in the light of Aino studies*, Tokyo: Tokyo Imperial University, 1887, pp. 43, 74-5; E. Morse, *Japan day by day*, Boston: Houghton Mifflin Co., 1917, vol. 2, pp. 1, 26.

Few who read these lines have ever seen the lower stages of human savagery and barbarism, still less have they an adequate conception of the physical and moral condition, or the manner of life, which characterises the lower types of human existence ... To know how miserably a savage lives, one must see him in his house.[8]

These men and women were fascinated by the idea of a lost 'white race' surviving in a remote corner of northeast Asia. As teachers and experts, they directly influenced the first generation of Japanese scholars trained in the Western scientific disciplines at Tokyo Imperial University in the 1880s. Edward Morse, for instance, conducted the first archaeological investigations in Japan and helped establish the Tokyo Anthropological Society (*Tōkyō Jinruigakkai*) in November 1884. Between 1886 and 1890, Basil Hall Chamberlain, already well established in Japan, inaugurated the study of linguistics while Professor of Japanese and Philology at Tokyo University. The main question that occupied these Western scholars and their young Japanese students was the 'racial' *(jinshuteki)* origins of the Japanese, a debate that was also underway among intellectuals such as Inoue Tetsujirō and Kume Kunitake, concerned with locating and defining the emerging national identity.[9]

It was Philipp-Franz von Siebold, resident physician in the Dutch settlement at Nagasaki during the late Tokugawa period, who first presented the theory that the Ainu were the original inhabitants of the archipelago. Morse argued against this on the basis of evidence from his excavations of the Ōmori shell mound near Tokyo in 1877 that the neolithic (*Jōmon*) inhabitants produced pottery, unlike the Ainu. One of Morse's students was Tsuboi Shōgorō, a founder member of the Anthropological Society and later Professor of Anthropology at Tokyo Imperial University. Tsuboi unearthed an Ainu legend about a dwarf-like people who had occupied the area when their ancestors arrived, the *koropokkuru*, which he used to back up Morse's theory of a non-Ainu neolithic people. This was strongly opposed by Koganei Yoshikiyo, the

---

[8] Hitchcock, 'Ainos of Yezo', pp. 442–3.

[9] S. Tanaka, *Japan's Orient: Rendering pasts into history*, Berkeley and Los Angeles: California University Press, 1993, pp. 70–86. *'Jinshu'* was the Japanese word used to translate 'race' in the scientific sense (*shuzoku* was also occasionally used), while in nationalist and popular discourse, notions of the Japanese 'race' and 'nation' were expressed by the multivalent term *minzoku*.

first Professor of Anatomy at Tokyo University, who argued, based on skeletal remains, that the Jōmon people were Ainu. Koganei was a follower of Erwin von Baelz, who introduced physical anthropology to Japan and with Wilhelm Dönitz of the Faculty of Medicine at the Tokyo Imperial University stimulated interest in the racial classification of the Japanese and the Ainu. Torii Ryūzō, known for his studies on the Kurile Ainu, proposed a variation on the theory with his argument of a later migration of an iron-using people (later known as the *Yayoi*) from the Asian continent. The debate was fought out in the *Jinruigaku Zasshi* (Anthropological Journal) till the death of Tsuboi in 1913, with Koganei and his supporters gradually gaining the upper hand.

With the growth of literacy in the late Meiji period (1868-1912), already higher than in most European countries even before the Restoration, the debate over racial origins reached a wide audience. Over 200 articles on the 'dwarf people' and other Ainu topics appeared in the *Tōkyō Jinruigakkai Zasshi* (Tokyo Anthropological Journal) and its successor alone during the last twenty-five years of the Meiji period, and the debate spilled over into other journals and popular publications. There was widespread interest in such issues at a time when increasing intellectual activity was devoted to forging a Japanese 'sense of nation', and most educated Japanese of the day, keen to absorb scientific knowledge and understanding, were familiar with the main propositions.

The image of the 'Ainu race' (*Ainu jinshu*) that this scholarly discourse promoted from the 1890s was that of the ignorant, primitive savage; an image that dressed the pre-modern barbarian in scientific clothing. Implicit in this categorisation was the obverse image of Japan as civilised, progressive and modern. Since both Ainu and elephants had large heads, noted Miyake Setsurei in 1891, large heads could not signify intelligence.[10] A similar view was expressed by the historian and philosopher, Inoue Tetsujirō, who argued that the absence of the Mongolian spot in European babies did not imply physical superiority since it was lacking in inferior Ainu babies as well.[11] Nitobe Inazō, in *The Japanese Nation* (1912), described the 'hirsute Ainu' as 'not yet emerged

[10] K. Pyle, *The new generation in Meiji Japan: Problems of cultural identity, 1885-1895*, Stanford University Press, 1969, p. 152.

[11] Tanaka, *Japan's Orient*, p. 77.

from the Stone Age, possessing no art beyond a primitive form of horticulture, being ignorant even of the rudest pottery'. The distinction between a modern, civilised Japan and 'primitive people' was even more explicitly drawn in the chapter on 'Japan as Coloniser' which dwelt on the benefits of Japanese colonial rule in Taiwan.[12]

CHARACTER, BLOOD AND SMELL: AINU STUDIES, 1912–1945

By the early Taishō period (1912–26) a new generation of scholars were involved in Ainu studies. Along with research into racial origins went a growing interest in the preservation of the material and spiritual culture of the 'dying Ainu' (*horobiyuku Ainu*). Ainu Studies was now a field attracting international interest; besides the early involvement of foreign scholars, Ainu had been displayed in 'native villages' at the Louisiana Purchase Exposition (St Louis, 1904) and the Anglo-Japanese Exhibition of 1910.

The master narratives of progress and civilisation adopted from the West legitimised the colonisation of Hokkaidō and the subordination of the Ainu. According to the first official history of Hokkaidō, edited by the noted Ainu scholar Kōno Tsunekichi and published in 1918, responsibility for the colonisation had fallen to the Japanese 'as no other superior race' (*yūtō jinshu*) was in contact with the Ainu.[13] The scientific 'objectivity' of scholars was therefore not in any sense neutral but embedded within these structures of power. Colonial domination ensured that Ainu could not protect their ancestral and sacred grave sites from widespread destruction, or prevent scholars from entering their communities and homes with impunity. Any action could be justified in the name of science. Some Ainu scholars began turning their expertise to the investigation of the colonised in Japan's other possessions. This became a wider trend in the 1930s when many scholars joined research bodies like the *Tōa Kenkyūjo* (East Asia Research Institute), a supposedly neutral establishment

[12] I. Nitobe, *The Japanese nation: Its land, its people, its life; with special consideration to its relations with the United States*, New York and London: G.P. Putnam's Sons, 1912, pp. 86–7, 248–53.
[13] Cited in M. Kaiho, *Shiryō to kataru Hokkaidō no rekishi* (The history of Hokkaidō told by historical records), Sapporo: Hokkaidō shuppan kikaku sentā, 1985, p. 13.

whose research contributed to government policies towards colonised peoples.[14]

Within this framework of domination, scholars began refining their classification of Ainu inferiority. A major trend of the 1920s and 1930s was the increasing interest in such pseudo-scientific disciplines as eugenics and serology. Two scholars instrumental in initiating and popularising research into blood-types from the 1920s were Furuhata Tanemoto and Furukawa Takeji. The notion that racial identities (*minzokusei*) existed and were inheritable encouraged scholars to search for the characteristics carried by Ainu blood. Furukawa himself participated in this research, contributing an article on the racial characters of Ainu and Taiwanese aborigines to the journal *Hanzaigaku Zasshi* (Journal of Criminology) in 1931. Identifying two broad character types, an Active Type (blood groups O and B) and a Passive Type (A and AB), Furukawa then turned to an analysis of the 'violent and cruel' Taiwanese aborigines. Their 'stubborn' and energetic natures were due to a high proportion of O blood type, which meant that 'it will be necessary to exert an enormous amount of energy to civilise [*tokka*] them'. The Ainu, on the other hand, 'not far from extinction', were predominantly B type, happy to live in the present 'with little care for the past or future'.[15] Over a decade later a Hokkaidō Imperial University team also carried out a survey on Ainu character; although based this time on a psychological questionnaire, it did not question the underlying assumption that racial character was objectively quantifiable. Their results found that the Ainu 'were strong of body, but weak in spirit'. Ainu were also introverted, jealous, suspicious of each other's success, and backward in such social feelings as public justice.[16]

Ainu intelligence also became an object of scientific curiosity. In 1926 research on Ainu and Japanese children in Karafuto (southern Sakhalin) found that Ainu children were inferior on

---

[14] Tanaka, *Japan's Orient*, pp. 239-62.

[15] T. Furukawa, 'Ketsuekigata yori mita Taiwan banjin to Hokkaidō Ainujin no minzokusei' (The racial character of Taiwanese aborigines and Hokkaidō Ainu viewed through blood-type), *Hanzaigaku zasshi*, vol. 4, no. 2 (March 1931), pp. 130-6.

[16] T. Ishibashi, F. Oka and T. Wada, 'Ainu no seikaku: Seishōnen ni okeru chōsa ni mototsuite' (Ainu character based on a survey of young people), *Minzoku eisei*, vol. 12, no. 6 (Nov. 1944), p. 352.

almost all the tests carried out.[17] A detailed survey was conducted in wartime by a Hokkaidō Imperial University team. To a certain extent, their report in *Minzoku Eisei* (a eugenics journal, official English title *Race Hygiene*) acknowledged that deterministic notions of Ainu 'racial' inferiority were not universal among scholars since there were those who thought that Ainu backwardness was due to adverse factors in the social environment such as disease and discrimination in education. However, the report stressed that Ainu inferiority was due instead to 'innate' (*sententeki*) and 'characteristic' (*sōshitsuteki*) difference. Nature vanquished nurture. In intelligence tests, Japanese children performed best, followed by 'mixed-blood children' (*konketsu jidō*); 'full-blood children' (*junketsu jidō*) were consistently at the bottom in all tests. The report commented on the influence of mixed blood:

> Mental ability clearly displays a racial [*jinshuteki*] difference, and this difference is reduced by the mixing of blood. Through mixing of blood, superior ability is lowered, while inferior ability is raised ... If our race [*waga minzoku*] has no choice but to mix blood, we should choose a race [*shuzoku*] that has a mental ability not inferior to ours, or at least a race possessing some special mental characteristics.[18]

Yet another study made an attempt to link the Ainu with the 'white race', who 'as a race possess a strong body odour'. The research found that 'the Ainu are a smelly race' (*nioi jinshu*). The scientific research method involved was the placing of the nostrils close to the half-naked body of an Ainu in a room overheated by a roaring stove; one of a series of experiences with Ainu odour that led the researcher to muse that 'it's tough for those engaged in ethnology [*jinshugaku*]'.[19]

Popular myths and stereotypes dating from Tokugawa times were now backed up by scientific authority. By portraying cultural difference as 'natural' and inevitable, scientific research reconciled

---

[17] Y. Kubo, 'Karafuto ni okeru Ainu jidō to Nihon jidō tono hikkaku' (A comparison of Japanese and Ainu children in Karafuto), *Jidō kenkyūsho kiyō*, vol. 9 (1926), pp. 415-17.

[18] T. Ishibashi *et al.*, 'Ainu jidō no chinō chōsa: Chinō no jinshuteki sai oyobi chinō ni oyobasu konketsu no eikyō ni kansuru – chiken' (Survey of intelligence among Ainu children: Racial difference in intelligence and the influence of mixed blood on intelligence – an opinion), *Minzoku eisei*, vol. 10, no. 4 (Aug. 1942), pp. 288-94.

[19] J. Kanazeki, 'Ainu no wakiga' (Ainu body odour), *Seirigaku kenkyū*, vol. 11, no. 8 (1934), pp. 542-6.

popular images of Ainu inferiority with theoretical science, and located both within a wider common-sense understanding in which the categories of 'race' and nation overlapped. Even in scientific discourse, the distinction between *jinshu* and *minzoku* was often not clearly drawn, as can be seen in the passage above. Conversely, the discourse of scientific knowledge itself was proof of Japan's status as a modern nation of superior attributes. The power relations that underlay this ability to classify the primitive were seen, if acknowledged at all, as the workings of the scientific principle of the survival of the fittest.

PROTECTION AND EDUCATION, 1890–1930

While scholars were instrumental in fixing the Ainu within the discourse of 'race' and spreading this awareness among the intellectual élites, those who were actually in closest contact with the Ainu were the colonial officials in charge of their welfare. In the early days of colonial administration in Hokkaidō, the Ainu were perceived broadly through the stereotypes of the Tokugawa period as ignorant, half-human barbarians. By the 1890s these Confucian-inspired stereotypes of civilised and barbarian were undergoing transformation to conform to the new paradigms for the explanation of difference and inequality: 'race' and the 'survival of the fittest'. The widespread acceptance of these ideas by government officials can be clearly seen in the parliamentary debates that accompanied the various attempts to introduce a Protection Act. Although exploitation by Japanese immigrants (known as *wajin* or *naichijin*) was occasionally discussed, it was seen as a natural result of the laws of nature; in effect, the Ainu themselves were to blame.

Not all agreed with this view. The first proposal in the Diet for a Protection Act came from Katō Masanosuke in the 5th Imperial Diet in 1893. In his opening statement, Katō referred to the argument put forward by some that

> The survival of the fittest is a natural feature of the world. The Ainu race [*Ainu jinshu*] is an inferior race, while our Japanese race [*naichi jinshu*] is a superior race. The superior race says that the inferior Ainu race will naturally die out ... and that there is no need to protect them.[20]

---

[20] First Reading of Hokkaidō Natives Protection Act, House of Representatives, 29 Nov.

Although Katō argued that the Ainu were not an inferior race,
other Dietmen, however, were worried that 'because they are
innately stupid they will spend any money they are given on
alcohol', or would eat any seeds given to them instead of planting
them. The bill failed.[21]

After failing again in 1896, a draft Protection Act was put
forward by the government in the 13th Imperial Diet in 1898.
During committee deliberations, one member asked how half-
breeds (*ainoko*) were identified. Admitting that it was sometimes
difficult to tell, the government spokesman Shirani Takeshi replied
that they were recorded as Ainu if ancestry was known. If this
was unclear, phenotypical criteria were employed; 'only those
whom anyone can clearly recognise [as Ainu] are treated as Ainu,
Former Natives.'[22] Shirani was well placed to argue for the legislation; in a previous appointment as an educator and Hokkaidō
government (*Dōchō*) official he had been active in the original
movement for a Protection Act. In a speech in 1894, Shirani
argued that Ainu extinction could not be avoided, but that welfare
was necessary since 'it is against human nature not to extend
a helping hand to our neighbours', although 'we must definitely
not undertake the preservation of the race'.[23]

The Protection Act was duly enacted, and the Imperial Diet
only occasionally considered the Ainu thereafter. One exception
to this trend was the 1907 debate on the extension of the domestic
legal system to the new colony of Karafuto. Special consideration
had to be given to the status of the indigenous inhabitants, including
Ainu, who had not been granted Japanese citizenship. Giving
details of the natives, the committee member representing the
government pointed out that 'the term "natives" means Ainu,
and besides them the most inferior races, Gilyak, Orochon, Tungus
and Yakutsk'. Since they were such 'extremely inferior races'

1893. 'Teikoku gikai gijiroku' (Transcripts of Imperial Diet proceedings), in Hokkaidō Utari
Kyōkai Ainu Shi Henshū Iinkai (ed.), *Ainu shi shiryō shū 3: Kingendai shiryō 1* (Collected
materials on Ainu history 3: Modern and contemporary materials 1), Sapporo: Hokkaidō utari
kyōkai, 1990, pp. 32-3. Hereafter cited as *ASS3*.

[21] *ASS3*, pp. 44, 47.

[22] House of Representatives, 21 Jan. 1899; *ASS3*, p. 99.

[23] Cited in M. Ogawa, 'The Hokkaidō Former Aborigines Protection Act and assimilatory
education' in N. Loos and T. Osanai (eds), *Indigenous minorities and education: Australian and
Japanese perspectives of their indigenous peoples, the Ainu, Aborigines and Torres Strait Islanders*,
Tokyo: Sanyūsha, 1993, p. 239.

(*goku rettō no jinshu*) the application of domestic law to them was clearly inappropriate.[24] Racial inferiority justified legal inequality.

Besides legislators and bureaucrats, educators were also prominent in the campaign for a Protection Act. For instance, Iwaya Eitarō, a member of a committee involved with Ainu education, was well within mainstream opinion when he argued in 1891 that the decrease in Ainu numbers was the result of the 'principle of the survival of the fittest' since the Ainu were an 'inferior race' (*rettō naru jinshu*).[25] In a 1901 article, referring again to the survival of the fittest, Iwaya argued that it was the duty of the 'Yamato race' (*Yamato jinshu*) to extend their sympathy and compassion to protect the Ainu.[26] In 1903 Iwaya again addressed the topic of Ainu policy, concluding that assimilation was the 'safest and most appropriate doctrine'. This was to be carried out in two stages, hybridisation (*konwa*) and fusion (*yūgō*). As 'intercourse between the Former Natives and the Wajin becomes intimate', Wajin would naturally stop cheating the Ainu, mutual trust would develop, and Wajin would teach them Japanese customs. Sympathy and education would then lead to fusion, although assimilation of this 'different race' was not something that would happen in only ten or twenty years.[27]

But there were others who considered the whole programme of Ainu welfare and education a waste of time and money. In a 1918 essay the arguments for and against protection of the Ainu were put forward by a former governor of Karafuto, Hiraoka Sadatarō. Hiraoka was clearly influenced by the new pseudo-science of eugenics. Opening with a discussion on 'racial reconstruction' (*jinshu no kaizō*) and its importance for national survival, Hiraoka presented the arguments for leaving the Ainu to fend for themselves. For many, 'race' and nation had clearly become coterminous:

[24] Special Committee on the Laws for Karafuto, House of Peers, 23 March 1907, *ASS3*, pp. 189-90.

[25] E. Iwaya, 'Ainu no genshō' (The decrease in Ainu numbers), *Hokkaidō kyōiku zasshi*, no. 6 (1891), p. 11.

[26] E. Iwaya, 'Hokubei dojin hogohō a ronjite Ainu jinshu hogohō ni oyobu (2)' (On the Protection Act for the North American natives with reference to the Protection Act for the Ainu race, part 2), *Hokkaidō kyōiku zasshi*, no. 88 (May 1901), pp. 1-3.

[27] E. Iwaya, 'Kyūdojin kyōiku dan' (On Ainu education), *Hokkaidō kyōiku zasshi*, no. 125 (June 1903), pp. 29-33.

The world is a stage on which the strong devour the weak. [...] As Darwin wrote in *The Origin of Species*, the so-called idea of the survival of the fittest is a principle that rules the whole world of nature. From the phrase 'survival of the fittest' it follows that those unadapted for life are oppressed. The Ainu are unadapted members of humanity. [...] The Ainu today have nothing to contribute to the happiness of humanity; consequently their survival or extinction should be left to nature. In particular, artificial preservation through human agency is unnecessary and, moreover, is said to be impossible. Another view [in favour of letting the Ainu die out] argues from the standpoint of the Yamato race [*Yamato minzoku*]. Our country is proud of the purity of our ancient race, and the long-term preservation of this racial purity [*shuzoku junsui*] is our nationalism. [...] If interbreeding with Ainu introduces Ainu blood into Japanese, it will violate the movement to preserve our national essence [*kokusui*].[28]

However, interbreeding between Ainu and Wajin was already occurring in Hokkaidō. In 1916 the Dōchō used racial categories to classify the Ainu population into 13,557 'recognised full-bloods', 4,550 'recognised mixed-bloods', and 714 'Yamato race' (*wajinshu*), those Wajin children who had been adopted as infants and brought up by Ainu.[29]

Fusion and the Mixing of Blood: Ainu Policy, 1930-1945

By the early 1930s, Ainu leaders had become active in a movement for self-help and the revision of the Protection Act, in particular the system of discriminatory education that was now viewed as an obstacle to assimilation. An Ainu organisation, the *Ainu Kyōkai*, had been formed in 1930 in cooperation with officials of the Social Section of the Hokkaidō government to further these aims. These officials took it upon themselves to encourage the movement.

---

[28] S. Hiraoka, 'Ainu jinshu shobun ron' (On the management of the Ainu race), appendix in T. Aoyama, *Kyokuhoku no bettenchi* (The different world of the extreme north), Tokyo: Nippon Seinen Tsushinsha, 1918, pp. 4-6.

[29] Hokkaidō-chō, *Kyūdojin ni kansuru chōsa* (Survey of the Former Natives), Sapporo: Hokkaidō-chō, 1922, p. 115.

'The Ainu are not racially [*jinshuteki*] inferior in any way; merely culturally backward, having been separated by the Tsugaru Straits'. This was the opinion of the Director for Social Welfare Projects at the Dōchō in 1931.[30] Wajin prejudice against Ainu, he argued, was not 'racial' and would be alleviated by increased assimilation as Ainu furthered their knowledge and social standing. Another attempt to challenge the dominant discourse of Ainu 'racial' inferiority current in educated circles (but not the idea of 'race' itself) was made by Kita Masaaki, the official most involved in Ainu welfare. Like Hiraoka, Kita based his argument on eugenics, but to make an altogether different point: 'Based on the principles of eugenics, mixed-blood children take after the superior race, and are born almost as Wajin'.[31]

For those involved in this movement, one of the primary means of assimilation was seen as being intermarriage and subsequent miscegenation. To overcome the widespread distaste for interbreeding, some officials used the imagery of Ainu blood merging and 'fusing' (*yūgō*) with that of the Yamato race. At the same time, this image could be used to deny the assertion of a 'dying race'. Ainu blood was not dying out, but would continue to flow in the veins of the Yamato race. This represented progress for the Ainu.

> The natives are being gradually Japanised. Assimilation and intermarriage – for these two reasons the natives are gradually losing their primitive appearance. The volume of their blood is swiftly fusing into the Yamato race and increasing. [...] As time goes by the Hokkaidō natives are assimilating. Assimilation [*dōka*], that is the transformation of customs and appearance, is not the so-called extinction that people believe; rather, we can say that they are a race that is developing and progressing, uniting and fusing with the Yamato race.[32]

The author of the above was Kita Masaaki, who often expressed such views in the articles he wrote in the journal devoted to social welfare in Hokkaidō, *Hokkaidō Shakai Jigyō*. Another to

---

[30] T. Nishida, 'Kakusei o nozomu' (Wishing for awakening), *Ezo no hikari*, no. 2 (March 1931), p. 21.

[31] Kita Kōyō (M. Kita), 'Dojin hogo no enkaku to Hogohō no seishin' (A history of native welfare and the spirit of the Protection Act), *Hokkaidō shakai jigyō*, no. 15 (July 1933), p. 27.

[32] Kita, 'Dojin hogo no enkaku', p. 28.

take up this theme was the chief of the Dōchō Social Section, Okabe Shirō, although in a more cautionary tone:

> Year by year, through the mixing of blood between the two parties, integration [*yūwa*] is taking place, and we are unaware that it is forming the superior Yamato race of which we are so proud. Even if, for instance, the pure Ainu race dies out, should we feel sadness at the extinction of a race? Ah, what is the meaning of racial preservation? In the present century the policies in Nazi Germany for the preservation of the blood of the pure German race are moving racial problems forward into a new area, although I do not have time to refer to this now.[33]

In 1937 these supporters of the Ainu self-help movement were instrumental in achieving revision of the 1899 Protection Act. Many officials of the Dōchō had now come to believe that assimilation of the Ainu would eventually be achieved through intermarriage, miscegenation and fusion, and their policies aimed to encourage this. Unfortunately, this view was not shared by the public at large on whom they relied to do the job for them.

IMAGES OF THE 'DYING RACE'

So far the discussion has concentrated on the images of the Ainu held by a relatively narrow circle of élite intellectuals and bureaucrats. The images that informed the understanding of this élite group shaped policies towards the Ainu that served to perpetuate their subordinate status for all to see. Moreover, the discourse of 'race' and consequent categorisation of the Ainu in these terms reached a far wider audience through such media as newspapers, popular journals and school textbooks. These ideas combined with the widely-held folk images of the Other to explain the reality of economic, political and social marginalisation of the Ainu to the 'average person' (*ippanjin*) who encountered them.

The press was a major vehicle for the transmission of the discourse of 'race' from scholarly and official circles to a wider audience. Reporting on the Ainu was characterised by the use

---

[33] S. Okabe, 'Kyūdojin zakki (2): Jinkō ron to iseki hozon' (Notes on the Former Natives no. 2: Population and preservation of relics), *Hokkaidō shakai jigyō*, no. 60 (May 1937), p. 50.

of the epithet 'dying race' (*metsubō naru jinshu, horobiyuku minzoku*). Almost without fail, articles mentioned in the manner of a routine preamble that Ainu destitution and population decline were the result of scientific principles:

> According to the principle of the survival of the fittest, as civilisation advances superior races succeed while inferior races die out. [...] This can clearly be seen these days in the case of the Aino, that is to say the natives.[34]

Within this Darwinian framework, a range of stereotypes characterised the Ainu as ignorant, alcoholic, disease-ridden, dirty and lazy. Rather than being the invention of journalists, these stereotypes owed their origins to both the 'primitive savage' of scholarly discourse and the images of the barbarian formed in the trading posts of pre-Restoration Hokkaidō, images which still enjoyed widespread currency within rural Hokkaidō society. In Tokachi, it was reported in a typical article in 1910, the natives still had not escaped from their old customs and relied on nature, lacking a sense of accumulation (*chozōteki kannen*) and interest in agriculture. The men were lazy and loved alcohol, leaving their wives to earn a living.[35] A similar situation existed among the survivors of the Kurile Ainu relocated to the barren island of Shikotan; reports on their plight sometimes managed to include all these negative images within the space of a single article.[36] As for health, one report informing the public of the situation of the Ainu in 1918 ended with the words: 'These days the natives themselves are a splendid congealed lump [*katamari*] of tuberculosis and syphilis.'[37] In the issues they reported and the tone they used, newspapers served to promote a negative image of the Ainu among the reading public. The emphasis on welfare issues underlined the dependence and subordination of the Ainu as 'protected' or 'welfare people' (*hogomin*). This was linked to their lack of civilisation and progress which would ultimately doom them to extinction. Such articles gave the Japanese public

---

[34] *Hakodate shinbun*, 3 Sept. 1886.

[35] 'Tokachi no dojin' (The Tokachi natives), *Hokkai taimusu*, 12 March 1910.

[36] For example, see 'Chishima Shikotan no dojin' (The natives of Shikotan), *Hokkai taimusu*, 19 June 1923; 'Horobitsutsu aru Shikotan dojin no konshaku' (The past and present of the dying Shikotan natives), *Hokkai taimusu*, 18 March 1930.

[37] 'Kyūdojin jōtai' (The situation of the Former Natives), *Hokkai taimusu*, 18 March 1918.

an opportunity to reflect on the modernity and progress of the nation. In the words of one official, 'whenever journalism opens its mouth on the Former Natives it talks sorrowfully about the "dying race" to tempt the reader to pathos.'[38] Another vehicle for the propagation of the image of the 'inferior race' among the general public was the exhibition or exposition (*hakurankai*). The first display of Ainu in a 'native village' occurred at the notorious Hall of Mankind (*Jinruikan*) at the Fifth Industrial Exhibition at Osaka in 1903. The Jinruikan was the brainchild of Tsuboi Shōgorō, and took its cue from the native villages that had become a regular fixture in these events since the 1889 Paris Exposition. Although plans to display Chinese, Koreans and Okinawans were dropped after many objected strongly to the humiliation of being portrayed as primitives, nobody raised doubts about the primitive status of the Ainu.[39] Before long, the image of the Ainu as primitive and subordinate colonial subjects was strikingly reinforced by their display at the Colonial Exposition (*Takushoku Hakurankai*) of 1912 in Tokyo, which featured a native village to display the 'natives of the new territories'. These included Ainu from both Karafuto and Hokkaidō. A commemorative album of photographs of the Exposition shows traditionally dressed and unhappy-looking Ainu and Nivkh from Karafuto standing beside their native dwellings behind stout fences, surrounded by crowds of grinning onlookers dressed in the latest modern fashions.[40] The contrast between subordinate and inferior natives, and the modern, civilised Japanese, and the power relations that underlay such a representation itself, were starkly portrayed in the clothes, buildings and fences within which the indigenous peoples of the Empire were enclosed. Whether overtly articulated or not, the discourse of 'race' and the Darwinian notions that underlay colonial expansion found concrete expression in these displays. These images were effectively conveyed to large numbers of ordinary Japanese: 4,351,000 people, for instance, visited the Osaka Exhibition during

---

[38] Okabe, 'Kyūdojin zakki', p. 48.

[39] Y. Kaiho, *Kindai hoppō shi: Ainu minzoku to josei to* (Modern history of the northern regions: The Ainu people and women), Tokyo: Sanichi shobō, 1992, pp. 157–62.

[40] Meiji Kinenkai (ed.), *Takushoku hakurankai kinen shashin chō* (Commemorative photographs of the Colonial Exposition), Tokyo: Meiji kinenkai, 1912. The quotation is from one of the captions.

the five months it was open.[41]

School textbooks used in the standardised system of primary education set up in 1872 also conveyed stereotyped images within a racialised context. A textbook of 1887 introduced the Ainu as the 'Ezo, or Aino, natives who have lived in Hokkaidō from ancient times', then described their hair and tattoos and how they lived off the flesh of fish and beasts, before concluding: 'Although they used to be a wild people, they now have a gentle character and are well mixed in with mainlanders.'[42] After 1901, Ainu were included in the section on 'Races' (*jinshu*) in the chapter on the Japanese Empire.[43] All of these books included illustrations of Ainu in traditional dress beside their traditional dwellings. Ainu leaders and their supporters during the following decades considered such descriptions influential in spreading the image of their people as a backward 'race' throughout the younger generations. Since it was part of a widespread tendency in elementary school textbooks to propagate the official ideology of Japanese 'racial' superiority and colonial mission, especially after 1910, it is likely that the first encounter of most Japanese schoolchildren with the Ainu through textbooks such as these would have led to the formation of just such a stereotyped image.[44]

Tourism, while localised, also contributed. Although mass tourism had not yet developed, those with the money and inclination to travel were sufficient in number to turn at least two Ainu villages, Shiraoi and Chikabumi, into regular tourist attractions in the early twentieth century. A guide published in 1941 gave a hint of attitudes encountered by the Ainu performing for tourists:

Money goes a long way here as well as elsewhere, it is true; but even here it is not omnipotent. Many thoughtful Ainu people are ashamed to perform the old manners of their ancestors for money amid the laughter of spectators. They consider it

[41] S. Yoshimi, *Hakurankai no seijigaku: Manazashi no kindai* (The politics of expositions: The modern gaze), Tokyo: Chūkō Shinsho, 1992, p. 127.

[42] S. Akiyama, *Nihon chiri shōshi* (Outline of Japanese geography), Tokyo: Chūōdō, 1887, vol. 2.

[43] For example, Fukkyūsha Henshūsho, *Shōgaku chiri* (Elementary geography), Tokyo: Fukkyūsha, 1901, vols 2 and 4.

[44] H. Yamanaka, 'Shōkokumintachi no shokuminchi' (The colonies of the little citizens) in Iwanami Kōza, *Kindai Nihon to shokuminchi (7): Bunka no naka no shokuminchi* (Modern Japan and the colonies (7): The colonies in culture), Tokyo: Iwanami Shoten, 1993, pp. 57-79.

disrespectful to their forefathers. You are therefore requested, while looking at them, to refrain from laughing without any reason or assuming an attitude of mockery.[45]

The Native Schools set up under the Protection Act of 1899 were also on the itinerary of many a tourist, encouraged by the Dōchō which recommended to visitors, in an official guide to Hokkaidō, that they visit the villages of Shiraoi and Chikabumi and also a Native School, where they could observe the efforts being undertaken to civilise the Ainu.[46] In this way tourism served as yet another means of contrasting the primitive with the civilised. Ainu destitution and the fringe camp nature of the villages were displayed to the public, not as the direct result of the appropriation of Ainu land and resources for colonial development, but as a showcase of the primitive, which the casual visitor could fleetingly observe and then leave, confident of his or her own modernity and civilisation.

While it is a relatively straightforward matter to trace these means by which images of the 'dying race' were diffused among the *ippanjin*, or general public, it is another to determine to what extent these notions were rejected or adopted within the common-sense categories that people used to understand the everyday world around them. Most of the residents of the island who entered in the period of mass immigration after 1890 actually had little contact with the indigenes since government policy had confined most Ainu to quasi-reservations. This social distance and the depersonalisation it engendered is hinted at in a 1928 article about a rail journey through the Hidaka region:

Some Ainu got on. There was a *menoko* [woman] carrying a child, one who looked like her husband [*sono otto rashii no*] and one who looked like the grandmother, four in all. On the face of the old woman there was a large tattoo around the mouth that seemed to symbolise the loss of all happiness and hope in the world. [...] The Ainu are like splendid horses

[45] K. Kindaichi, *Ainu life and legends*, Tourist Library no. 36, Tokyo: Board of Tourist Industry, Japanese Government Railways, 1941, pp. 76–81.

[46] M. Ogawa, 'Hokkaidō kyūdojin hogohō, Kyōdojin jidō kyōiku kitei no shita no Ainu gakkō' (Ainu schools under the Hokkaidō Former Natives Protection Act and the Regulations for the Education of Former Native Children), *Hokkaidō daigaku kyōikugakubu kiyō*, no. 58 (1992), p. 232.

turned loose to graze; autumn was slowly deepening on the road to Hidaka and brought to mind the sparseness of human habitation.[47]

But there were also many Wajin who lived close to Ainu villages, and evidence suggests that intimate contact encouraged highly negative attitudes. The memories of Ainu who grew up in the early twentieth century are full of incidents of cheating and manifestations of the overt prejudice that was rife among the rural poor. As the British missionary John Batchelor pointed out in 1919, while Japanese were polite among themselves and to Westerners, they treated the Ainu as 'outside the brotherhood of man', referring to the continued belief that they were descended from dogs.[48] Although immigrant attitudes were complex and defy simplistic categorisation, it appears that many members of the professional classes, on the other hand, treated the Ainu considerately, perhaps motivated by feelings of pity.[49] But among the lower orders in both military and civilian life, physical mistreatment of Ainu was common, often stemming from Wajin perceptions that they tended to forget their inferior status. For Ainu children, school became a torment whenever they were a numerical minority. This was illustrated by an official report from Kasai District in 1923, which found that Ainu children who attended mainly Wajin schools were 'clearly affected by racial [*jinruiteki*] prejudice', and that absenteeism was high.[50] With such attitudes widespread, it is no surprise that despite the official rhetoric of intermarriage and 'fusion', records of the time indicate that enthusiasm for this was not widely shared in rural Hokkaidō society. Relationships between Wajin men and Ainu women tended to be temporary liaisons, with the women often being abandoned after a winter of cohabita-

[47] K. Sasaki, 'Hidaka yuki' (Bound for Hidaka), *Hokkaidō kyōiku shinbun*, no. 37 (Nov. 1928), p. 26.

[48] 'Ainu ni taisuru Nihonjin no jinshuteki sabetsu taigū' (Racially discriminatory treatment of the Ainu by Japanese), *Hokkai taimusu*, 25 Oct. 1919.

[49] Ogawa, 'Protection Act and assimilatory education', p. 243. See also the recollections of K. Sunazawa, *Kusukup orishipe: Watashi no ichidai no omoide* (The story of my life), Tokyo: Fukutake Shoten, 1990, p. 311.

[50] Cited in M. Ogawa, 'Ainu kyōiku seido no haishi: Kyūdojin jidō kyōiku kitei haishi to 1937-nen Hokkaidō kyūdojin hogohō kaisei' (The end of the Ainu education system: The abolition of the Regulations for the Education of Former Native Children and the 1937 revision of the Hokkaidō Former Natives Protection Act), *Hokkaidō daigaku kyōikugakubu kiyō*, no. 61 (1993), p. 59.

tion. Individuals of mixed ancestry were overwhelmingly
categorised as Ainu, or 'mixed-blood Ainu' (*konketsu Ainu*), but
never as 'mixed-blood Wajin', indicating that identity was es-
sentially determined by 'racial' notions of inferior blood. This
was helped by the fact that thinking about 'race' meshed easily
with established social customs, in particular those surrounding
the institution of marriage and incorporating folk attitudes towards
blood lines and pollution.[51]

From the 1880s onwards, the Ainu had increasingly come to
be perceived as a 'dying race', an image that encompassed both
folk images of the Other and the deterministic notions of popular
social Darwinism. This in turn was part of a larger process in
Japanese society in which the boundaries of 'race' and nation
had overlapped in the context of modernisation and the expansion
of a colonial empire inhabited by inferior 'racial' Others. By
the 1930s the expression 'dying race' had become so commonly
used whenever the Ainu were mentioned that it provoked extreme
annoyance among those like Kita Masaaki who were attempting
to promote their assimilation.

> Ainu! Whenever this word is written, it is attached without
> fail to the phrase 'dying race'. Ainu! Whenever the average
> person [*ippanjin*] hears this word, preconceptions of 'primitives,
> hairy men, simpletons' flash like lightning through his mind
> and echo there.[52]

For Kita, the problem was that the association of the Ainu with
a primitive 'dying race', if not seen as actual scientific truth,
was certainly part of the practical worldview of the 'average person'.
Building on earlier notions of difference, premodern stereotypes
had been adapted and reproduced within the discourse of 'race'
alongside the language of Darwinism. Whether Ainu were consciously perceived by individual Wajin through the lens of 'race'
or not, common-sense understanding ensured that an essential
Otherness excluded the Ainu from membership of the superior

[51] For ritual pollution and blood, see C. T. Hayashida, 'Identity, race and the blood ideology of Japan', unpubl. Ph.D. diss., University of Washington, Seattle, 1976, pp. 120-3.

[52] M. Kita, 'Ainu yo izuko e iku (1)' (Ainu, where are you going? Part 1), *Hokkaidō shakai jigyō*, no. 63 (Aug. 1937), p. 44.

'Yamato race'. Although less explicitly stated than in the discourse of the scholars, educators and officials of the colonial administration, for the 'average person' too, Ainu subordination and inequality were matters of 'blood'. And since such racialised understanding contributed to the differentiation, exclusion and domination of the Ainu under a colonial order, it deserves to be considered as racism.

RETHINKING RACE FOR MANCHUKUO
SELF AND OTHER IN THE COLONIAL CONTEXT[1]

Louise Young

The emergence of a Japanese discourse on race in the late nineteenth and twentieth centuries represented one of the many dramatic consequences of Japan's integration into the world system. With intellectual opening, the sudden infusion of Western ideas on race stimulated the emergence of new schools of thought that grappled with the problem of racial taxonomies and Japan's place within them. This racial discourse was shaped in fundamental ways by the new kinds of social interactions between Japanese and foreigners. In their encounters with Europeans, for example, Japanese experienced forms of social relations which were conditioned, as they saw it, by racial difference. This view emerged out of the history of Japanese-European interactions in the treaty ports, as well as in the European settlement societies in the Americas and the Pacific to which Japanese attempted to emigrate. Japan's own empire-building created a different context in which Japanese interacted with foreigners. Within their growing empire in East Asia, and domestically, with immigration of Chinese and Koreans into Japan, Japanese began to draw racial boundaries between themselves and other Asians. Here the Asian Other was socially encountered and culturally constructed within the contexts of institutionalised violence, economic exploitation, and Japanese monopolies of political power and social privilege. Social interactions with non-Japanese thus produced two axes of racial differentiation: Japanese and Europeans on the one hand, and Japanese and Asians on the other.

[1] Funds for travel to Hong Kong in November 1994 to participate in the Racial Identities Conference were generously provided by Georgetown University.

This chapter takes up the latter of these and, using Japanese-ruled Manchukuo in the 1930s and '40s as a case study, explores the forms of thinking on race that emerged in this colonial context. Beginning with the Manchurian Incident of 1931, Japanese imperialism entered a new and critical period. During this phase of empire-building, aptly characterised by John Dower as 'go-fast imperialism',[2] Japan moved aggressively to expand its overseas territories, occupying first China and then Southeast Asia, and initiating a series of military conflicts against the Nationalist and Communist forces in China, the Soviet Union, the United States and the British empire. For Japan's sphere of influence in the provinces of Northeast China, known as Manchuria, this signalled a dramatic transformation of the imperial project. In a series of military campaigns between 1931 and 1933, known as the Manchurian Incident, Japan's Kwantung Army drove the warlord armies of Zhang Xueliang out of Northeast China, set itself up as the new political authority in the region, and declared the new state of 'Manchukuo' independent of China. Seeking to tie the Manchurian economy into an autarkic imperial production sphere, the Japanese initiated a programme of colonial development, pouring money into the construction of the railways, factories, dams and mines deemed essential to unlock Manchuria's fabled treasure-house of resources. And to extend Japanese control into Manchuria's rural hinterlands, they inaugurated a programme of mass Japanese rural settlement, dispossessing Chinese and Korean farmers to make way for Japanese colonists. These changes in the technologies of domination also transformed the context of racial interactions between Japanese and the mostly Chinese inhabitants of Northeast China. After 1931, interactions between the coloniser and the colonised were more frequent and direct, and more violent, appropriative and exploitative. Such interactions engendered, in Japanese racial discourse, an intensification of the rhetoric of difference: they breathed new life into old cultural stereotypes and generated new ones, accelerating the growth of racist attitudes.

Ideas of race in Manchukuo emerged out of a long-standing discourse on race and colonialism. It is often mistakenly assumed that Japanese race thinking was entirely derivative – that Japanese

---

[2] J.W. Dower, *Empire and aftermath: Yoshida Shigeru and the Japanese experience, 1878-1954*, Cambridge, MA: Council on East Asian Studies, Harvard University, 1979, p. 85.

imported racial categories wholesale from the West and simply applied them to other Asians. The reality was more complicated, involving two interrelated processes. Racial discourse in Japan was structured, first, by the selective assimilation of European ideas into an existing framework for comprehending relations between Japanese and others. Secondly, their ideas about race developed, over time, in the context of the experiences of the Japanese themselves with colonialism. From the first steps towards empire in the 1870s to the go-fast imperialism of the 1930s and '40s, the processes of cultural assimilation and colonial expansion gave a distinctive shape to the Japanese discourse on race.

The first phase of this dual process occurred in the late nineteenth century, when Confucian ideas about 'proper place' in social hierarchies and Shinto beliefs in the divine ancestry of the Japanese were overlaid with the framework of Western racial science. Seeking to defend themselves against the Western threat by building their own empire in Asia, the Japanese began to rethink their relationships with Chinese and Koreans. They constructed a justification for positioning themselves at the head of an East Asian 'family of nations' by appropriating legitimations of hierarchy from their own and the Western tradition. The point is not that the Japanese learned to think in alien racial categories from the West, but rather that such categories made sense precisely because they resonated with home-grown notions of hierarchy.

Beginning in 1895, the acquisition of a colonial empire stimulated the formation of an academic and official discourse on colonial rule, marking a new juncture in Japanese intellectualisations of race.[3] Here, too, Japanese formulations borrowed heavily from European models. Policy discussions over the strategies of colonial rule appropriated European debates on the relative merits of racial assimilation or association. But whereas European colonial theory tended to gravitate towards the associationist position, for Japan the rhetoric of assimilation fit better with an emerging colonial mission to usher Asia into the modern age. Thus, the Japanese deployed the assimilationist vocabulary to justify the forced export of those institutions regarded as the engines of their own successful modernisation: a new system of land tenure, a network of railways,

---

[3] For a brief treatment of Japanese colonial discourse, see Mark R. Peattie, 'Japanese attitudes toward colonialism, 1895-1945' in Mark R. Peattie and Ramon H. Myers (eds), *The Japanese colonial empire, 1895-1945*, Princeton University Press, 1984, pp. 262-92.

a police system, and so on. In the process, colonial policy and colonial theory reinforced Japanese conceptualisations of racial difference between themselves and other Asians in terms of 'levels of civilisation', providing the context for Japanese to continually reaffirm their cultural advance against the putative backwardness of their colonial subjects. At the same time, assimilationist theory suited the particular needs of Japanese colonialism. In Taiwan and Korea initial Japanese interventions met with fierce resistance; assimilationist rhetoric justified the creation of the heavily bureaucratised colonial administration necessary for Japan to impose its will on reluctant subjects.

In the 1930s, the start of a new aggressive phase of military expansionism in Asia set in motion a rethinking of the question of race and empire. On the one hand, the need to mobilise colonial populations for an increasingly demanding war effort led to an intensification of efforts towards racial assimilation. In Taiwan and Korea, colonial officials instituted the so-called *kōminka* (imperialisation) policy, which attempted to force racial assimilation through coercive diffusion of Japanese language and names as well as shrine Shinto. At the same time, the deterioration of relations with Western powers in Asia led to an escalation in the rhetoric of racial hostility towards the West. The Japanese appropriated European vocabularies of racial fear (the yellow peril) and racial mission (the white man's burden) and turned them against the West, calling on Asians to join forces against the 'white peril' and proclaiming their intent to liberate Asia from the shackles of white imperialism. Thus the colonial phase of the 1930s brought about a racialisation of the language of international relations and colonial policy.

In the context of Manchukuo, the racialisation of the imperial project began with the military campaigns of the Manchurian Incident. While the Kwantung Army was overrunning Manchuria, at home the Japanese greeted the news of the occupation with an outburst of racial vituperation. In narrative encounters on the battlefields of imagination, the Japanese reinvented their racial Others to accommodate a more aggressive and confrontational style of empire-building.[4]

[4] This discussion is adapted from Louise Young, *Japan's total empire: Manchuria and the culture of wartime imperialism*, Berkeley: University of California Press, 1997 (in particular chapter 3: 'Cowardly Chinese and Western bullies').

In the autumn of 1931, war fever swept Japan as news of the fall of one Manchurian city after another came in over the wires. These seemingly effortless victories over the Chinese unleashed a wave of self-congratulatory articles in the mass media about the beating Japan was giving China and the ineptitude of the Chinese soldiers. This was not the first time that such sentiments had found expression in Japan, nor was it the country's first war fever. During the first Sino-Japanese war of 1894-5, in woodblock prints and popular songs, in newspapers and magazines, in speeches and popular rallies, the Japanese let loose a torrent of anti-Chinese invective.[5] Such an outpouring of abuse marked a profound disjunction with the past. Since the period of intense cultural borrowing from the continent in the sixth and seventh centuries, China had represented a standard of high civilisation to which the Japanese aspired. The awareness that China was the source of Japan's writing system, the philosophical traditions of Buddhism and Confucianism, and a host of other institutions and ideas nurtured a sense of cultural debt. Although the intrusion of the West into Asia in the nineteenth century and the spectre of China's defeat in the Opium War began to shake Japanese faith in Chinese superiority, as late as 1890 Japanese greeted the visit of a Chinese fleet to Japan with fear and respect. But when war broke out in 1894, victory for the Japanese side inspired contempt and derision for the vanquished, shattering the image of China as a model of civilisation.

Even so, the passions stirred up by the first Sino-Japanese War did not completely erase Japanese reverence for China, which remained embedded in a variety of sinified artistic, philosophical, scholarly and other cultural practices. As Japan joined the ranks of Western powers carving China into spheres of influence, these manifestations of Chinese cultural influence provided a constant reminder of an earlier time and a different relationship. The discomfort of living with such a contradiction perhaps explains the explosive force of the hostility towards China that erupted in the war fever of 1931-3, as producers of Japanese culture sought to wash out lingering feelings of cultural debt with a wave of hatred.

---

[5] Donald Keene, 'The Sino-Japanese War of 1894-5 and Japanese culture' in Donald Keene, *Landscapes and portraits: Appreciations of Japanese culture*, Tokyo: Kōdansha, 1971, pp. 259-99.

As in the war fever of 1894-5, reports of the military engagement between Japanese and Chinese forces in 1931 sought to portray the success of the Japanese occupation as evidence of racial superiority. Popular accounts lavished praise on Japanese military prowess, while constructing a stereotype of the Chinese soldier as weak and cowardly. Thus, Japanese reports of the Manchurian Incident invariably showed Chinese soldiers in the act of 'bolting', 'escaping', 'running off', 'hiding' or, in one striking phrase, 'fleeing pell-mell like scattering spider babies'.[6] Journalists derisively reported hearing of Chinese officers hiding from the Japanese, describing, in one account, the shocking sight of 'officers creeping out from under the floors' when the Japanese Army 'set fire to the Chinese barracks to smoke out hiding enemy soldiers'.[7]

Although the Japanese chose to depict the Chinese retreat as an act of collective cowardice, in fact Zhang Xueliang's soldiers were following orders. On the advice of Chiang Kaishek, head of the Guomindang central government to which Zhang Xueliang declared allegiance in 1928, Zhang's army responded to Japanese aggression with 'non-resistance', while Guomindang diplomats appealed to the League of Nations for diplomatic intervention in the Sino-Japanese dispute. But incessant boasting about the '10,000 Japanese' taking on '200,000 Chinese' ignored the fact that the majority of the Chinese were voluntarily withdrawing from the path of the advancing Japanese. Instead, the Japanese interpreted these numbers as meaning that each Japanese soldier was worth twenty of the enemy. As major military targets such as Mukden (Shenyang) and Jilin province were occupied almost without bloodshed, in magazines like *Shōnen kurabu* (Boy's Club) voluntary withdrawal, voluntary disarmament and other forms of 'non-resistance' were transformed into a cowardly and disorganised retreat.

In order to justify continued military action against an enemy that refused to fight back, official Japanese army pronouncements began to circulate a new stereotype of the Chinese soldier – the 'soldier-bandit' (*heihi*). An army propaganda pamphlet explained

[6] Suzuki Gyōsui, illustration captioned 'Teki no shōkō ressha o kōgeki suru waga hikōki' (Our planes attack the train of the enemy officers), *Shōnen kurabu* (Feb. 1932).

[7] Takinaka Takeo, 'Shōnenkan no mite kita Manshū senchi no hanashi: tetchō kara' (A youth's view of the Manchurian battlefield: From the notebook of an eyewitness), *Shōnen kurabu* (Feb. 1932), p. 109.

that as Chinese forces retreated, 'although some retained their
unity ... most scattered to the four winds. Having scattered, Chinese
soldiers will, as always in the past, quickly turn to banditry.'[8]
These soldier-bandits then proceeded to commit 'looting and
violence' and other 'atrocities' against 'Japanese subjects and
Japanese rights and interests all over Manchuria', thus 'disturbing
the peace and menacing the Railway Zone'.[9] In this way, the
army transformed Zhang and his allies into disorganised gangs
of thugs, at the same time insinuating that any type of armed
resistance to the Japanese occupation was a form of banditry.

The mass media eagerly embraced this racial stereotype of the
Chinese soldier. An article written for children on 'The Chinese
Soldier in Manchuria' explained: 'Bandit-soldiers are just like flies
– no sooner do you drive them off than they come right back
out again.' Depicting them as outlaws, Japanese accused Chinese
soldiers of employing unscrupulous and dishonourable methods
of warfare. As the author of 'The Chinese Soldier' declared: 'Because the Chinese Army loses if it fights in an open and sportsman-
like manner, it uses this cowardly method to harass the Japanese
Army.'[10]

What Japanese in 1932 were calling 'banditry' reflected the
emergence of guerrilla resistance among troops not answering
to the command of Zhang Xueliang. To counter such resistance,
Japanese military operations began to target rural villages and other
civilian populations suspected of giving aid to 'banditry'. These
operations provided cover for mass murder, rape and other
atrocities. Although government pressure and self-censorship kept
reports of the summary execution of entire village populations
out of the Japanese media, accounts of individual acts of brutality
appeared with remarkable frequency. These accounts reflected,
on the one hand, the routine nature of atrocities committed against
civilians and, on the other, the indifference with which Japanese
regarded such treatment of Chinese.

[8] Rikugun-shō, *Mantetsu fuzokukchi-gai shutsudō butai hikiage no fukanō naru yuen ni tsuite* (Why
it is impossible for Japan to withdraw troops stationed outside the Manchurian railway zone),
Tokyo: Rikugun-shō, 1931, p. 3.

[9] Ibid.; Rikugun-shō, *Chō Gakuryō Kinshō seiken no tai Nichi Kōsen junbi ni tsuite* (Zhang
Xueliang's preparations for an attack on Japan from his base in Jinzhou), Tokyo: Rikugun-shō,
1931, p. 92.

[10] Imamura Kakichi, 'Manshū no Shina hei' (The Chinese soldier), *Shōnen kurabu* (Feb.
1932), pp. 76-7.

One round-table discussion among Manchurian Incident veterans published in the magazine *Ie no hikari* (The Light of the Home) provided a striking example of this. Explaining that they had orders not to kill 'friendly' Chinese, one soldier confessed 'You just can't tell them apart', and a comrade added: 'You wouldn't believe the numbers of Chinese who are really soldiers. You can basically consider anyone out on the street in Manchuria as a plain-clothes soldier. They say in Jinzhou alone there were more than 300,000 of them.'[11] These words conveyed to the home population the impression that Japanese soldiers in Manchuria were surrounded by Chinese enemies, all disguised as civilians.

Under such circumstances, the soldiers explained, they had developed a simple technique for telling friend from foe:

'When you see someone coming, you put your gun on them. If they cry or run away, they're friendly. If they put their hands up, you know they are soldiers in urban dress. But as one personal anecdote demonstrated, you could never be too careful.

Everybody thinks that only men are plain-clothes soldiers. But there are women, kids, all kinds. Once a young woman of twenty-two or twenty-three came up to me looking very friendly. There in front of her house stood a crippled old grandmother, again smiling in a friendly way so naturally I thought they were good people. But then I had a bad feeling about one of them and I shouted out a warning. The old woman ran hobbling off. I strip-searched the girl ... she couldn't understand me so I gestured with my hands. Underneath her clothes she was wearing two pairs of panties. Hidden inside, sure enough, there was a pistol. I did not want to kill her but she tried to hit me with the gun and that was why she died. She said something abusive first. Afterwards I felt sorry about her, but at the time if I had not handled it right I would have been done for. I was provoked.'[12]

Such words revealed the intense fear and mistrust felt by the Japanese towards Chinese civilians in occupied Manchuria. The anecdote recounted the story of an atrocity: the murder of a

[11] 'Jissen ni sanka shita gunjin no zadankai' (Round table discussion of soldiers who saw action), *Ie no hikari* (July 1932), pp. 50-1.

[12] Ibid., pp. 50-1.

Chinese woman. It communicated to the home front the bullying
and terrorising of the civilian population that was standard operating
procedure during the occupation; Chinese life was cheap. The
matter-of-fact retelling of this story in a popular magazine showed
that to the soldiers, the editors and probably the audience, the
murder was unexceptional. In this way the ruthless nature of
imperialism brutalised not only its practitioners – the soldiers who
actually wielded the bayonets – but also the cultural consumers
who took a vicarious part in the violence.

Another dimension of the Chinese stereotype constructed in
the context of the Japanese war fever was the idea that the Chinese
(unlike themselves) lacked patriotism. At a time when the rise
of organised Chinese nationalism posed a serious challenge to
Japan's position on the continent, the Japanese told themselves
stories of the self-absorbed indifference of the masses to the fate
of the nation. The popular travel writer Gotō Asatarō frequently
commented on the absence of 'national feeling' among the
Chinese. 'Chinese coolies', wrote Gotō in 1932, 'are happy to
build sandbags for the Japanese Army because they can get money
for it. The next day they sit on top of the sandbags, drinking
sorghum wine and watching their own soldiers being destroyed
by the Japanese, saying "Wow! Look at that!"'[13]

Accounts of Chinese corruptibility similarly attempted to
derogate Chinese nationalism. Unlike the stereotype of cowardice,
that of Chinese venality did not date back to the first Sino-
Japanese War but had emerged, rather, through the 1910s and
'20s. Bribing their way through a string of warlord allies, Japanese
representatives sold their patronage for the biggest concession and
sold out their friends. Perceived as an indication of Chinese venality,
the experience of Japan's China hands became the basis for an
additional dimension to the Chinese national character. The mer-
cenary theme was given wide play in 1931-3. An article on 'ordinary
crimes of bribery and betrayal' illustrated the character of the
Chinese soldiers with a drawing of two Chinese warlords, one
with a giant 'money' magnet pulling the army off the other warlord's
weaker magnet. The accompanying text read: 'Civil wars occur
often in China but it is rare for these conflicts to be resolved
by a decisive military victory. Rather, victory is decided through

[13] Gotō Asatarō, 'Shina no heitai' (Chinese soldiers), *Kingu* (April 1932), p. 53.

one side purchasing the betrayal of the enemy with money. [...] According to Japan's code of war it is shameful to allow yourself to be bought off by the enemy', but Chinese change sides 'the minute they are handed some money'.[14]

In the context of war fever, the assault on the Chinese national character reinvented the idea of 'China' in Japanese popular imagination. As they had done repeatedly in the past, the Japanese reworked the symbolic meaning of their relationship with China – a country which had in elemental ways given shape to their own culture. In the latest phase of this process, the new imperialism of the 1930s engendered the reinvention of the Chinese Other in several ways. The new racial contempt for China produced by the war fever helped to overlay any lingering sense of cultural debt that stood in the way of empire-building on the continent. Moreover, by fostering racial hatred, the new views of China in the mass media inured people to the brutality of imperial warfare and accustomed them to increasingly violent encounters with Chinese. Since the Meiji period, pejorative racial depictions of China had provided a foil against which Japan constructed its own national identity. To this end, the disparaging racial portrayals of the Chinese soldiers that circulated in the early 1930s represented indirect praise of the Japanese character, helping to reforge a national identity appropriate to a more aggressive military imperialism. Go-fast imperialism, in short, required high-growth racism.

What was true for the military occupation was equally apparent in other dimensions of the imperial project in Manchuria. The Manchurian colonisation programme, which undertook to resettle impoverished Japanese tenant-farmers in rural Manchuria, used racial appeals to mobilise popular support of an enterprise of extraordinary ambition. There were plans to export to the empire, within the space of twenty years, 5 million farmers, equivalent to one-fifth of the 1936 rural population. Though only 300,000 Japanese were resettled before the programme was halted by defeat in 1945, its impact went far beyond the settlers themselves. The Manchurian colonisation programme involved an unprecedented government expenditure and an enormous expansion of bureaucracy to facilitate the population transfer, as well as the

[14] Shimonaga Kenji, 'Shina hei mandan' (Stories of Chinese soldiers), *Kōdan kurabu* (May 1933), p. 84.

mobilisation of rural Japanese society to aid in the exodus of the village poor. Representations of the Manchurian colonisation project in government propaganda and the mass media justified this prodigious effort with the invention of a Japanese racial mission to expand.

The first articulation of this racial mission emerged in the context of public discussions over Manchurian migration that took place in the early 1930s, when the so-called 'Manchurian migration debate' invited input from bureaucrats, academics and social activists on the feasibility of a government-sponsored mass migration programme to Manchuria. In the course of this debate a new rationale for empire in China began to emerge. Amid discussions of emigration as the solution to the long-standing problem of rural poverty, the expansionist imperative coalesced around a racial mission, what came to be known as the 'continental development of the Japanese race' (*Nippon minzoku no tairiku hatten*). As Professor Nasu Kō of Tokyo University expressed it, the new imperial project in Manchuria was 'not simply an economic movement but a racial movement ... not a capitalist advance but a racial advance.' The new view of what constituted imperial control required 'large numbers of people who share the same racial consciousness', for imperialism now meant racial expansionism.[15]

The new mandate for racial expansionism in Manchuria resuscitated a language of race and empire circulated on the eve of the annexation of Korea in 1910. Reworking the argument, introduced by the politician Okuma Shigenobu in 1906, that 'Korea is the touchstone which determines whether the Japanese race possesses the ability for assimilation',[16] academics in 1932 used Darwinian theories to depict Manchurian settlement as a kind of test of racial hardiness. As one writer explained, racial struggle historically determined who dominated Manchuria. In recent years three races had competed for control – the Chinese, the Japanese

---

[15] Nasu Kō, 'Manshū nōgyō imin no jikkō hōhō ni tsuite' (Methods for implementing Manchurian farm emigration), *Shakai seisaku jihō*, 140 (May 1932), p. 157, 'Tai Manmō keizai seisaku no konpon hōshin' (The fundamental principles of Manchurian-Mongolian economic policy), *Ekonomisto* (1 April 1932), p. 20.

[16] *Tōkyō keizai zasshi* (Tokyo economic journal), no. 1330, (31 March 1906), cited in Karl Moskowitz, 'The creation of the Oriental Development Company: Japanese illusions meet Korean reality', Occasional Papers on Korea, no. 2, Joint Committee on Korean Studies, American Council of Learned Societies and the Social Science Research Council, March 1974, pp. 80-1.

and the Russians – but the real contest today was between the
Chinese and Japanese peoples:

> The advance of the Japanese people into Manchuria is relatively
> recent and their roots are still shallowly planted. Buttressed
> by a superior military, political and cultural position, our national
> strength can be used to wield limitless pressure on the Chinese
> people. [...] But no matter how superior the Japanese race,
> with these tiny numbers we cannot resist being overwhelmed
> by the masses of Chinese people.[17]

Empire-building in Manchuria now involved demographic expansion, which was justified in the language of racial mission.
For promoters of the 'racial mission' thesis, it was imperative
that settlers be 'selected carefully' from among the 'superior elements of society' so that Japan would win the 'racial struggle'
with China: Manchuria must not become a dumping ground
for 'inferior elements' – the poor or unemployed, who represented
the 'losers in the struggle for existence'.[18] In fact, this line of
reasoning contradicted the oft-repeated argument that mass migration was the solution to Japan's overpopulation problem. It was
nothing new for promoters of Japanese emigration to argue at
cross-purposes with one another. Such contradictions reflected
the diversity of interests among them, some being interested in
promoting emigration to resolve domestic social problems, while
others saw it as the means to improve Japan's position internationally. In the debate over Manchurian colonisation, even more
knots were added to this tangled web of logic when support
gathered for the proposition that Manchurian settlers represented
'true colonists' who, unlike emigrants in the past, were 'expanding
the national territory of Japan'. Although Japanese settlements
in Brazil and Peru had long been advertised as model communities
of overseas Japanese, 'migrants to South America' were suddenly
dismissed in 1932 as 'human discards' (*kimin*).[19] *Ekonomisto* (The

---

[17] Nakajima Jinnosuke, 'Manmō imin mondai no tenbō' (The outlook for emigration to
Manchuria-Mongolia), *Shakai seisaku jihō*, 140 (May 1932), pp. 96–7.

[18] Hijikata Seibi, 'Manshū imin to jinkō mondai' (Manchurian immigration and the
population problem), *Shakai seisaku jihō*, 140 (May 1932), p. 45; Nakajima Jinnosuke,
'Manmō imin mondai no tenbō' (The outlook for emigration to Manchuria-Mongolia),
Shakai seisaku jihō, 140 (May 1932), p. 105.

[19] Satō Yasunosuke, 'Manshūkoku e no imin seisaku' (Emigration policy to Manchukuo),
Ekonomisto (1 April 1932), p. 69.

Economist) phrased the distinction between the old and new colonists as follows: 'South American emigrants are the detritus of human society [*jindō ni modoranai kimin*] but Manchurian emigrants represent a kind of national investment.'[20]

When Manchurian colonisation was adopted as national policy by the Japanese government in 1936, administrators picked up the idea of racial mission to justify pouring government resources into the effort to transplant millions of Japanese farmers to the new empire.[21] The literature on colonisation frequently referred to Manchuria as a 'brother country to which Japan has given birth' (*Nihon ga unda kyōdaikoku*).[22] The idea that Japan and its colonies represented a 'brotherhood of nations' was, of course, a stock image in Confucian-inspired representations of the Japanese empire. Manchurian colonisation took this one step further, re-inforcing the Confucian family metaphor with the Shinto-inspired idea of the family-state. Enshrined in the Meiji Constitution and disseminated through primary school textbooks, the concept of a family-state rested on the mytho-historical account of a common racial ancestry. Classical texts traced the origins of the Japanese people back to the divinely descended Emperor Jimmu, founder of the Japanese state at Yamato in 660 BC and mythic progenitor of what was called the Yamato race. In these terms, the nation constituted an extended family linked by blood, and the imperial head of state was also the paternal head of this extended national household. When emigration propaganda applied the biological language of kinship to the colonisation of Manchukuo, the empire was brought into the racial embrace of the family-state. As one article explained, Manchukuo was not just a colony of Japan, but kin by blood. The imperial relationship became an extension of the Japanese family system where 'Japan is the stem family and Manchuria is the branch family'. Observing the hierarchical relations maintained between stem and branch, Japan acted as 'parent' to the infant nation of Manchukuo, rearing it to become

---

[20] 'Tai Manmō keizai seisaku no konpon hōshin' (The fundamental principles of economic policy toward Manchuria-Mongolia), *Ekonomisto* (1 April 1932), p. 20.

[21] The following discussion is drawn from Louise Young, *Japan's Total Empire*, chapter 8 ('Racial Expansionism').

[22] Hatta Yoshiaki, 'Tairiku no yokudo wa maneku' (The fertile soil of the continent beckons), *Ie no hikari* (April 1939), p. 35; Koiso Kuniaki, 'Ichi kuwa no chikara' (The strength of one hoe), *Ie no hikari* (Oct. 1939), p. 31.

a 'splendid nation just like Japan'.[23] Thus, in the new language of colonisation, colonies became kinsmen and the family-state became the family-empire.

The policy of recruiting second and third sons to set up branch families in Manchuria reinforced this idea of colonial kinship. Recruiting literature stressed that 'the rich soil of the continent beckoned', especially to second and third sons whose 'bleak expressions registered their despair at making a life for themselves on the family farm'.[24] In similar fashion, the language of the village colonisation programme literally signified the creation of a 'branch village' (*bunson*). As one caption urged, 'Set up a branch family in Manchuria through village colonisation' (*bunson imin de Manshū e bunke*).[25] In this way, the metaphors of reproduction and family were invoked to suggest a new connection of race and blood between coloniser and colonised.

In keeping with the idea of racial seeding, emigration promoters strongly sounded the youth theme. Echoing Horace Greeley's famous admonition 'Go west young man', Baron Ōkura Kinmochi of the Manchurian Emigration Council instructed Japanese youth 'Go to the continent young man', for 'a new land awaits the village youth'.[26] In popular settlement songs the 'frontier spirit' overflowed, invariably, 'with the blood of youth'.[27]

The prominence of images of youth in colonialist discourse and the representation of Japanese overseas expansion in the figure of a virile young man can be traced back to the embrace of the idea of progress in the 1870s and 1880s and the self-representation of a youthful and progressive Japan guiding decrepit Asian neighbours down the path to Western-style civilisation and enlightenment. In the 1930s, the cultural content in the metaphor of nation as youth thinned, and was replaced by biological and physiological meanings. Anthems of the Patriotic Youth Brigade, a Manchurian colonisation programme that recruited teen-aged

---

[23] 'Tokugō –tairiku wa maneku Manshū kaitakusha mondō' (Special series: The continent beckons – questions and answers for prospective Manchurian colonists), *Ie no hikari* (April 1939), p. 141.

[24] Hatta Yoshiaki, 'Tairiku', p. 35.

[25] 'Tokugō', p. 145.

[26] Ōkura Kinmochi, 'Seinen yo tairiku ni idō seyo' (Go to the continent, young men!), *Ie no hikari* (Jan. 1938), p. 34.

[27] Shimada Keita, 'Kaitaku damashii' (The colonial spirit), *Ie no hikari* (Sept. 1941), pp. 34-5.

boys, eulogised the physical vigour and power of the young –
qualities needed to plant the race on the continent. Lyricist
Hoshikawa Ryōka referred to the 'capable fists' and 'strength'
of youth in his prize-winning tune 'We are the Young Volunteers'.
The song 'Frontier March' popularised phrases like 'stalwart sons
of the holy land' (*shishū no kendanji*), and the 'Patriotic Youth
Brigade Song' proclaimed:

> *With our young lives*
> *We are Japan's advance guard on the soil.*
> *Our emotion burns bright,*
> *We come gripping hoes,*
> *So we will open up the land*
> *The great land of Manchuria.*[28]

There were, of course, practical reasons for advocates of colonisation
to pay particular attention to recruiting young people. Literature
on Manchurian colonisation laid great stress on the responsibility
of Japan's youth to seed the new empire with the Yamato race
and expand the nation's living space on to colonial soil. In the
words of a colonisation manual, Japanese youth were uniquely
capable of founding a new continental generation and a 'new
continental Japan'.[29] Under the caption 'The Joy of Becoming
a Progenitor' one article asked: 'What could be better than creating
a new country and becoming the founding fathers of that country?
There is no life more worth living. There is no task more worth
doing.'[30] In the pages of *Ie no hikari* (The Light of the Home),
joyful settlers declared their burning desire to 'bury our bones
in an unknown land ... and build a paradise for the children
and grandchildren yet to be born'.[31]

The racial overlay to the colonising mission in Manchukuo

[28] Hoshikawa Ryōka's 'Wareware wa wakaki giyūgun' and Tobishi Aiko's 'Kaitaku yuki' shared first prize in a song contest held by Hirake Manmō (Opening Manchuria-Mongolia) for the official anthem of the Youth Brigade. Shimao Atsunari wrote 'The Patriotic Youth Brigade Song' (*Seishōnen giyūgun no uta*). Sakuramoto Tomio, *Manmō kaitaku seishōnen giyūgun* (The Manchurian-Mongolian Patriotic Youth Brigade), Tokyo: Aoki shoten, 1987, pp. 53-4, 101.

[29] Miura Etsurō (ed.), *Manshū ijū dokuhon* (Manchurian emigration manual), Tokyo: Kaizōsha, 1939, p. 34.

[30] Katō Takeo, 'Seishōnen giyūgun no seikatsu' (The life of the youth brigade settlers), *Ie no hikari* (Dec. 1938), pp. 231-2.

[31] 'Tairiku no hanayome' (Continental brides), *Ie no hikari* (July 1938), p. 27.

involved more than a *Lebensraum*-like idea of racial expansionism. It also drew on the racial conceptualisation of the relationship between Japanese and other Asians that was the product of the colonial experience in Taiwan and Korea. Applying the racial definitions of difference to the so-called land of 'racial harmony', colonisation literature reinforced and invigorated ideas of a natural hierarchy of race and power in Asia.

In the representations of the interactions between Japanese and the other Asian inhabitants of Manchukuo, race was everything. The frequency with which propagandists felt compelled to assert 'the superiority of the Japanese race' was as noteworthy as their ingenuity in varying the iteration of this concept. The position of the 'Yamato people' was expressed variously as 'heart' (*kakushin*), 'pivot' (*chūjiku*) and 'axis' (*chūsū*) of the 'five races' (Japanese, Chinese, Korean, Manchurian and Mongolian). The Japanese described themselves as in the 'position of leadership' (*shidōteki chii*), the 'guiding role' (*shidōteki yakuwari*), 'leader of the Asian continent' (*Ajia tairiku no meishu*), 'head of the five races' (*gozoku kyōwa no sentō*), the 'driving force of racial harmony' (*gozoku kyōwa no suishinryoku*), or all of these at once. Since the early Meiji period, advocates of empire had trumpeted Japan's right to assume the 'leadership of Asia' by virtue of its success in creating a modern civilisation. Now cultural superiority was signified in the biological language of race.

Race also prescribed the duty of Japanese settlers to 'lead and enlighten' (*shidō keihatsu*) the other races of Manchukuo, and undertake their 'moral reform' (*tokka*) and 'guidance' (*yūeki*).[32] Detailing the task of racial enlightenment, literature on Manchurian colonisation catalogued the racial characteristics that separated Japanese from other Asians. In Japan, as in other colonising societies, the perception of technological backwardness became a key measure of the racial gap.[33] Books and magazine articles on Manchukuo paid particular attention to the level of material culture among the native Chinese population, contrasting it negatively with Japan.

[32] For examples of these slogans as well as those cited in the preceding paragraph, see Miura Etsurō (ed.), *Manshū ijū dokuhon* (Manchurian emigration manual), Tokyo: Kaizōsha, 1939, pp. 31-5; 'Tokugo', pp. 141-2; Ishiwara Jirō, *Manshū imin to seinendan* (Manchurian colonisation and youth groups), Tokyo: Dai Nippon rengō seinendan, 1937, p. 40.

[33] For an account of science, technology and imperial ideologies, see Michael Adas, *Machines as the measure of men: Science, technology, and ideologies of Western dominance*, Ithaca, NY: Cornell University Press, 1989.

Describing a visit to the home of a wealthy Chinese landlord, one writer 'thought it peculiar' that the home was decorated with empty glass bottles, because he had heard that 'glass products were highly prized in Japan about a hundred years ago when Japan was first exposed to Western culture'. When he saw those bottles, he realised that the Chinese were 'about a hundred years behind the Japanese' farmers.[34]

The belief that levels of technology reflected racial development led some writers to rearrange the facts in order to maintain the myth of Japanese racial superiority. While in Manchuria the Japanese settlers were frantically trying to learn local cultivation practices from Chinese and Korean farmers, as home settlement propaganda was instructing Japanese farmers of the burning need to go to the new paradise to disseminate superior Japanese farming methods. One pamphlet, noting that Manchurian farm villages were in an appalling state, which the Manchukuo government was 'working diligently to improve', explained that 'no matter how many times things are explained to them [Chinese farmers] they do not understand'. To 'overcome their failings', the pamphlet counselled the 'necessity to bring a superior race well-trained in agricultural techniques to guide these backward Chinese farmers in the field'.[35]

In addition to the question of technology, colonisation literature drew attention to standards of personal hygiene as a measure of racial difference. One writer, in his 'First Look at a New Settlement', described at length the revulsion he suffered from the 'foul' body odour of a 'crowd of Chinese coolies'.[36] On their return from a tour of the settlements, a husband and wife team reported enthusiastically of their success in disseminating hygienic practices among the Chinese. Stressing the special role of Japanese women in promoting racial harmony through bathing instruction, Mrs Koshio observed: 'As everybody knows, Manchurians are a very dirty race and there are many of them who only take a bath two or three times in their life. But while

[34] 'Manshū imin mura hōmon ki (ge)' (Record of a visit to a Manchurian settlement, part two), *Ie no hikari* (March 1937), pp. 63–4.

[35] Ōkura Kinmochi, *Nōson seinen shokun no funki o unagasu* (An inspirational message for village youth), Tokyo: Manshū ijū kyōkai, 1936, p. 12.

[36] 'Manshū ijū mura hōmon ki (jō)' (Record of a visit to a Manchurian settlement, part one), *Ie no hikari* (Feb. 1937), p. 61.

they are mixing with Japanese women, they begin to imitate our bathing customs and learn how to get rid of "Nanjing vermin" [bedbugs].[37] Mr Koshio followed this with his own illustration of the 'dirty racial habits' of the Chinese, explaining how settlers had 'struggled to promote the use of lavatories' through a 'prize contest'. While the men were out bringing law and order to the land with guns and swords, Mrs Koshio felt that this instruction brought about 'what I would call true pacification'.[38]

Such stories were important because they reinforced the sense, for Japanese, of their proper place in the social hierarchy of Manchukuo. By transplanting a rural underclass to the empire, Manchurian colonisation raised disturbing questions of the relationship between the social hierarchy at home and in the empire: moving into the Manchurian context the socially inferior suddenly became the socially superior. To smooth over the contradictions between domestic underprivilege and colonial overprivilege, propagandists highlighted racial hierarchy and the putative civilisation gap between Chinese and Japanese, using a racial construction of difference to obscure what poor farmers of both nationalities had in common.

As such reports from the frontier informed readers back home, the Japanisation of Manchuria implied not only filling the country with Japanese, but also the cultural Japanisation of the native population. Thus advocates of Manchurian colonisation defined racial expansionism in terms both of demographic expansion and of cultural assimilation. In choosing to frame their appeals in the language of race, they helped to reinvent the ideology of Japanese expansion. This process of reinvention reflected the profundity of the changes engendered by Japan's new imperialism. As the Manchurian colonisation movement brought Japanese into new forms of social contact with colonial subjects, colonisation literature began to express a new sense of intimacy between Japan and Manchukuo. Imperial propagandists conveyed this in their depictions of an empire 'turning Japanese' – painting fanciful pictures of mass Chinese conversion to a Japanese way of life, and of Japanese settlements in hues of bucolic familiarity.

At a more basic level, the imperative of racial expansionism

[37] 'Otoko to onna no tachiba kara Manshū kaitaku mura o miru' (A man's and a woman's view of a Manchurian settlement), *Ie no hikari* (Oct. 1939), p. 139.
[38] 'Otoko to onna', pp. 137, 139.

provided a mission for the proliferating institutional apparatus of Manchurian colonisation. Thus a racialised colonial mission legitimated the extension of the colonial project into a new sphere of activity, even as it allowed enormous government budgets, an army of bureaucrats and mountains of paper to be generated.

In both the new militarism of the Manchurian Incident and the demographic transformations of the Manchurian colonisation campaign, go-fast imperialism led to the cultural reconstruction of race. The brutality and violence of the military occupation gave rise to new expressions of racial hatred and fear, helping to erase public memories of a previous era when Japanese venerated China as the wellspring of civilisation. Appeals to a *Lebensraum*-like racial mission to expand were the justification for a grand scheme of social engineering which linked social policy in Japan and Manchukuo. While Japanese settlers were establishing a new social hierarchy of race and power in the Manchurian countryside, at home the export of rural poverty made the 'living space' of the empire the instrument of racial revitalisation. In both cases the social transformation in the relationship between coloniser and colonised involved the production of a new language of race. As the dynamics of expansion brought Japanese into more sustained, intense and intimate contact with Chinese, it became necessary to draw the racial boundaries that separated them more sharply. Thus in the 1930s, as before, Japanese racial discourse was tied inextricably into the process of empire-building. Ideologies of difference were the product of particular institutions of colonial violence, domination and exploitation, and in turn they helped to reproduce and reshape those same institutions.

ANTI-SEMITISM IN JAPAN
ITS HISTORY AND CURRENT IMPLICATIONS

David G. Goodman

In January 1995, just two months before it attacked passengers on the Tokyo subway system with the deadly sarin gas, killing twelve people and making an estimated 5,500 others ill, the Aum Shinrikyō religious cult dedicated a special issue of its organ, *Vajrayāna Sacca*, to a vehement attack on the Jews. The 95-page tract, titled 'Manual of Fear', began with a 'declaration of war' on the Jewish enemy: 'On behalf of the earth's 5.5 billion people', the editors wrote, '*Vajrayāna Sacca* hereby formally declares war on the "world shadow government" that murders untold numbers of people and, while hiding behind sonorous phrases and high-sounding principles, plans to brainwash and control the rest. Japanese, awake! The enemy's plot has long since torn our lives to shreds.'[1]

The same month *Marco Polo*, a monthly magazine published by the powerful and prestigious Bungei Shunjū company, the publisher of Anne Frank's *Diary*, ran an article that denied the Holocaust. Titled 'There Were No Nazi "Gas Chambers"'; it was timed to coincide with the fiftieth anniversary of the liberation of Auschwitz. 'January 27 will be the fiftieth anniversary of the "liberation" of the Auschwitz concentration camp', the editors wrote in their preface to the article, endorsing its assertions. 'But this event conceals the greatest taboo of the postwar period. The fact of the matter is that significant doubt is now being cast on the "Holocaust", the theory that there was a mass murder of the Jews.'[2]

---

[1] *Vajrayāna Sacca*, ed. Aum editorial staff, no. 6, 25 Jan. 1995, p. 3.

[2] Nishioka Masanori, 'Nachi 'gasu-shitsu'' wa nakatta' (There were no Nazi 'gas chambers'),

177

These two incidents are only the most recent in a long and complicated history of Japanese thinking about Jews. Attitudes towards Jews in Japan have evolved over the past two centuries as a complex accretion of images derived from diverse sources. In order to understand such recent phenomena as the Aum Shinrikyō 'Manual of Fear' and the Holocaust denial published in *Marco Polo*, this complex accretion must be examined.[3]

CULTURAL ORIGINS

Japanese attitudes to Jews are rooted in Japanese culture and reflect Japanese attitudes towards foreigners in general. These attitudes are characterised by a profound ambivalence, which sees outsiders alternatively as threatening demons and awesome gods. Japanese religion and artistic practice embody these attitudes; they are replete with rituals that seek either to propitiate or to exorcise gods from afar. Underlying the fact that Jews are simultaneously feared and admired in Japan, therefore, is this basic pattern of Japanese culture.

Partly because of their island nation's geographical isolation, people in Japan have had little experience with intercultural exchange. Instead, they have historically conducted monologues about foreign peoples among themselves, manipulating the images of foreigners for domestic political, social and psychological purposes. This pattern is especially evident in Japan's premodern relationship with China, where the power and authority of Chinese civilisation were constantly invoked but the Chinese people were seldom engaged.[4] This way of conceptualising the outside world is not unique to Japan, as Edward Said has shown in his influential study *Orientalism*, which reveals how the West has conducted a self-interested monologue about the Middle East throughout the modern period, but the Japanese have been particularly susceptible to it and have been slow to develop alternatives.

Marco Polo, Jan. 1995, p. 170.

[3] The following account is based on David G. Goodman and Masanori Miyazawa, *Jews in the Japanese mind: The history and uses of a cultural stereotype*, New York: The Free Press, 1995.

[4] See David Pollack, *The fracture of meaning: Japan's synthesis of China from the eighth through the eighteenth centuries*, Princeton University Press, 1986; and Ronald P. Toby, *State and diplomacy in early modern Japan: Asia in the development of the Tokugawa bakufu*, Princeton University Press, 1984.

Attitudes to Jews in Japan are also deeply rooted in the anti-foreignism that was formulated in its modern form during the first decades of the nineteenth century. In 1825, the nativist thinker Aizawa Seishisai articulated the basic outlines of this xenophobia in his influential treatise, *New Theses*, emphasising his conviction that an alien, occult religion posed a mortal threat to Japan. Aizawa argued that the adherents of this occult religion were conspiring to conquer the world and intended to subvert every area of Japanese culture in order to further their scheme. Trade and finance were the conspirators' major weapons, Aizawa wrote, and their ultimate goal was to destroy Japan's national identity in order to create a single world order that they alone would control. The 'occult religion' Aizawa had in mind was Christianity, not Judaism, but a century later his arguments were applied to the Jews.[5]

The raw material of Japanese ideas about Jews came from abroad. The foreign reference works Japanese writers depended on for their early information about the outside world routinely carried derogatory definitions of the word 'Jew', like the following from the *Concise Oxford Dictionary of Current English* (1914): 'Jew: Person of Hebrew race; extortionate usurer; trader who drives hard bargains'. These defamatory definitions continue to appear in Japanese dictionaries and have affected the basic Japanese image of Jews.

However, this raw material has been filtered and shaped by Japanese culture – a process exemplified by the career of Shakespeare's *Merchant of Venice*. First performed in 1885, it was the first play by Shakespeare to be staged in Japan and it was the one most frequently performed throughout the twentieth century, being used as a text in Japanese high schools into the 1980s. Every educated Japanese is expected to know the play, which is why in 1985 Iwai Katsuhito, a prominent economist at Tokyo University, was able to publish a serious and commercially successful study of modern capitalism based entirely on it.[6]

The Merchant of Venice became popular in the late nineteenth

---

[5] See Bob Tadashi Wakabayashi, *Anti-foreignism and Western learning in early-modern Japan: The New Theses of 1825*, Cambridge, MA: Council on East Asian Studies, Harvard University, 1986.

[6] Iwai Katsuhito, *Benisu no shōnin no shihonron* (The theory of capitalism in *The Merchant of Venice*), Tokyo: Iwanami shoten, 1985.

century because of contemporary Japanese interest in trials and
money-lending. It was first staged as a typical *kabuki* drama set
in Japan with all the characters recast as Japanese. Shylock was
renamed Gohei and diverged in no significant detail from the
standard miser character in *kabuki*. In this and other ways the
Japanese projected on to Shylock their own concerns and preconceptions, so this character who in Japan is routinely taken as
a prototypical Jew is in important respects actually a reflection
of an indigenous cultural imagination.

Be that as it may, Shakespeare's play and especially the image
of Shylock have had a profound impact on Japanese conceptions
of the Jews. As one journalist writing in 1923 put it, 'I received
the strong impression that the Jews had always been a despicable
race like Shylock, who was best described as stingy, greedy, cruel,
cold-blooded and heartless.'[7]

JAPANESE CHRISTIAN THEOLOGY

The Christian scriptures were also a major source of Japanese
images of the Jews. However, it was the image of the Jews not
as Christ-killers, which had played such a significant role in Europe,
but as God's 'chosen people' that captured the Japanese imagination.
The Judaic notion that God would choose a particular people
to be His instrument in human history, and the Christian innovation
that this mantle of election was transferable, enthralled Japanese
theologians, who used it to establish their parity with the West
or even superiority to it. The *Japanese* were God's chosen people,
these theologians claimed, and the mantle of election had now
passed to them. As one theologian put it in 1924,

> Japan has leapt from the ignoble position of an isolated island
> in the Far East, nay, a nation of pagans, to the status of a
> world-class empire blessed by God. The right to look down
> upon the countries of the West that profess Christianity is
> ours. It is high time they discovered that Japan is God's sacred
> repository ... a divine nation with no need of their arrogant
> missionising.[8]

[7] Watanabe Minojirō, *Yudaya minzoku no sekai-teki katsudō* (The global activities of the Jews),
Tokyo: Ōsaka Mainichi shimbun and Tokyo Nichinichi shimbun, 1923, p. 1.
[8] Sakai Katsuisa (a.k.a. Sakai Shōgun), *Sekai no shōtai to Yudayajin* (The true nature of the

Exposed to British Anglo-Israelism, these theologians also developed syncretic theories of Japanese-Jewish common ancestry, which in various configurations cast the Japanese as descendants of the Ten Lost Tribes of Israel or, alternatively, as the true Jews. In their origin and consequence these theories have much in common with Christian identity beliefs, which have been used to justify acts of racist violence in the United States, including the bombing in Oklahoma City on 19 April 1995.[9]

THE PROTOCOLS OF THE ELDERS OF ZION

In the early 1920s *The Protocols of the Elders of Zion* entered Japan. This anti-Semitic tract, which purports to document a clandestine Jewish plot to take over the world, was forged by the Russian secret police about the time of the Dreyfus affair in France and subsequently became a staple of anti-Semitism around the world, including Japan, where it continues to be republished and is available in every major bookstore.

The Protocols was introduced to Japan following the Russian Revolution, when Japan sent troops into Siberia as part of an international attempt to reverse the revolution. Before they withdrew in 1922, Japanese troops reached a maximum strength of 72,000. White Russian soldiers in Siberia were being issued with copies of *The Protocols* to familiarise them with the enemy they were supposedly fighting. Japanese soldiers also received copies. The tract was quickly translated into Japanese and used to explain not only why the Russian Revolution had taken place, but why the Japanese military had been powerless to reverse it. However, an important reason why *The Protocols* seemed so plausible and became so popular in Japan was its close resemblance to the occult religious conspiracy against which Aizawa Seishisai and others had warned a century before.

The way *The Protocols* interacted with Japanese nativist ideology and Christian theology was epitomised in the thought of Sakai Katsuisa (a.k.a. Sakai Shōgun), a nationalist ideologue and fundamentalist Christian who attended the Moody Bible Institute

---

world and the Jews), Tokyo: Naigai shobō, 1924, pp. 218-19.

[9] For a description of Anglo-Israelism, its origins and relations to contemporary American racism, see Michael Barkun, *Religion and the racist right*, Chapel Hill: University of North Carolina Press, 1994.

in Chicago. As a Christian, Sakai accepted the election of the Jews, but as a nationalist he asserted that the Japanese were God's *true* chosen people; and as a believer in *The Protocols* he subscribed to the notion that an international conspiracy of Jews was threatening Japan's unique national polity. This concatenation of ideas led to the kind of ambivalent thinking that henceforth came to characterise Japanese attitudes towards the Jews. It identified with Jews even as it rejected them, and envied their power even as it feared it. As Sakai wrote in 1924,

> Today the world is a battlefield. Japan is under attack from savage external threats and internal confusion. What we should fear most is not cannonballs but ideological deviation, not battleships but conspiracy. Like the Jews, I am an advocate of the restoration of Divine Rule and a Zionist. Nevertheless, I do not wish their conspiracy to succeed anywhere in Japan or for it to contaminate our Imperial Land, for I believe that Imperial Japan has no need of their conspiracy and in fact is in a position to enlighten them. However, since the people of Japan have not yet roused themselves from their infatuation with foreign cultures, the black hand of [the Jews'] great conspiracy has already begun to invade their thinking.[10]

NAZISM AND WARTIME ANTI-SEMITISM

Anti-Semitism in Japan is the chimerical belief in a global Jewish conspiracy bent on destroying Japan based on indigenous xenophobia, Western literary and reference works, certain varieties of Japanese Christian theology, and *The Protocols of the Elders of Zion*. This pre-existing anti-Semitism was legitimated by the rise of Nazi Germany in the 1930s and Japan's alliance with it. With Nazi reinforcement, what had been a far-right eccentricity in the 1920s grew to become an integral part of Japanese ultra-nationalist ideology in the 1940s and resulted in what the historian John Dower has called 'an outburst of anti-Jewish race hate' that was particularly noticeable at the beginning of the war.[11]

[10] Sakai Katsuisa, *Yudaya minzoku no daiinbō* (The great Jewish conspiracy), Tokyo: Naigai shobō, 1924, p. 77.

[11] John W. Dower, *War without mercy: Race and power in the Pacific war*, New York: Pantheon, 1986, p. 258.

'The Jews are the curse of mankind,' inveighed Tokutomi Iichirō, the doyen of Japan's ultra-nationalist writers, in a typical statement. 'Under the guise of democracy they wield their plutocratic hegemony in the United States. American democracy has become a Jewish den.'[12] It was against this 'evil and ugly plutocracy' that Japan was fighting, Tokutomi claimed.[13]

Japanese schoolchildren were indoctrinated with anti-Semitic ideas in school. 'During the war, all the knowledge we had about Europe and America was what we could glean from our Western history and world geography textbooks,' the historian Saitō Takashi has recalled. 'Books describing "the Jewish global conspiracy" and "the Masonic threat" were available, and our knowledge was so poor that we readily believed the theories they presented.'[14] Likewise, the respected liberal historian Irokawa Daikichi later confessed with admirable candour that he had made the following entry in his diary while a student in high school.

> Stalin, Chiang Kaishek, Roosevelt and Churchill are all puppets of International Jewry; the roots of their strategy lie in secret organisations of Jewish military industrialists, international businessmen, finance capitalists, members of secret societies, speculators and the like; Hitler and the Nazis are the saviours of mankind for combating them. [...] Japan has also been victimised by the Jews, who initiated the present war. Any Japanese with an ounce of sense knows that we are not imperialists. [...] Our theory of 'eight corners of the world under one roof' [*Hakkō ichiu*] is far greater, more introspective, and sublime than the theory of 'the absolute superiority of the German *Volk*'. [...] Hitler is the hero of the century, an agent of Nietzsche, the saviour of Western civilisation, and anything but an imperialist![15]

The purpose of Japanese wartime anti-Semitism was not to

[12] Tokutomi Iichirō, *Hisshō kokumin tokuhon* (A citizen's reader for certain victory), Tokyo: Mainichi shimbunsha, 1944, pp. 69-71; 139-40. Quoted in Ben-Ami Shillony, *Politics and culture in wartime Japan*, New York: Oxford University Press, 1981, p. 161. Tokutomi is referred to as 'the dean of Japan's nationalist writers' in Ryusaku Tsunoda *et al.* (eds), *Sources of Japanese tradition*, vol. 2, New York: Columbia University Press, 1964, p. 291.

[13] Cited in Dower, *War without mercy*, pp. 224-5.

[14] Saitō Takashi, 'Rekishi to no deai' (Encounter with history), *UP*, Sept. 1975.

[15] Irokawa Daikichi, *Aru Shōwa-shi: jibunshi no kokoromi* (One man's history of the Shōwa era: An attempt at a self-history), Tokyo: Chūō kōronsha, 1975, pp. 91-2, 115.

persecute Jews but to suppress domestic dissent and promote the war effort. The more than 20,000 Jews under Japanese control in Shanghai during the war were not harmed, because they were valuable hostages who, it was hoped, could be convinced to put the resources of the international Jewish conspiracy at the disposal of Imperial Japan.[16] Domestically, however, the Japanese government actively promoted anti-Semitism as an instrument of thought control, and it was promulgated through Japan's newspapers, which the government strictly controlled. All of Japan's major newspapers carried anti-Semitic articles, and, according to Takeda Seigo, author of the 1944 book *Newspapers and the Jews*, Japan's newspapers were 'a weapon of war to destroy the Anglo-American-Jewish enemy.' The role of Japan's newspapers was 'to expunge Anglo-American-Jewish influence completely' and 'join forces with the news organs of our ally Germany to launch a frontal assault on the journalistic plots of the Anglo-American-Jewish foe'.[17]

The Japanese government also promoted anti-Semitism through the Association for International Politics and Economics, which it funded through the Foreign Ministry. Shiratori Toshio (1887-1949), ambassador to Italy from December 1938 to 1940 and one of the principal architects of the Tripartite Pact, was the most prominent Foreign Ministry official to act as liaison between the Ministry and the Association.[18]

This government-sponsored anti-Semitism was used to suppress ideological non-conformists. In particular, Japanese Christians who identified with the Jews were persecuted for their beliefs. For example, ninety-six members of the three branches of the Holiness Church, a fundamentalist sect, were arrested on 26 June 1942, and imprisoned for 'thought crimes'. Additional arrests were made in February and April the following year, bringing the total number of detainees to 111. Of this number more than half were prosecuted; nineteen were sentenced to jail terms, and several died in jail.

---

[16] For details on the Jewish relationship with the Japanese in Shanghai, see David Kranzler, *Japanese, Nazis and Jews: The Jewish refugee community in Shanghai, 1938-1945*, New York: Yeshiva University Press, 1976; Ernest G. Heppner, *Shanghai refuge: A memoir of the World War II Jewish ghetto*, Lincoln: University of Nebraska Press, 1993; and James R. Ross, *Escape to Shanghai: A Jewish community in China*, New York: The Free Press, 1994.

[17] Takeda Seigo, *Shimbun to Yudayajin* (Newspapers and the Jews), Tokyo: Ōa Tsūshinsha, 1944, pp. 256-59.

[18] Kase Hideaki, 'Nihon no naka no Yudayajin' (Jews in Japan), Chūō kōron, May 1971, pp. 238-40.

In justifying its actions, the government alleged that the Holiness believers

> not only deny our National Polity and are unrepentant in their profanation of the Great Shrine [of Ise, symbol of the imperial family], but they also regard the Jews as 'God's Chosen People' and delude themselves with visions of reconstructing a Jewish state. [...] Finally, they preach the heresy that the purpose of the Great Pacific War is to construct a Jewish state, which distorts and obscures the significance of our Holy War. They are seditious elements susceptible to exploitation by our enemies and a great obstacle to the prosecution of the war.[19]

POSTWAR IDENTIFICATION AND DENIAL

Anti-Semitism went out of fashion after the war, along with the nationalist ideology of which it was a part, but it did not disappear, and a bifurcated situation developed. On the one hand, a new understanding of Jews and Jewish history developed. Numerous books that objectively described the Jewish experience were written and translated, like Anne Frank's *Diary of a Young Girl,* which was published in Japanese in 1952 and immediately became a bestseller – today it has sold over 4 million copies. Many Japanese intellectuals repudiated anti-Semitism and actively debated the causes and implications of the Holocaust. The Japanese people closely followed the trial of Adolf Eichmann in Jerusalem in 1961-2, and reports by Japanese journalists covering the trial were avidly read. In 1960, the Japan Association for Jewish Studies (*Nihon Isuraeru-bunka kenkyūkai*) was founded to promote the study of Jewish civilisation in Japan.

At the same time, however, anti-Semitic attitudes persisted in altered form. As the Cold War began and the United States determined to build Japan up as a bulwark against communism in Asia, many conservative politicians and former military men who had been responsible for Japan's prewar anti-Semitism were rehabilitated and transformed into 'liberal democrats' in what came

---

[19] Wada Yōichi *et al.* (eds), *Tokkō shiryō ni yoru senji-ka no Kirisuto-kyō undō* (The Christian movement in wartime Japan as seen in the records of the Special Higher Police), vol. 2, Tokyo: Shinkyō shuppansha, 1972, p. 143.

to be known as 'the reverse course'. Foremost among these was Kishi Nobusuke (1896-1987), who had held several wartime cabinet positions and had been detained as a Class 'A' war criminal after the war. Kishi was rehabilitated late in the Occupation and went on to become Japanese prime minister from 1957 to 1960.

In a similar fashion, wartime anti-Semites like Inuzuka Koreshige (1890-1965), the naval officer responsible for the Jews in Shanghai from 1939 to 1942, were transformed in the 1950s into 'friends of the Jews'. Inuzuka had been the author of numerous anti-Semitic tracts before and during the war, yet in 1952 he founded several 'pro-Jewish' organisations, including the Japan-Israel Association (*Nihon-Isuraeru Kyōkai*), which he headed till his death in 1965. He successfully obscured his anti-Semitic past, presenting his belief in a global Jewish conspiracy as awe at Jewish vitality, and his wartime sins were overlooked by Jews grateful to anyone who had saved Jewish lives during the Holocaust, regardless of their motive.

Increasingly in the postwar period, the Japanese accepted the revisionist, amnesiac mentality that Kishi and Inuzuka represented. They reformulated the Second World War as a sort of natural disaster, the causes of which were unfathomable and outside their control. In this new formulation, the Japanese had been the victims, not perpetrators, of the war. The popularity of Anne Frank in Japan may be attributed in part to her identity as an innocent, non-threatening victim; identification with her helped to justify this self-image. The bombing of Hiroshima, in which the Japanese had indeed been victims, came to be viewed as a synecdoche for the entire Japanese war experience. This Japanese-as-victims mentality in turn gave rise to the linking of Hiroshima and Auschwitz and the equation, without historical justification, of the Japanese wartime experience with that of the Jews.

LEFT-WING ANTI-ZIONISM

There was a gradual re-emergence of antipathy towards Jews in Japan following the 1967 Six Day War and particularly after the Arab oil embargo of 1973-4. Part of this was the re-emergence of 'traditional' anti-Semitism represented by *The Protocols of the Elders of Zion*, which was reissued in 1971 under the title *The*

Jews and World Revolution.[20] However, a far more significant force at this time was left-wing anti-Zionism, which denied Jewish peoplehood and depicted Israel as a Nazi racist state.

Left-wing anti-Zionism was common around the world following Israel's victory in the 1967 Six Day War. In the eyes of the international left, Israel had ceased to be the underdog in the Middle East conflict and revealed itself as the oppressor of the Palestinian people. Japanese anti-Zionism found its most violent expression on 20 May 1972, when three Japanese terrorists attacked disembarking (mostly Puerto Rican) tourists at Tel Aviv's Lod airport, killing twenty-four and injuring seventy-six. Leftist anti-Zionist ideology also provided the intellectual rationale for the Japanese government's economically motivated pro-Arab foreign policy in the 1970s and '80s and justified its refusal on 10 November 1975, to oppose the infamous UN General Assembly resolution defining Zionism as a form of racism.[21] That the Jews were not a people and that Israel was the illegitimate product of an international imperialist cabal came to be widely accepted in Japan, and by the early 1990s some, like the journalist Hirose Takashi, had taken the leftist position to its logical extreme, asserting that a worldwide Jewish conspiracy controlled the world economy, had engineered the 60 per cent drop in the Japanese stock market in 1989, and was threatening Japan's very existence.[22]

THE RECRUDESCENCE OF ANTI-SEMITISM IN THE 1980s

Certainly not all criticism of Israel has an anti-Semitic motive, nor are all left-wing critics of Israel anti-Semites. By consistently

---

[20] Nagafuchi Ichirō, *Yudayajin to sekai kakumei* (Jews and world revolution), Tokyo: Shinjinbutsu Ōraisha, 1971.

[21] On 16 Dec 1991, Japan voted with the United States and 109 other states to repeal the resolution.

[22] Hirose Takashi, 'Introduction' in Hirokawa Ryūichi and the Committee for Palestinian and Jewish Studies (eds), *Daiyamondo to shi no shōnin: Isuraeru no sekai senryaku* (Merchants of diamonds and death: Israel's global strategy), *Yudayajin* (The Jews), vol. 2, Tokyo: Sanyūsha, 1986, p. 5; 'Kinkyū keikoku: "kabuka ichiman-en" de "Yudaya shihon" ni nerawareru Nihon kigyō' (Urgent alert: Japanese industry threatened by 'Jewish capital' when stock prices hit ¥10,000), *Shūkan Post*, 10 July 1992, pp. 31-5; and 'Isuraeru-PLO no "rekishiteki wakai" wa "akai tate" Rosuchairudo-ke no shōchū de okonawareta' (The 'historical reconciliation' between Israel and the PLO was engineered by the 'red shield' of the Rothschilds), *Sapio*, 28 Oct 1993, pp. 18-22.

depicting the Jews as villains and denying legitimacy to Jewish culture, however, the Japanese left helped to lay the groundwork for the recrudescence of anti-Semitic ideology in Japan in the mid-1980s, when dozens of flagrantly anti-Semitic books began to sell millions of copies.

A survey commissioned by the Anti-Defamation League of B'nai B'rith (ADL) in 1988 documented just how prevalent anti-Semitic stereotypes were in Japan at this time. It found that 'in the area of personal traits, Jews tended to be seen by large pluralities as unfriendly and greedy. Small marginal groups also saw them as unclean and deceitful.' The survey found that Jews were seen as inferior to Christians and Buddhists in most categories and, along with Muslims, Arabs, and Blacks, defined as unattractive types. The state of Israel 'ranked at or near the low point in perceptions held of its trustworthiness, commitment to peace, straightforwardness in business dealings, generosity to other countries, and level of economic advancement.' Significantly, the survey found that the college-educated, affluent and younger respondents were more likely to harbour such negative views than others, in part owing to the devaluation of Jewish culture by influential left-leaning intellectuals.[23]

The most popular and prolific of the anti-Semitic authors who appeared at this time was Uno Masami, a fundamentalist Christian minister who published two books in 1986 alone claiming that the United States was a 'Jewish nation' ruled by a clandestine Jewish 'shadow government'. He denied the Holocaust, defended Hitler, and asserted that an international Jewish conspiracy was manipulating the world economy to destroy Japan.[24] Far from being criticised for his ideas, Uno was quoted approvingly in the mass media, including the *Yomiuri shimbun*, Japan's most widely-read daily newspaper, which cited them as a plausible explanation

---

[23] William Watts, 'Anti-Semitism in Japan: A survey research study – A report to the Anti-Defamation League of B'nai B'rith', December 19, 1988, pp. 3-4, 18. This survey was conducted in November 1988 by the Nippon Research Center, an affiliate of Gallup International Research Institutes, and collected data through direct interviews with 1,365 Japanese adults aged eighteen and over.

[24] Uno Masami, *Yudaya ga wakaru to sekai ga miete kuru* (If you understand the Jews, you will understand the world), Tokyo: Tokuma shoten, 1986; and Uno Masami, *Yudaya ga wakaru to Nihon ga miete kuru* (If you understand the Jews, you will understand Japan), Tokyo: Tokuma shoten, 1986.

for the country's economic woes.[25] Uno was also invited to speak
at a Constitution Day rally sponsored by a faction of the ruling
Liberal Democratic Party chaired by a former prime minister,
Kishi Nobusuke.[26] Uno energetically mined the accumulation of
Japanese stereotypes of Jews that had grown up over the past
hundred years, and this accounted for the popularity of his ideas
and the alacrity with which so many Japanese readers accepted
them.

Economic frustration and nationalist resentment also accounted
for the resurgence of anti-Semitic thinking at this time. Japan
had emerged as an economic superpower. By 1989 it dominated
high-tech industries like cameras, video recorders, silicon memory
chips and robotics, and it was producing one out of every four
automobiles in the world. However, while Japanese workers toiled
incessantly, earning themselves a reputation as 'economic animals',
they received few tangible or even spiritual rewards for their
efforts. By the mid-1980s, half of those Japanese surveyed reported
dissatisfaction with the quality of their lives, and one in three
office workers was said to be having treatment for a stress-related
illness.[27] The anti-Semitic conspiracy theories of Uno Masami
and others that appeared at this time were an expression of the
nationalist resentment this situation bred.[28]

INSECURITY AND ANTI-SEMITISM IN THE 1990s

In 1990 the Japanese economy entered the worst recession of
the postwar period, and by April 1995 the unemployment rate
had risen to an unprecedented postwar level of 3.2 per cent.
During the same period, the collapse of the Soviet Union and
the end of the Cold War introduced an element of uncertainty
into Japanese politics that had not existed since the early 1950s.
In the July 1993 Diet elections, the Liberal Democratic Party
lost control of the government for the first time since 1955,
and a year later Murayama Tomiichi, leader of the Social Demo-

[25] 'En: Haisui no kōbō' (The yen: Last ditch defence), *Yomiuri shimbun*, 17 Jan 1987.

[26] 'Backers, protesters mark Constitution's 40th Year', *Japan Times*, 4 May 1987.

[27] 'Rich man, poor man in Japan: Not an economic party for all', *New York Times*, 26 Dec.
1988; 'Feeling Poor in Japan', *Economist*, 11 June 1988.

[28] See Ian Buruma, 'A new Japanese nationalism', *New York Times Magazine*, 12 April 1987,
pp. 22-9, 38.

cratic (Socialist) Party, on becoming head of the coalition government, repudiated the entire platform that had guided the opposition
through the postwar period. These changes and the lack of political
scruple they showed increased cynicism among Japanese voters.
Politics became a joke, and voters rejected party nominees in
the 9 April 1995 regional elections, choosing instead the comedians
Aoshima Shigeru and Yokoyama Knock as the governor of Tokyo
and Osaka respectively.

Economic and political insecurity caused an escalation in anti-
Semitic rhetoric and activity. Writing in 1992, Ōta Ryū (born
1930) traced the Jewish plot to destroy Japan back 1,200 years
to the Nara period.[29] In 1993 'Jacob Morgan', possibly a pseudonym
for his 'translator' Oshino Shōtarō, charged that the Japanese Ministry of Finance and the Bank of Japan were controlled by Jews
and that 'Jewish' insignia that ridiculed the imperial family could
be found on Japanese paper money.[30] Early in 1995, two books
appeared which even blamed the Jews for the Kobe earthquake
on 17 January that year.[31]

Mainstream journalistic and political organisations did little to
criticise this anti-Semitic thinking and often promoted it. For
example, the mass circulation *Asahi* and *Nihon Keizai* (*Nikkei*)
newspapers both promoted the Morgan books by carrying large,
garish ads for them, and the *Nikkei* reacted angrily when challenged
about the propriety of doing so.[32] In May 1994 Ogai Yoshio,
a forty-five-year-old official in the Tokyo branch of the Liberal
Democratic Party, published a book with the party's prior approval,
advocating the electoral strategies of Adolf Hitler.[33]

[29] Ōta Ryū, *Yudaya sekai teikoku no Nihon shinkō senryaku* (The Jewish world empire's plot to invade Japan), Tokyo: Nihon bungeisha, 1992. See also Ōta Ryū, *Ima Nihon ga abunai! Yudayaka nyūmon* (Japan is in danger now! An introduction to the Jewish peril), Tokyo: Nikkei kikaku shuppankyoku, 1992.

[30] Jacob Morgan, *Saigo no kyōteki Nihon o ute: zoku Yudaya sekai shihai no giteisho* (Get Japan, the last enemy: The Jewish protocols for world domination, continued), tr. Oshino Shōtarō, Tokyo: Daiichi kikaku, 1993.

[31] Sasagawa Eisuke, *Akuma kara no keikoku* (Warning from the devil), Tokyo: Daiichi kikaku, 1995; and Koishi Izumi, *Sekai o ugokasu Yudaya-kyō no himitsu* (The secret of Judaism which moves the world), Tokyo: Daiichi kikaku, 1995.

[32] 'Anti-Semitic book ad assailed', *Japan Times*, 31 July 1993. The *Nikkei* ad appeared on 27 July 1993; the *Asahi* ad appeared on 31 March 1993 (international satellite edition).

[33] Ogai Yoshio, *Hitoraa senkyo senryaku —gendai senkyo hisshō no baiburu* (Hitler's election strategy: A bible for certain victory in modern elections) Tokyo: Chiyoda Nagata shobō, 1994. See also 'Japanese book praises Hitler for politics', *New York Times*, 8 June 1994; and

In the early 1990s, Japanese anti-Semites also became politically active for the first time since the war, and bright red handbills emblazoned with swastikas appeared regularly on lamp-posts in Tokyo and surrounding areas. One such handbill posted on 25 May 1993, near the Israeli embassy in Tokyo by the League of National Socialists (*Kokka shakaishugisha dōmei*) read, 'Remember *Kristallnacht*! Get the illegal aliens who threaten Japan's security! Fight the Zionist occupation government! Smash international Jewish power and free the world from diabolical Judaism!' The *Asahi* reported in April 1993 that 3,500 such handbills were being posted each Sunday in Tokyo and the adjoining Saitama prefecture.[34]

Japanese anti-Semites did not limit themselves to sloganeering. In the July 1992 Upper House Diet elections, the overtly anti-Semitic Global Restoration Party (*Chikyū ishin tō*) fielded candidates in Tokyo, Osaka-Kobe and Gumma prefecture, and, as a recognised party, received national television time and newspaper space to promote its message. That message, according to the campaign literature for Fujinami Norio, one of the party's candidates, was to 'smite the traitors who are selling out Holy Japan to the diabolical Jewish cult'. 'The Global Restoration Party', a campaign notice read, 'denounces the ambitions of the Jews (Pharisees) to conquer the world and turn it into a global pasture for the human race and promotes the establishment of a world order under the rule of the Emperor and the Imperial Principle of Universal Brotherhood [*hakkō ichiu*].' The Global Restoration Party polled only 11,883 votes or a tiny 0.03 per cent of the electorate and was one of several unconventional parties to participate in the election, but its presence on the ballot signaled a new activism among anti-Semitic groups that foreshadowed the Aum poison gas attack on 20 March 1995.[35]

THE *MARCO POLO* AFFAIR

It would be a mistake to depict anti-Semitism as a significant force in Japanese society; in intellectual life it is a decidedly minor

---

'Hitler book is withdrawn by Japanese', *New York Times*, 15 June 1994.

[34] *Asahi shimbun*, international satellite edition, 7 April 1993.

[35] Election results from the *Asahi shimbun*, 27 July 1992.

strain. Nevertheless, a long and coherent tradition of intellectual anti-Semitism does exist in Japan, where anti-Semitic ideas have greater currency today than in any other advanced industrial society and their logical consequence is murder.[36] It is in this context that the expressions of anti-Semitism in *Marco Polo* and Aum Shinrikyô should be viewed.

Nishioka Masanori's Holocaust-denying article, 'There Were No Nazi "Gas Chambers"' which appeared in the February 1995 issue of *Marco Polo*, is an unremarkable rehashing of Holocaust revisionist theories from the United States and Europe. Its acknowledged sources are the fraudulent Institute for Historical Review in California and the infamous Holocaust-deniers, Paul Rassinier, Arthur Butz, Fred Leuchter and others.[37] In preparing his article Nishioka, a neurologist at a sanatorium outside Tokyo, consulted no primary sources, interviewed no survivors and spent less than four hours at Auschwitz on a guided tour.[38] So patently ludicrous was the article that it was rejected by dozens of publications before *Marco Polo* finally accepted it in July 1994.[39] *Marco Polo* not only published it, but to heighten its impact timed its release to coincide with the fiftieth anniversary of the liberation of Auschwitz and endorsed its assertions with an editorial preface printed over a photograph of the mangled corpses of concentration camp victims.

This scurrilous piece of journalism at first went unnoticed in the Japanese press but drew protests from Israeli diplomats and Jewish groups; they were summarily rebuffed during a meeting by an assistant editor of *Marco Polo*, who invoked the privilege

[36] David G. Goodman, 'Han-Yudayashugisha to shite no Momotarô' (Momotarô as anti-Semite), *Sekai*, January 1988, pp. 329-39. This article is reprinted in a slightly altered version in my *Hashiru Kokusaika jidai no chichioya-jutsu* (Running: Fatherhood in an international age), Tokyo: Iwanami shoten, 1989, pp. 148-64. The reference to the murderous implications of Japanese anti-Semitic ideas is on page 153 of the later text.

[37] For a thorough analysis of the doctrines of the Institute for Historical Review and the work of Rassinier, Butz, Leuchter and others, see Deborah Lipstadt, *Denying the Holocaust: The growing assault on truth and memory*, New York: The Free Press, 1993.

[38] Ugaya Hiromichi, 'Nachi Holocaust wa taboo na no ka' (Is the Nazi Holocaust a taboo subject?), *AERA*, 27 February 1995, pp. 21-3; Iwakami Yasumi, 'Mujaki na Holocaust revisionist' (A guileless Holocaust revisionist), *Takarajima 30*, April 1995, pp. 18-27.

[39] Ochiai Nobuhiko reports that Nishioka submitted his article to 200 publications, but the number is probably closer to seventy. See Ochiai Nobuhiko, '"Marco Polo haikan" sôdô no ura de kokka ni yoru genron tôsei ga shinobiyotte kuru' (Behind the uproar over the closing of *Marco Polo*, state censorship nears), *Sapio*, 9 March 1995, p. 36.

of press freedom.[40] Earlier complaints against the *Nikkei* newspaper and Daiichi Kikaku publishers had met with similar stonewalling.[41] But when Volkswagen, Cartier, Mitsubishi Motors and other firms acceded to a call by the Los Angeles-based Simon Wiesenthal Center for an advertising boycott of *Marco Polo*, and when that ban threatened to spread to the company's other periodicals, Bungei Shunjū immediately announced that unsold copies of *Marco Polo* would be recalled and the magazine would be permanently closed. The announcement came on 27 January, just two weeks after the offending issue appeared on the news-stands, and a joint news conference by Bungei Shunjū's president Tanaka Kengo and Abraham Cooper, associate dean of the Simon Wiesenthal Center, was held in Tokyo on 2 February to make the formal announcement and answer questions about the affair.[42]

The decision to close *Marco Polo* was presented as a conscientious response to international criticism of Nishioka Masanori's article, and the maximum use was made of it by Bungei Shunjū for its publicity value to prove the company's good faith. Bungei Shunjū was, after all, the publisher of Anne Frank's *Diary* and had profited handsomely from it. But neither the Simon Wiesenthal Center nor any other Jewish group had ever suggested that *Marco Polo* be shut down, and subsequent events made it clear that the decision to close the magazine was part of a struggle within Bungei Shunjū to unseat Tanaka Kengo as president of the company.[43]

During his long tenure in the firm, Tanaka had helped give

[40] 'Japanese criticized for Holocaust denial story', *Chicago Tribune*, 25 January 1995.

[41] 'Anti-Semitic book ad assailed', *Japan Times*, 31 July 1993.

[42] A full chronology of the events leading up to the news conference of 2 February may be found in '"Marco Polo" haikan: irei-zukume no tenkai', *Mainichi shimbun*, 5 Feb. 1995. A transcript of the news conference appears in "Marco Polo' jiken no shōgen' in *Seiron*, April 1995, pp. 60-75.

[43] The sources for this account include 'Bunshun shachō jinin: rosen hihan shōshū ni hairyō ka' (Bungei Shunjū president resigns: An attempt to contain criticism of his policies?), *Asahi shimbun*, 15 February 1995; Yamazaki Masahito, '"Marco" haikan no uragawa de tenkai sareta Bungei Shunjū "coup d'état" geki no tenmatsu' (Details of the Bungei Shunjū 'coup d'état' drama played out behind the closing of *Marco Polo*), *Uwasa no shinsō*, May 1995, pp. 40-7; Onodera Akio, ' "Marco Polo" haikan: hyōmenka shita "Hanada meibutsu henshūchō" no shanai hyōka' (The closing of *Marco Polo*: Star editor Hanada's reputation within the company surfaces), *Shūkan yomiuri*, 19 February 1995, pp. 156-8; Shinoda Hiroyuki, 'Bungei shunjū, Tanaka Kengo zen-shachō no yūutsu' (The melancholy of Tanaka Kengo, former president of Bungei Shunjū), *Tsukuru*, April 1995, pp. 134-9; ' "Marco Polo" jiken no shōgen' (The *Marco Polo* affair testimony), *Seiron*, April 1995, pp. 60-75.

Bungei Shunjū a reputation for scandal-mongering and unscrupulous journalism. As an editor, he had helped the firm weather the financially difficult 1970s by publishing muckraking articles in the company's flagship publication, *Bungei Shunjū*. In 1985, as publishing director, he had founded Nesco, a subsidiary that published, among other works, four books by Uno Masami, Japan's most prolific anti-Semite. And it was as company president that he created *Marco Polo* in 1991. It resembled the American *Esquire* in being a glossy magazine pitched at an affluent, well-educated male audience. However, after three years the size of its readership disappointed the owners and thus in April 1994 Tanaka named his protégé, Hanada Kazuyoshi, editor to turn the foundering publication around. Hanada was a highly successful editor who had revitalised another Bungei Shunjū periodical, *Shūkan Bunshun*, making it the country's best-selling weekly magazine (circulation 760,000). He accomplished this feat by running a series of scandal-mongering articles that sold magazines but also deeply embarrassed the company. Once, *Shūkan Bunshun* was banned from sale in the vital kiosks in the JR East national railway stations because of an offensive article about the railroad's management; and on another it was forced to make a public apology for an article criticising the imperial family.

Running a tasteless essay denying the Holocaust on the fiftieth anniversary of the liberation of Auschwitz was thus an extension of existing Bungei Shunjū publishing policy and entirely in character for Tanaka Kengo and Hanada Kazuyoshi. But sentiment had been growing within Bungei Shunjū that this tabloid style of journalism no longer benefited the firm, and the advertising boycott of *Marco Polo* finally convinced members of the company's upper management, including North American bureau chief Shioya Kō and presidential assistant Saitō Tadashi, that Tanaka would have to go. On 14 February, less than three weeks after *Marco Polo* had been shut down, Tanaka was forced to resign as president of Bungei Shunjū, and on 9 March his successor, Andō Mitsuru, conducted a company-wide personnel shake-up that deprived Tanaka of his power base and severely curtailed his influence.

The *Marco Polo* affair and its aftermath were in many ways typical of Japanese publishing and thinking about Jewish subjects. The decision to close the magazine made front-page news, and a deluge of press reports followed, including special numbers of several monthly magazines. The special issues of two magazines, *Takarajima 30* and *Brutus,* were especially thoughtful and constructive attempts to deal with anti-Semitism and the Holocaust, as well as with more general Jewish culture and history.[44] But for the most part, journalism dealt introspectively with questions raised by the affair, focusing almost exclusively on the quality of Bungei Shunjū's journalism and what it implied about the state of Japanese society.[45] Despite the fact that the entire affair had supposedly been precipitated by a deep affront to Jews, virtually no attempt was made to engage Jews in a dialogue and only one article by a non-Japanese observer appeared.[46] This failure to engage foreigners but instead to conduct an intense, solipsistic monologue about them was typical of the way many Japanese have dealt with the outside world for centuries.

AUM'S POISON GAS ATTACK

The self-centred, inner-directed way Japanese writers and editors treated the *Marco Polo* affair helps us understand how anti-Semitism relates to the Aum poison gas attack on the Tokyo subway.

It is frequently asked what harm anti-Semitism does in Japan, which has virtually no Jewish population and where Jews are treated as well as or better than other foreigners. But the question misunderstands the issue. Since the early nineteenth century, dire warnings of imminent subversion by an alien religious cult have been used by Japanese xenophobes to instil a siege mentality and galvanise support for their reactionary cause. Japanese anti-Semitism has inherited this xenophobia, and during the Second World War it was used to suppress dissidents and bolster support for Japan's aggressive war in Asia. The real victims of Japanese anti-Semitism have therefore always been the Japanese themselves and the millions of Asians who fell victim to their ultra-nationalist ideology. This was the case once again during the Aum poison gas attack on the Tokyo subway.

Aum was part of Japan's anti-Semitic subculture. Its paranoia was multifaceted and cannot be reduced to the fear of any single

[44] *Takarajima 30,* April 1995; *Brutus,* 1 July 1995.

[45] See, for example, *Seiron,* April 1995.

[46] David G. Goodman, 'Nihon no "han-Yudayashugisha"-tachi' (Japan's 'anti-Semites'), *Takarajima 30,* April 1995, pp. 28–36.

imagined enemy, but Jews figured prominently among its many demons. The 'Manual of Fear' published in *Vajrayāna Sacca* two months before the gassing documented this terror fully.[47] In each of its six chapters, it quoted at length from *The Protocols of the Elders of Zion* and other anti-Semitic works. It accused Jews of promoting mindless popular culture and fomenting endless wars of attrition in order to weaken the gentile nations of the world and turn non-Jews into docile cattle. It presented the Talmud as a homicidal, racist tract that guides the Jews' nefarious plot to subjugate the world. Jews, it asserted, are not Jews at all but descendants of the Khazars, a Turkish people who flourished on the Volga River in the Middle Ages; the Second World War was Hitler's defence against an attempt by these latter-day Khazars to recapture their ancient homeland.[48] It charged that Jews were responsible for mass murder in Cambodia, Bosnia and Rwanda and are planning similar massacres in the near future in a premeditated effort to reduce the world's population by three *billion* people by the year 2000.

However, Jews *per se* were not Aum's primary concern. The Aum believers were predictably fearful, not of Jews as such but of 'Jewish Japanese', who threatened the vital substance of Japan from within. Aum listed the leaders of this 'black aristocracy' in a special section of its 'Manual of Fear'.[49] Included were the politicians Ozawa Ichirō and Hosokawa Morihiro, the philanthropist and *éminence grise* Sasakawa Ryōichi, the former prime minister Nakasone Yasuhiro, the business consultant Ohmae Ken'ichi, and the UN envoys Akashi Yasushi and Ogata Sadako; also the present emperor and crown princess. The taint of internationalism is what linked these individuals together as 'Jews' in Aum's addled mind.

---

[47] Aum also devoted a 65-page section of *Vajrayāna Sacca*, no. 10, 25 May 1995, to its obsession with the Jews.

[48] On the anti-Semitic origins and intentions of this theory, see Robert Singerman, 'The Jew as racial alien: The genetic component of American anti-Semitism' in David A. Gerber (ed.), *Anti-Semitism in American history*, Urbana: University of Illinois Press, 1986, pp. 103–28. See also Barkun, *Religion and the racist right*, pp. 136–42. The myth of the Jewish Khazars is widely accepted in Japan. For example, Professor Ochi Michio of Meiji University, who otherwise displays an admirable grasp of Jewish history, repeats this canard. See Ochi Michio, ' "Eien no hisabetsusha"-zō wa naze "saikyō no kagaisha"-zō ni henbō shita ka' (Why did the image of [the Jew as] 'eternal victim' change to 'most ruthless victimiser'?), *Sapio*, 23 March 1995, pp. 18–19.

[49] *Vajrayāna Sacca*, no. 6, pp. 16–18.

'Jews' were not confined to the Japanese élite. Ikeda Daisaku, head of Sōka Gakkai, a major neo-Buddhist sect, and Sun Myung Moon, founder of the Unification Church, were also included on *Vajrayāna Sacca*'s list of enemies. Sōka Gakkai and the Unification Church were actually *Jewish* sects, Aum inveighed, and Ikeda and Moon had surreptitiously converted their millions of followers to Judaism. Don't look now, Aum warned, but your apparently Japanese neighbour might actually be a Jew in disguise![50]

That the Aum leadership was palpably terrified of Jewish power was borne out on 23 April 1995, following the fatal stabbing of Murai Hideo, Aum's 'minister of science and technology'. With his dying breath, Murai blamed the Jews for taking his life,[51] and as the novelist Nosaka Akiyuki recognised, this accusation gave special weight to the suspicion that Aum was motivated by anti-Semitism.[52] After all, if the Jews were plotting to exterminate 3 billion people in the next five years, and if 'Jews' are actually internationalised Japanese, then a pre-emptive strike against a high concentration of them in the heart of Tokyo's cosmopolitan business district made a kind of perverse sense. And what better weapon in such an attack than poison gas, a tried and true defence against the Jewish peril that the Nazis had used to such devastating effect?

As always therefore, it was the Japanese themselves who suffered most from Japanese anti-Semitism, but the international affinities of this doctrine of hate should be noted. Aum was founded in 1984 and incorporated as a religious body in 1989. Its grotesque image of Jews derived from the plethora of anti-Semitic books that appeared at this time, including the works of Uno Masami and Hirose Takashi, who are duly credited in its 'Manual of Fear'.[53] Uno is head of the Japanese branch of the Liberty Lobby, a Washington-based hate group the Anti-Defamation League has described as the most active anti-Semitic organisation in the United

[50] Ibid., pp. 16–18, 36–7.

[51] *Vajrayāna Sacca*, ed. Aum editorial staff, no. 10, 25 May 1995, pp. 186–7; 'Top Aum spokesman: Murai uttered "Judea" after he was stabbed', *Mainichi Daily News*, 28 March 1995. Note that in contemporary Japanese discourse the term *Yudaya* always refers to 'the Jews' and never to the biblical kingdom of Judea.

[52] Nosaka Akiyuki, 'Aum ni totte sarin wa han-Yudaya no shōchō datta no ka' (So sarin was a symbol of anti-Semitism to Aum!), *Shūkan bunshun*, 25 May 1995, pp. 52–3.

[53] *Vajrayāna Sacca*, no. 6, pp. 22–3 Hirose; 84 Uno. A list of Aum's sources, which includes Akama Gō, Gary Allen and others, appears on p. 34.

States.[54] Uno publishes the Japanese edition of *New American View*, the newsletter of the Liberty Lobby, in addition to *Enoch*, his own anti-Semitic monthly.

To argue, as many have, that Japanese anti-Semitism is an isolated eccentricity with no history and no consequences is thus a mistake. Aum was inspired by Uno Masami who in turn was inspired by the Liberty Lobby; the latter backs men like James 'Bo' Gritz, who are the leaders of the Christian Identity and militia movements, and all the evidence seems to indicate that it inspired the blowing up of the Alfred P. Murrah Federal Building in Oklahoma City on 19 April 1995.[55] While no terrorist, the Christian evangelist Pat Robertson repeats the same anti-Semitic conspiracy theories that so fascinate Japanese readers in his 1991 tome *The New World Order*.[56] Robertson leads the Christian Coalition, one of the most powerful constituencies in the Republican Party, which won control of both houses of the US Congress in November 1994. To dismiss anti-Semitism and Holocaust denial in Japan as marginal phenomena without consequences and without relevance to the West is therefore a dangerous error. They are in fact bloody evidence of the re-emergence of anti-Semitic thought and violence around the world.

[54] Anti-Defamation League of B'nai B'rith, *Extremism on the right*, New York: Anti-Defamation League of B'nai B'rith, 1988, p. 35. See also Lipstadt, *Denying the Holocaust*, pp. 144-53.

[55] See Barkun, *Religion and the racist right*, pp. 211-12; and 'Idaho community built on hatred and fear', *New York Times*, 5 October 1994.

[56] Pat Robertson, *The new world order*, Dallas: Word Publishing, 1991. See also Michael Lind, 'Rev. Robertson's grand international conspiracy theory', *New York Review of Books*, 12 Feb. 1995, pp. 21-5; and Jabob Heibrunn, 'His [Robertson's] anti-Semitic sources', *New York Review of Books*, 20 April 1995, pp. 68-73.

THE DISCOURSE ON BLOOD
AND RACIAL IDENTITY IN
CONTEMPORARY JAPAN[1]

Kosaku Yoshino

Studies of race and ethnicity have tended to concern themselves with multi-ethnic societies, neglecting the cases of supposedly homogeneous societies such as Japan. This essay attempts to bridge this gap. It focuses on a number of relevant issues on race in Japan, in particular, the Japanese perception of themselves as a distinct 'racial' community. This perception is characteristically expressed by the imagined notion of 'Japanese blood'. The main aim of the essay is to inquire into the notion of 'Japanese blood' as a metaphor of racial identity and the way in which it is associated with the cultural identity of the Japanese.

THE 'JAPANESE RACE' AS AN IMAGINED COMMUNITY

It is essential at the outset to clarify the usage of the concept of 'race', since this term has been used in various ways and can be quite misleading. Even after the biological concept of race was refuted some decades ago, 'race' has continued to be used in everyday social relations, and this has led sociologists and anthropologists to acknowledge the existence of socially constructed races. On this point, Rex remarks that 'sociology being the kind of discipline it is, any attempt to define its field without taking into account actors' own subjective definitions of the situation

---

[1] Certain of the arguments in this essay were originally presented in Kosaku Yoshino, *Cultural nationalism in contemporary Japan: A sociological enquiry*, London and New York: Routledge, 1992.

must be seriously inadequate'.[2] 'Race' may therefore be defined as a human group that perceives itself and/or is perceived by other groups as different from other groups by virtue of innate and immutable phenotypical and genotypical characteristics. Race is, first and foremost, socially constructed. Using Benedict Anderson's insight of the nation as an 'imagined community', we may say that 'race' is also imagined, in the sense that it has no real biological foundation and that the members of the 'race' do not actually know most of their fellow members, 'yet in the minds of each lives the image of their communion'. 'Race' is imagined as limited in that its members perceive its boundaries, beyond which lie other races. 'Race' is an imagined community having a common and unified sense of comradeship.[3]

Although there is no 'Japanese race' that can be said to exist in any objective sense, the Japanese have a strong tendency to perceive themselves as a distinct 'racial' group. In British and American race relations, race tends to be equated with physical differences. Perception of phenotypical differences, however, is not the only basis on which a group can be racialised. Imagination of genotypical differences can also be a basis for racial categorisation. Lee and De Vos remark, concerning Koreans in Japan, that 'although most Koreans are physically indistinguishable from Japanese, they nonetheless continue to be considered racially distinct by Japanese.'[4] The idiom 'Japanese blood' is commonly used to refer to that aspect of their identity which the Japanese tend to perceive as immutable. Indeed, in Japanese perceptions of their national identity, a belief in their unchanging quality is no less important than the belief in the distinctiveness of Japanese culture. '*You have to be born a Japanese* to understand Japanese mentality', a statement often made by Japanese, illustrates the salience of the racial dimension of their identity.

The notion of Japan as an imagined racial community originated in the late nineteenth-century nationalist ideology that conceived it as a 'family-nation' or 'family-state' (*kazoku kokka*) of divine

---

[2] John Rex, *Race relations in sociological theory*, London: Routledge and Kegan Paul, 1970, p. 161.

[3] Benedict Anderson, *Imagined communities: Reflections on the origins and spread of nationalism*, London: Verso, 1983, pp. 6-7.

[4] Chansoo Lee and George De Vos, *Koreans in Japan: Ethnic conflict and accommodation*, Berkeley: University of California Press, 1981, p. 356.

origin.[5] In this family-nation, members were perceived as being related 'by blood' to one another and ultimately to the emperor. Here we have an example of what Armstrong calls 'the racialisation of the imagined community'.[6] Kinship, race and religion were‑fused together to produce an intensely felt collective sense of 'oneness'. Being the ideological backbone of pre-war and wartime nationalism, the notion of family-nation came under strong attack following the country's defeat in 1945 and has disappeared from the main ideological scene. Yet in the subconsciousness of Japanese people, the nation as imagined kinship remains alive and well. This kin-oriented in-group mentality is epitomised in the racial metaphor of 'Japanese blood'.

The fictive notion of 'Japanese blood' reveals much about the way in which the Japanese perceive their supposedly 'immutable' difference. As Wallman remarks, the 'differences observed and the way they are interpreted say as much about the classifier as about the classified'.[7] In British and American race relations, ethnicity is often concerned with positive identification of 'us' in contrast to race, which tends to be associated with negative categorisation of 'them'.[8] 'Race', however, can become a source of positive identification of the in-group, as with the notion of 'Japanese blood', which is used for the positive identification of 'us' Japanese. Generating a symbolic image and evoking collective sentiments, 'race' stakes out a very effective boundary. I have elsewhere described the symbolic power of this concept as follows:

> The symbol of 'Japanese blood' evokes the stable sense of 'us' and 'our' identity by representing a complex set of meanings and emotive associations concerning Japanese identity. If eth‑ nicity is a collectivity of people defined by virtue of belief in shared culture and history, race focuses upon, and exaggerates,

[5] The Japanese word *kokka*, which consists of two characters meaning 'country' and 'family', means both nation and state. This dual meaning is indicative of the Japanese historical situation in which the state came to be identified with the nation as symbolised by the central political and socio-cultural authority, the emperor. On the notion of *kazoku kokka* (family-nation), see Kosaku Yoshino, *Cultural nationalism in contemporary Japan*, pp. 90-2.

[6] Bruce Armstrong, 'Racialisation and nationalist ideology: The Japanese case', *International Sociology*, 4, no 3 (1989), pp. 329-43.

[7] Sandra Wallman, 'Ethnicity and the boundary process in context' in John Rex and David Mason (eds), *Theories of race and ethnic relations*, Cambridge University Press, 1986, p. 229.

[8] See Michael Banton, *Racial and ethnic competition*, Cambridge University Press, 1983, p. 106.

a particular aspect of ethnicity, that is, kinship and kin lineage. Here, race is a marker that strengthens ethnic identity. The symbol of 'Japanese blood' generates, and is generated by, an image that 'we' are members of the extended family that has perpetuated its lineage. Furthermore, the notion of 'Japanese blood' assumes the existence of distinct racial groups, which is predicated upon the assumption of breeding isolation. This assumption enhances psychological distance between the in-group and others, generating the sense that 'we' Japanese people have been formed within 'our' own circles and in isolation from others and that 'we' are the product of this special formative experience. The symbol of 'Japanese blood' thus facilitates the idea that the Japanese possess unique qualities.[9]

If a Japanese person is given an opportunity to think *consciously* about 'Japanese blood', he/she would certainly deny its existence. It should, therefore, be emphasised that 'Japanese blood' is socially invented *not* to refer to genetic traits as such *but* to mould and channel psychological responses concerning 'we'-ness and 'them'-ness. 'Japanese blood' is, first and foremost, a case of *social construction* of difference.

THE ASSOCIATION OF RACE AND CULTURE, BUT NOT GENETIC DETERMINISM

The second salient feature of racial discourse in Japan is a connection between race and culture in perceptions of national identity. Of course, a strong connection between race and culture is not unique to the Japanese. In racial discourse generally, racial and cultural differences are often closely associated. Genetic determinism is one common form of such association: genetically transmitted traits are considered to determine (or condition) cultural traits. In fact, genetic determinism has often been equated with racism.[10] Ruth Benedict, one of the first scholars to use the term critically and extensively, defined racism as 'the dogma that one ethnic

---

[9] Yoshino, *Cultural nationalism*, pp. 26-7.

[10] Consider, for example, Robert Knox's *The races of men* (Renshaw, 1850) and Gobineau's *The inequality of human races* (trans. of part of *Essai sur l'inégalité des races humaines* [1853-5]), (Heinemann, 1915) and a number of other publications from the second half of the nineteenth century up till the end of the Second World War.

group is condemned by nature to congenital inferiority and another group is destined to congenital superiority'.[11] Michael Banton writes that the core of racist doctrines is found in the assertions '(a) that people's cultural and psychological characteristics are genetically determined; and (b) the genetic determinants are grouped in patterns that can be identified with human races in the old morphological sense that envisaged the existence of pure races'.[12] Banton then defines racism as 'the doctrine that a man's behaviour is determined by stable inherited characters deriving from separate racial stocks having distinctive attributes and usually considered to stand to one another in relations of superiority and inferiority'.[13]

There is sentiment among the Japanese that their mode of thinking and behaving is unique and that non-Japanese therefore cannot understand it, still less acquire it. Such a sentiment often obstructs foreign residents' adaptation to social life in Japan. For example, foreigners may experience the barrier of 'No foreigners, please' in apartment-hunting due to the assumption that because foreigners are intrinsically different and are unable to adjust to the Japanese way of life, problems will arise. In research conducted by the present author on fairly well-educated sections of the Japanese population, the majority of respondents expressed the view in one way or another that foreigners, including those born in Japan, could not become fully part of Japanese social life because they would never be able to understand and adjust to the distinctive Japanese patterns of behaviour and thought.[14]

A comparison of Japanese perceptions of the two types of 'not so obviously foreign' foreigners – namely, Japanese-Americans and Koreans – are of particular interest here. Most respondents did not foresee any serious obstacles for Japanese-Americans, born and socialised in the United States, in integrating culturally in Japan, remarking that, because they have 'Japanese blood', they can eventually learn to behave and think like 'us' after the initial

---

[11] Ruth Benedict, *Race and racism*, London: Routledge and Kegan Paul (orig. 1942), 1983, p. 97.

[12] Michael Banton, 'The concept of racism' in S. Zubaida (ed.), *Race and racialism*, London: Tavistock, 1970, pp. 17-18.

[13] Ibid.

[14] For the methods and findings of my research, see Yoshino, *Cultural nationalism*, esp. chapters 6 and 7.

phase of trying. By contrast, Koreans are supposed not to be able to behave and think like 'us' because, it was claimed, they do not have 'Japanese blood'. This comparison reveals the racialised nature of Japanese cultural identity.

If the Japanese are strongly aware of their 'racial' and cultural distinctiveness from other peoples and closely associate 'race' and culture, one would be tempted to conclude that this is genetic determinism. However, this notion fails to capture the exact nature of Japanese race thinking. The notion of 'property', that is possession, is a more accurate rendering of the Japanese sense of their uniqueness; exclusive *ownership* of certain aspects of Japanese culture is claimed. The essential characteristic of the Japanese racial discourse lies in the perception that particular cultural traits should belong to, or are the exclusive property of, a particular group with distinct phenotypical and genotypical traits. This 'racially exclusive possession of a particular culture' may be contrasted with genetic determinism.

One can find abundant examples of Japanese culture being perceived as belonging exclusively to the 'Japanese race'. In the discourse on Japanese uniqueness (*nihonjinron*) prevalent in the 1970s and 1980s, many writers drew attention to the 'uniquely Japanese' mode of thinking by citing various untranslatable Japanese phrases.[15] They assume that such phrases defy translation and hence that a person has to be born a Japanese to be able to grasp the intricate and subtle nature of the Japanese language. Probably the most explicit view is supplied by Watanabe Shōichi, professor of English literature, who writes that the spirit of the Japanese language is 'as old as our blood'.[16] He writes that, although he knows of some Europeans whose Japanese is accurate and quite fluent, and some Korean residents in Japan have won literary awards for their Japanese prose or fiction, he knows of no foreigner who can write good *waka*, or traditional thirty-one syllable Japanese poetry.[17] In an attempt to reveal the 'racistic' thinking of Watanabe, Wetherall characterises him as saying that 'the spirit of Japanese language and its poetic expression is all but *genetically transmitted*'.[18]

---

[15] On the *nihonjinron*, see K. Yoshino, *Cultural nationalism*.

[16] Watanabe Shōichi, *Nihongo no kokoro* (The soul of the Japanese language), Kōdansha, 1974, p. 8.

[17] *Ibid.*, pp. 105-6.

[18] William Wetherall, 'Public figures in popular culture: Identity problems of minority heroes' in C. Lee and G. De Vos (eds), *Koreans in Japan*, Berkeley: University of California

But Watanabe does *not* go so far as to say this; what he suggests is that it 'belongs exclusively' to the Japanese in the sense that it can be truly appreciated only by the Japanese. The analytical distinction I have proposed above may be illustrated here. (However, it goes without saying that Watanabe's remark is chauvinistic. The ability to write good *waka* does not derive from being a Japanese but from one's willingness and efforts to perfect one's poetic expression.)

Let us return to the Korean case to consider this point further. The first reactions of our respondents to the Korean case were generally negative, suggesting in one way or another that, however long they live in Japan, they cannot claim to have acquired Japanese culture to the same extent that any Japanese person can. None the less, when their attention was drawn to examples of many former Koreans who had become naturalised and already passed as Japanese, including well-known entertainers and figures in sport, most respondents agreed that Koreans could 'become Japanese' unless reminders of their foreign origin such as names were presented. A lack of systematic thinking is not unusual in racial discourse. Indeed, systematic thinking is impossible here because, as discussed earlier, 'Japanese blood' is a social construct designed to shape and channel emotional responses along the lines of 'us'–ness and 'them'–ness. 'Japanese blood' symbolises the sense that 'we', members of the in-group, have interacted among 'ourselves' in isolation from others. This sense of psychological distance between 'us' and 'them' maintains and enhances the notion that only 'we' can share with one another 'our' distinctive modes of thinking and behaving.

Racial, cultural and national categories virtually overlap in the Japanese perception of themselves. They often use the convenient term *tan'itsu minzoku* to describe their homogeneity as a people, without specifying whether they are referring to their racial or cultural features.[19] (*Tan'itsu* means 'one' or 'uni-', and *minzoku* is a multivocal term which, reflecting the Japanese situation, means not only 'race' but 'ethnic community' and 'nation'.) In the literature on Japanese uniqueness (*nihonjinron*), widely read by well-

---

Press, 1981, pp. 299-300, emphasis added.

[19] On the myth of Japanese homogeneity, see Kosaku Yoshino, 'The changing discourse on race, ethnicity and nationalism in Japan', *The ASEN Bulletin*, no. 8 (winter 1994/5), pp. 10-13.

educated sections of the Japanese population in the 1970s and
'80s, the notion of *tan'itsu minzoku* was often used as an easy
and tautological explanation for so-called distinctively Japanese
characteristics such as group harmony, consensual human relations
and non-confrontational patterns of interpersonal communica-
tion.[20] Such conceptual ambiguity surrounding the relation between
race and culture underlies Japanese perceptions of national identity.
It would thus be unrealistic to attempt to establish a deterministic
relationship between race and culture with reference to those
perceptions. Rather, this way of relating race and culture may
best be called 'perceptual association'.

The notion of 'racially exclusive possession of a particular
culture' is an apt characterisation of the 'particularistic' cultural
sentiment of the Japanese, who have long perceived themselves
as being in a 'peripheral' relation to the 'central' civilisations of
China and the West where the 'universal' norms exist. By contrast,
genetic determinism as an ideology to rationalise Western
dominance points to the more universal (and superior) aspects
of human ability and activity that are perceived as having comprised
the base of the 'universal' civilisation of the West. Viewed in
terms of universal criteria, difference between Westerners
(Caucasians) and others is a difference in ability: hence, the 'vertical'
sense of superiority. The Japanese sense of difference, on the
other hand, is associated with the notion of 'racially exclusive
possession of a particular culture'. It is primarily 'horizontal' – a
difference of kind. The fact that Western civilisation has tended
to be perceived by Westerners and non-Westerners alike as
'universal' and associated with the 'white race' may well explain
why in the West racial sentiment is equated with genetic determinism.

This, however, is not to say that the Japanese sense of uniqueness
is exclusively one of difference of kind. Where intelligence level
is referred to, a sense of superiority comes into play. About half
of the respondents suggested that the Japanese intelligence level
is very high. They refer, for example, to cross-national comparisons
of students' math scores as well as the high performance – as they
perceive it – of Japanese scientific researchers working in the
United States. Nevertheless, there is no clear-cut evidence on

[20] Kamishima Jirō, 'Nihonshakai no tokusei' (The characteristics of Japanese society) in *Shin
Nihonjinron*, Kōdansha, 1980, pp. 64-76.

which to base a claim that their perception of Japanese intelligence is 'racial' in nature. Rather, it is vaguely suggested that their high intelligence level has much to do with the Japanese way of life that stresses diligence.

BLOOD DETERMINISM, BUT NOT EXACTLY RACISM

To argue that the 'racially exclusive possession of a particular culture' should be distinguished from genetic determinism does not necessarily mean that the latter is absent among the Japanese. Most Japanese have an active interest in the relationship between blood type and personality traits. This may be briefly mentioned.

Japanese studies of blood types in the early decades of the twentieth century were undeniably influenced by German proto-types, but the tradition of such studies had already existed in Japan.[21] In pre-war Japan, blood types were studied with the aims of classifying racial types and verifying the claim that the Japanese and the Koreans were of different races. There was also an attempt to link blood type with temperament and with ethnic (national) character. Following Japan's defeat in 1945, the subject of blood types fell from favour in scholarly circles. The lull continued until the 1970s, when post-war constraints on some of the themes asserted in pre-war and wartime Japan diminished. The reemergence of this topic in the 1970s did not meet with any significant criticism in Japan probably because Japan's post-war intellectual history lacked an actively conscious refutation of genetic determinism such as has taken place in the West. This difference may exist partly because Japan's pre-war ideologues did not for-mulate genetic determinism as explicitly and articulately as was done in the West.

The subject of blood types has made a come-back since the 1970s, helped along by the publication of a number of books on the topic early in that decade. It has now become common for popular magazines to carry information on blood type and its relation to various aspects of social life. Most contemporary Japanese are favourably and actively oriented to the topic of blood

---

[21] On pre-war studies on blood types, see Cullen T. Hayashida, 'Identity, race and the blood ideology of Japan', unpubl. Ph. D. dissertation, University of Washington, 1976, pp. 144-59.

type and personality traits.[22] In conversation, people often inquire about blood type when a person's personality and temperament are being discussed. In this sense it is not unlike the Western horoscope. The subject often comes up in daily conversation among friends and colleagues in connection with congeniality between the sexes, the ways of developing one's latent talents, and the social skills needed for dealing with persons with particular blood types in various settings. It is important to note that references in popular publications and everyday conversation are almost always to the relation of blood types to the personality traits of individuals and not to national character, with which it is hardly associated at all. This is shown by the fact that not many ordinary people know that blood type composition could vary from one ethnic/national group to another. Thus the contemporary interest in blood types should be distinguished from racist concerns in the pre-war period.

Potentially, however, discussions of personality traits can be extended to discussions of national character. This occurs in the writings of Nomi Masahiko, one of the post-war popularisers of the 'theory' of blood types: 'Considering that blood type is reflected in temperament at the level of the individual, it logically follows that it has something to do with ethnic character'.[23] Nomi argues that the Japanese are a well-mixed ethnic group with a highly uniform distribution of blood types throughout the country. Because type A has the largest representation within the national distribution, characteristics associated with type A tend to be strongly reflected in the Japanese character. Those characteristics include 'diligence, group consciousness, formalism, respect of tradition and customs, lack of individual assertion, superficial politeness and in-group exclusiveness, skills for practical improvements rather than creativity, and preference for situational ethics rather than ideology'.[24] Suzuki Yoshimasa, another post-war writer who has popularised the blood type 'theory', goes even further and remarks that the Japanese character has not changed much for the last hundred years because 'blood type is hereditary ... [and because]

---

[22] Nomi's survey shows that only five per cent of his respondents consider that there is no relation between blood type and personality. See Nomi Masahiko, *Ketsuekigata ningengaku* (The study of people through blood types), Tokyo: Sankei Shimbun, 1973, p. 256.

[23] Nomi, *Ketsuekigata*, p. 53.

[24] Ibid., p. 54.

the relative proportion of four blood types for an ethnic group remains almost constant. This means that ... national and ethnic character passes on in a hereditary manner from parent to child and from child to grandchild, thereby persisting indefinitely'.[25] Suzuki points out a relationship between blood types and national character by referring to the rank ordering of types A, B and O. (For example, OAB means that type O is most commonly represented among a particular group, followed by A and B.) Among the two common patterns, OAB and AOB, the former is typically represented by the Americans, the latter by the Germans and the Japanese. Suzuki suggests a number of similarities in national character between the Japanese and the Germans; for example, both are 'introverted, concerned with details, and emotional'.[26]

An interest in blood type in general suggests that genetic determinism exists among the Japanese, but this should not be confused with what one can call the 'racially exclusive possession of particular cultural characteristics' which best describes the Japanese perception of their *national* identity.

CHANGING BUT PERSISTENT FEATURES OF JAPANESE RACIAL IDENTITY

Even a short essay like this one cannot be complete without mentioning aspects of change. Circumstances surrounding perceptions and expressions of Japanese identity are now undergoing significant changes in the wake of globalisation. Among the many changes occurring in the arena of Japanese ethnic/racial/national identity, we may point out one set of phenomena directly relevant to our main theme.[27] The notion that Japanese culture is the exclusive property of the Japanese race is being challenged by the increasing presence of foreigners who, while clearly foreign in appearance, can speak Japanese just as naturally as 'the native Japanese', on the one hand, and, on the other, those Japanese returnees from abroad (*kikokushijo*) whose behaviour and use of the Japanese language appear 'unnatural'. These cases of 'very

[25] Suzuki Yoshimasa, *O-gata ningen* (O-type people), Tokyo: Sanshinsha, 1973, pp. 222-3.

[26] Ibid., p. 218.

[27] An earlier and partial version of this section appeared in Yoshino, 'The changing discourse on race'.

Japanese' foreigners and 'not very Japanese' Japanese has generated
a lack of fit between cultural and 'racial' boundaries, thereby
causing an inconsistency and inefficacy in the symbolic boundary
system that defines Japanese identity. The assumption that those
who speak and behave like the Japanese should be 'racially' Japanese
and vice versa is being increasingly buffeted by the rising tide
of globalisation, resulting in increasing occurrences of such 'boundary dissonance'. Racial and cultural boundaries do not exactly
coincide.

Despite changes brought about by globalisation, such as the
one just illustrated, racial and cultural nationalism has tenacious
roots in Japan. Ironically, nationalism is resurfacing in the process
of so-called internationalisation of Japan. The problems involved
in the debate about *kikokushijo* (returnee children) and foreign
workers are symbolic of this. Returnee children, with their acquired
foreignness, are often reported to experience a stressful process
of cultural readjustment in the so-called 'homogeneous' society
of Japan, and their cross-cultural plight has been defined as a
social problem. Partly because their predicament is blamed on
society and partly because of the recent trend to view returnees
as a catalyst for positive change in schools and society where
'internationlisation' is a national agenda, some measures have been
introduced to protect and, sometimes, over-protect them by, for
example, exempting them from highly competitive entrance examinations in order to facilitate their re-entry into Japan's education
system. The difficulties of readjustment among returnee children
are not specific to Japan, as many scholars claim, but in other
countries of Asia and Europe the presence of such types of people
is not categorised as a social problem but is simply viewed as
a case of unsuccessful readjustment on the part of each individual.
This suggests that the problematisation of the returnee issue in
Japan may itself be a kind of theatre in which educators, policy-
makers, the media and returnees themselves consciously or un-
consciously play their assigned roles in the drama of the reinvention
of the myth of Japanese uniqueness. An attempt to 'internationalise'
may paradoxically produce the unintended consequence of promoting cultural nationalism.

The legal status of particular types of unskilled foreign workers
is another noteworthy example. Japan's Immigration Law prohibits
the entry of unskilled workers, partly because of fear that such

an influx might endanger the racial harmony of Japanese society. Nevertheless, large numbers of illegal foreign workers have already entered Japan and taken jobs in low-wage manual sectors of the economy vacated by Japanese workers. While there is demand for migrant workers in the labour market, the government is unwilling to change the Immigration Law. One measure taken by the business community to cope with this dilemma is to recruit South Americans of Japanese descent, since the Law allows second- and third-generation Japanese-South Americans to work legally in Japan, provided that proof is submitted that one of their parents is of Japanese nationality. A number of questions may be raised here regarding Japanese perceptions of race and culture. A comparison may be drawn between the Chinese who are, by definition, 'racially' different but culturally similar (to the Japanese), on the one hand, and the Japanese-Brazilians and Peruvians who are 'racially' Japanese but culturally very different, on the other. Chinese migrant workers are illegal. The Japanese media simply take note of the difficulties of adjustment in the daily lives of Latin Americans of Japanese ancestry and do not problematise the racialised nature of the issue – one will always be Japanese by virtue of blood.

INDEX

AIDS *see* sexually transmitted diseases (STDs)

Ainu of Hokkaidō: 108, 110, 112-13, 114-5; in Japanese racial discourse 136-7; in early Japanese studies 137-42; in Japanese studies (1912-45) 142-145; 'barbarian' stereotypes of 138-140, 141-2, 145, 151, 153; 'original inhabitants of archipelago' 140-1; criticised by Western scholars 138-41; and serology (*q.v.*) 143; and eugenics (*q.v.*) 143-4, 149-50; and social Darwinism (*q.v.*) 145, 147-8, 151, 152, 156; under Japanese protectorate 145-8; interbreed with Wajin 147-8; popular images of 151-6; 'a dying race' 150-1, 156-7

Aizawa Seishisai, author of *New Theses*, 179, 181

anthropology 7, 140-141

anthropometry 19

anti-Semitism *see* Jews

archaeology 20, 84, 86-9, 91, 92, 94, 140; *see also* palaeoanthropology

Asahi newspaper 190

Aum Shinrikyō (religious cult) 177, 195-8

Baelz, Erwin von 141

Batchelor, John 155 *cit.*

Benedict, Ruth, author of *Race: Science and Politics* 98, 203 *cit.*

Bernier, François 12

Bird, I. 139 *cit.*

blood types *see* serology

Bo Yang 31 *cit.*

Boxer uprising 37, 38

Brutus magazine 195

Buckle, Thomas, author of *History of Civilisation in England* 108

Buddhism 14, 162, 197

Chamberlain, B.H. 139 *cit.*, 140

Chen Jianshan 20

Chen Tianhua 17 *cit.*

Chen Yucang 19 *cit.*

Chinese Communist Party (CCP) 10, 75-6, 79

Christianity: 100, 179, 180-1; fundamentalists imprisoned 184-5

Confucianism: 1, 6, 7, 14, 16, 18, 38, 44, 57, 64, 116, 118, 119, 126, 127, 129-30, 133-4, 138, 145, 160, 162, 170

craniology 17, 19

Dai Jitao 63

Dalai Lama 91 *cit.*

Darwin, Charles 36

Delitzsch, Friedrich, author of *Babel oder Bibel* 57

Deng Xiaoping 26, 30, 81, 90

DNA *see* genetics

dōbun dōshu (Japanese shared cultural heritage with China) 119-35

Dönitz, Wilhelm 141

dragon descent myth 75-8

Drumont, Edouard 63

Engels, Friedrich 93

ethnic minorities 76, 91-2; *see also* Tibetans; Ainu

eugenics: 23-5, 108; legislation in China 27-8, 32; and Jews (*q.v.*) 66-7; and Ainu (*q.v.*) 143-4, 147-8, 149-50

evolution 6, 7-8, 21, 36, 46, 84-9, 138; *see also* social Darwinism

Fang Zhongyou 31
Fei Xiaotong 92 *cit.*
Frank, Anne, author of *Diary of a Young Girl* 177, 185, 186
Fukuzawa Yukichi, author of *Sekai kunizukushi* (World Geography) 109
Fukuda Tokuzo 113
Furuhata Tanemoto 108
Furukawa Takeji 108

gender hierarchy 8
genetics: and race 5; research into 'Chinese gene' 28; *see also* racial identity
German 'racial identity' 1
Gobineau, Arthur de 6, 110
Gong Tingzhang 20
Gotō Asatarō 132, 133 *cit.*, 166 *cit.*
Great Dictionary of Zoology 20 *cit.*
Great Wall of China 89-91
Gu Shoubai 20 *cit.*
Guomindang 22, 79, 163

Haga Yaichi 128 *cit.*
Han: 15, 19, 76, 77, 82, 83
Hara Sōbei 133 *cit.*
Harmand, Jules 113 *cit.*
Hashikawa Bunzō 121
He Ziheng 68
Himmler, Heinrich 94 *cit.; see also* Nazis
Hitler, Adolf 188, 190; *see also* Nazis
Hiraoka Sadataro 115 *cit.*
Hirose Takashi 187, 197
History of Japan 98-9
Hitchcock R., 138-9 *cit.*, 140· *cit.*
Hong Jun 59
Hong Yuan 22
Hoshikawa Ryōka 172 *cit.*
Hou Dejian, writer of song 'Descendants of the Dragon' 76, 78
Hozumi Nobushige, author of *Ancestor Worship* 99
Hozumi Yatsuka 102
Hu Shi 65
Huang Zunxian, 13 *cit.*
human rights: 2, 75; abuses 6, 11; *see also* racial discrimination

Huxley, Thomas, author of *On Evolution* 36

Inoue Tetsujirō, 102, 141
Inside Story of Outer Mongolia's Independence, The 30
International Convention on the Elimination of Racial Discrimination 10
Inuzuka Koreshige 186
Irokawa Daikichi 183 *cit.*
Ito Hirobumi 108
Iwaya Eitarō 147 *cit.*

Japanese Nation, The 141 *cit.*
Jews: 9, 23-4; Chinese definition of 53-4; physical stereotypes of 55-6, 64; prejudice against 56-7; culture of 57-8; as 'moneylenders' 58-9, 179-80; in anti-white Chinese race concepts 59-60; statelessness and Chinese nationalism 60-3; and Zionism in Chinese anti-imperialism 62; as 'superior race' 65-7; and eugenics (*q.v.*) 66-7; seen as fellow oppressed by Chinese intellectuals 68; persecuted in Japanese-occupied China 69-72; as enemies in Mao era 72-3; assimilated in modern China 73-4; attacked by Aum Shinrikyō religious cult 177, 195-8; Holocaust denied 177-8, 188, 192-5; origins of Japanese anti-Semitism 178-82; Japanese wartime anti-Semitism 182-5; post-war Japanese attitudes to 185-6; left-wing anti-Zionism 186-7; contemporary anti-Semitism 187-91
Jia Lanpo 28, 31, 84, 87, 88; *see also* palaeoanthropology
Jiang Guanyun, 55, 57
jinshu (Japanese 'race') 3, 98, 107, 108

Kada Tetsuji 99 *cit.*
kanbun (Chinese classics in Japan) 118-35
Kang Youwei: 2 *cit.*, 15, 38; disputes

Takekoshi Yosaburo 115
Takeuchi Yoshimi 134-5 *cit.*
Tanaka Kengo 193-4
Tanaka Odo 103
Tanka (South China boat-dwellers) 19
Tang Caichang 16 *cit.*
Textbook of civic biology (1924) 24, *cit.*
Tibetans 10, 15, 29, 78, 82, 83; and Han (*q.v.*) 91-3
Tides of Zhejiang, Chinese nationalist journal, 17 *cit.*
Tōa Kenkyūjo (East Asia Research Institute) 142
Tokutomi Iichirō (Sohō) 113, 133 *cit.*, 183 *cit.*
Tokyo Anthropological Society (*Tōkyō Jinruigakkai*) 140
Tōkyō asahi newspaper 129 *cit.*
Torii Ryūzo 141
Tsuboi Shōgorō 114, 140
Tsubouchi Shōyō 123-4 *cit.*

Ueda Kazutoshi 103, 127 *cit.*, 128
Uighurs 10, 29-30, 83
Unification Church 197
United Nations 2, 75, 77, 187
Uno Masami 188 *cit.*, 189, 194, 197-8

Wang Fuzhi, author of the *Yellow Book* 12-13 *cit.*
Wang Jingwei, President, 69-70 *cit.*
Wang Tao 57-8
Watanabe Shōichi 204 *cit.*
Wen Yiduo 22-3 *cit.*
'wild man' research 30-1
Wu Dingliang 31
Wu Jie, editor of *Handbook of education in Chineseness* 30

Wu Qinyou 68 *cit.*
Wu Rukang 28
Wu Zelin 73 *cit.*

Xinmin Hui (People's Renovation Society) 69
Xue Fucheng 58 *cit.*

Yamagata Aritomo 130-1 *cit.*
Yellow Emperor: 1, 6, 9, 12, 15, 16-17, 34, 40; in revolutionary rhetoric 46-9; cult revival of 79-84; myth contested by minority intellectuals 83
Yi Jiayue 25 *cit.*
Yomiuri newspaper 121 *cit.*, 129, 188
Young-tsu Wong 35 *cit.*
Yoshikawa Akimasa 127
You Xiong 65 *cit.*
Young, Donald, editor of *The American Negro* 23
Yu Songhua 65 *cit.*, 66
Yuan Hongbing 28 *cit.*
Yunnan, journal 17 *cit.*

Zhang Binglin: 35; early anti-Manchu propaganda 36-8; promotes Han 'racism' as anti-Manchu ideology 39; defines lineage terminology 41; openly rejects Manchu government 42; arrested and tried 45; identifies Han surnames 45; and Yellow Emperor (*q.v.*) 46-9
Zhang Junmai 22
Zhang Xiangwen 55-6 *cit.*
Zhang Xueliang 163, 164
Zhao Tongmao 29, 30
Zionism *see* Jews
Zou Rong 9